PREACHING
THE
NEW COMMON
LECTIONARY

PREACHING
THE
NEW COMMON LECTIONARY

YEAR C

Advent, Christmas, Epiphany

Commentary by:

Fred B. Craddock
John H. Hayes
Carl R. Holladay
Gene M. Tucker

ABINGDON PRESS
Nashville

Preaching the New Common Lectionary
Year C Advent, Christmas, Epiphany

Copyright © 1985 by Abingdon Press

This book is printed on acid-free paper.

Library of Congress Cataloging in Publication Data

Main entry under title:
  Preaching the new common lectionary. Year C,
  Advent, Christmas, Epiphany.

  Includes index.
  1. Bible—Homiletical use. 2. Bible—Liturgical lessons,
  English. I. Craddock, Fred B.
  BS534.5.P734 1985 251 85-11123

ISBN 0-687-33848-4
(pbk.: alk. paper)

MANUFACTURED BY THE PARTHENON PRESS AT
NASHVILLE, TENNESSEE, UNITED STATES OF AMERICA

Contents

Epiphany

Special Days

Introduction

It might be helpful to the reader if we make a few remarks about our understanding of our task and what we have sought to accomplish in this volume. The following comments will touch on four topics.

The Scripture in Preaching

There is no substitute for direct exposure to the biblical text, both for the preacher in preparation and for the listener in worship. The Scriptures are therefore not only studied privately but read aloud as an act of worship in and of itself and not solely as prelude to a sermon. The sermon is an interpretation of Scripture in the sense that the preacher seeks to bring the text forward into the present in order to effect a new hearing of the Word. In this sense the text has its future and its fulfillment in preaching. In fact, the Bible itself is the record of the continual rehearing and reinterpreting of its own traditions in new settings and for new generations of believers. New settings and new circumstances are properly as well as inescapably integral to a hearing of God's Word in and through the text. Whatever else may be said to characterize God's Word, it is always appropriate to the hearers. But the desire to be immediately relevant should not abbreviate study of the text or divorce the sermon from the biblical tradition. Such sermons are orphaned, released without memory into the world. It is the task of the preacher and teacher to see that the principle of fidelity to Scripture is not abandoned in the life and worship of the church. The endeavor to understand a text in its historical, literary, and theological contexts does create, to be sure, a sense of distance between the Bible and the congregation. The preacher may grow impatient during this period of feeling a long way from a sermon. But this time of study can be most fruitful. By holding text and parishioners apart for a while, the preacher can hear each more clearly and exegete each more honestly. Then, when the two intersect in the sermon, neither the text nor the congregation is consumed by the other. Because the Bible is an ancient book, it invites the preacher back into its world in order to understand; because the Bible is the church's Scripture, it moves forward into our world and addresses us here and now.

The Lectionary and Preaching

Ever increasing numbers of preachers are using a lectionary as a guide for preaching and worship. The intent of lectionaries is to provide for the church over a given period of time (usually three years) large units of Scripture arranged according to the seasons of the Christian year and selected because they carry the central message of the Bible. Lectionaries are not designed to limit one's message or restrict the freedom of the pulpit. On the contrary, churches that use a lectionary usually hear more Scripture in worship than those that do not. And ministers who preach from the lectionary find themselves stretched into areas of the canon into which they would not have gone had they kept to the path of personal preference. Other values of the lectionary are well known: the readings provide a common ground for discussions in ministerial peer groups; family worship can more easily join public worship through shared readings; ministers and worship committees can work with common biblical texts to prepare services that have movement and integrity; and the lectionary encourages more disciplined study and advance preparation. All these and other values are increased if the different churches share a common lectionary. A common lectionary could conceivably generate a community-wide Christian conversation.

This Book and Preaching

This volume is not designed as a substitute for work with the biblical text; on the contrary, its intent is to encourage such work. Neither is it our desire to relieve the preacher of regular visits to concordances, lexicons, and commentaries; rather it is our hope that the comments on the texts here will be sufficiently germinal to give direction and purpose to those visits to major reference works. Our commentaries are efforts to be faithful to the text and to begin moving the text toward the pulpit. There are no sermons as such here, nor could there be. No one can preach long distance. Only the one who preaches can do an exegesis of the listeners and mix into sermon preparation enough local soil so as to effect an indigenous hearing of the Word. But we hope we have contributed to that end. The reader will notice that, while each of us has been aware of the other readings for each service, there has been no attempt to offer a collaborated commentary on all texts or a homogenized interpretation as though there were not four texts but one. It is assumed that the season of the year, the needs of the listeners, the preacher's own abilities, as well as the overall unity of the message of the Scriptures will prompt the preacher to find among the four readings the word for the day. Sometimes the four texts will join arm in arm, sometimes they will debate with one another, sometimes one will lead while the others follow, albeit at times reluctantly. Such is the wealth of the biblical witness.

A final word about our comments. The lections from the Psalter have been treated in the same manner as the other readings even though some Protestant churches often omit the reading of the psalm or replace it with a hymn. We have chosen to regard the psalm as an equal among the texts, primarily for three reasons. First, there is growing interest in the use of Psalms in public worship, and comments about them may help make that use more informed. Second, the Psalms were a major source for worship and preaching in the early church and they continue to inspire and inform Christian witness today. And third, comments on the Psalms may make this volume helpful to Roman Catholic preachers who have maintained the long tradition of using the Psalms in Christian services.

This Season and Preaching

This book deals with the Seasons of Advent, Christmas, and Epiphany. It is our hope that this three-in-one format will not lure the preacher into moving through these services with a kind of sameness of spirit that fails to acknowledge and embrace the various changes in the seasons of the spirit. For observing Advent, which begins the Christian year, we have biblical texts that speak of promise, preparation, hope, and anticipation. Those who preach on these texts will want to capture their moods of restrained excitement. Christmas differs from Advent as fulfillment differs from expectation, as today differs from both yesterday and tomorrow. Having is an experience quite different from hoping, for having moves the spirit down the road of reflection, asking, Now what? Then comes Epiphany, the celebration of the manifestation of Christ to the nations. Themes and images of light, revelation, and public proclamation abound in these texts. Nothing is subdued or veiled here; "This is my beloved Son" is the word from heaven. Advent's whisper in Bethlehem is now a shout in the streets of every city. Good preaching will not only say the words but will also attempt to carry the tune.

Fred B. Craddock (Gospels)
John H. Hayes (Psalms)
Carl R. Holladay (Epistles)
Gene M. Tucker (Old Testament)

First Sunday of Advent

Jeremiah 33:14-16; Psalm 25:1-10; I Thessalonians 3:9-13;
Luke 21:25-36

The year opens with promises and prayers, promises of
the coming reign of God and prayers that the people of
God will be ready for that reign. The texts set a tone of
hopeful expectation, but not without apprehension in view
of the awesome events to come. The Old Testament
reading is an announcement that the ancient promise of a
Davidic messiah will be fulfilled and Jerusalem will dwell
secure. The responsorial psalm is a prayer for help and
forgiveness, reaffirming the righteousness and faithfulness
of God already expressed in the reading from Jeremiah 33.
In the epistolary reading, Paul's prayer that he be allowed
to join the faithful in Thessalonica becomes a petition that
they be ready for the coming of the Lord. The Gospel
lection sets the Season of Advent into an eschatological
framework: the signs in the heavens indicate that the
kingdom of God is near.

Jeremiah 33:14-16

These verses from Jeremiah are located in the context of a
series of announcements of salvation. The chapter begins
with an introduction that attributes the words that follow to
Jeremiah "while he was still shut up in the court of the
guard" (33:1), during the Babylonian siege of Jerusalem.
However, there are numerous allusions in the chapter to the
circumstances of the Babylonian Exile or even later. The city
and nation seem to be destroyed (33:7, 10, 12), and then come
these unconditional promises of restoration. Moreover, the
fact that our reading is part of a section (33:14-26) not found in

11

the Septuagint version is further indication that it comes from a period later than that of the prophet Jeremiah.

Verses 14-16 in fact contain an exact quotation of lines already found in Jeremiah 23:5-6. They apparently are quoted here to provide a text for the explanation and interpretation that follow in Jeremiah 33:17-26, in the same way that preachers cite a biblical text as the foundation for a sermon. Thus in the context of our reading an earlier promise concerning the line of David is called to the attention of a new and later group of hearers who are assured that the hope will one day be fulfilled. The major addition to the text from Jeremiah 23:5-6 is the line "when I will fulfill the promise I made to the house of Israel and the house of Judah" (verse 14). The hearers must live in a time when there is no king in the line of David on the throne in Jerusalem, but it is not clear whether the "righteous Branch" is expected in the near or distant future.

These verses reach to the heart of the Old Testament messianic expectations, assuming the promise, recorded in II Samuel 7, of a perpetual kingship in the line of David. The "messiah" (or "anointed one") was the title applied to each new monarch. The Davidic monarchy and the assurance that it would be permanent were gifts of divine grace intended to guarantee the peace and security of the people of God (II Samuel 7:10-13). As the people experienced rulers who were less than just, the promise of a "righteous Branch" was heard through the prophets, and was reiterated after the Babylonians brought an end to the Davidic monarchy.

In Jeremiah 33:14-16 it is the Lord who will fulfill the promise and "cause a righteous Branch to spring forth for David." Divine intervention is expected, but through a human figure. The language which characterizes this figure occurs also in Isaiah 11:1 (compare also Isaiah 4:2). In Zechariah 3:8 and 6:12 "branch" may refer to a particular individual in the time of that prophet.

Most important here are the functions of the one whom the Lord will "cause . . . to spring forth." "He shall execute justice and righteousness in the land. . . . Judah will be saved and Jerusalem dwell securely" (verses 15-16). This language has become such a part of our abstract religious vocabulary that we must remind ourselves of its concreteness. Justice and righteousness—the most familiar pair of terms from the Old Testament prophets—refer to fair and equitable relationships among people, impartial lawcourts, the protection of the weak from the strong (justice), and the personal characteristics (righteousness) which make such conditions possible. To "save" Judah and cause Jerusalem to "dwell securely" do not refer in the first instance to religious experiences or practices, but to specific political circumstances: Judah will be free of foreign domination and Jerusalem from fear of invasion.

The functions, then, of the righteous Branch are in the realm of what we would call governmental, political concerns, both domestic and foreign. If the Old Testament lesson has a contribution to make to the beginning of Advent, it is to keep before us God's concern for such matters. The reign of God comes not only beyond time and this world, but also in history and in this world. The righteous Branch, the anointed one of God, comes in human form into a human world. That is not just an ancient Israelite hope, but the Christian expectation at Advent as well.

Psalm 25:1-10

Two general features should be noted about this psalm. First, like a few other psalms (9/10, 34, 37, 111, 112, 119, 145), this one is an alphabetic poem, sometimes called an acrostic. This means that the psalm flows through the alphabet with each successive verse commencing with the next letter of the Hebrew alphabet. Second, the composition is a lament of an individual, that is, it was originally written to be used in worship services in which an individual's needs were the focus of attention.

The psalm moves back and forth between the individual's petitions to the Deity (verses 1-7, 16-22), the priest or worship leader's address to the worshiper (verses 8-10, 12-14), and the worshiper's statement to the priest/worship leader (verse 15). Thus the psalm contains three types of material: petitionary prayer, confession, and priestly proclamation.

The lection for today is comprised of two of the psalm's

components: a prayer or petition addressed to the Deity (verses 1-7) and theological proclamation probably addressed by the priest to the worshiper (verses 8-10).

Two verbs are of fundamental importance in verses 1-7—"wait" and "remember"—and give expression to two of the basic Christian sentiments and postures of Advent—"waiting" and "remembering." Advent is a time of waiting, or expectation, of looking to the future, but it is also a time for remembrance, for recollection, for reflection.

The term "wait" appears in verses 3 and 5. In the former, it appears in a petitionary intercession on behalf of a group—"those that wait for thee." In the latter, it appears in a confessional statement expressing trust. Intercession and confession may thus be seen as two ways of waiting.

In the melody of the waiting, there lies however, a dissonant chord. The time of waiting is not simply the idle passing of the hour; it is a time of misery and trouble. Note, in verses 16-19, the cacophony of unharmonious notes: loneliness, affliction, a troubled heart, distresses, sin, innumerable foes, and violent hatred. The psalmist waits for God when all the evidence suggests that the waiting may be long and the pain and misery deep. Mere endurance, however, is not the goal of waiting. Note the counterbalance of requests over against the terms depicting misery: "turn," "be gracious," "relieve," "bring me out," "consider," "forgive," "guard," "deliver," and "let me not be put to shame." Quite a list of Christmas requests for so early in Advent! But isn't that part of what Advent and redemption are all about: recognizing and confessing the nature of the status quo and wanting and requesting a new status of being.

The psalmist also speaks about remembering. Three times the verb occurs in verses 6-7. (The first occurrence, the RSV translates "be mindful.") The request for remembrance here takes two forms: remembering and remembering not. The psalmist requests that God remember his mercy and steadfast love, those divine qualities that predispose the Deity toward human redemption. These are seen as the qualities possessed by God "from of old." On the other hand, there is the request to "remember not," that is, forget, the human past with its youthful sins (inadvertent errors and

14

wayward faults) and more adult transgressions (more deliberate and premeditated wrongs). In Advent, with its backward glance and future focus, there is stress on those eternal characteristics of goodness attributed to God and at the same time the human need to be burdened no longer by the past with its accumulated failures.

The final plea to remember is in verse 7*b* where the psalmist asks that God should, on the basis of his love and goodness, "remember me." Remember me, not my past, just me, as I am, waiting and remembering.

I Thessalonians 3:9-13

Even though the Season of Advent is frequently observed as a time of preparation for Christmas, and thus as a time when we direct our thoughts toward the Advent, or coming, of the incarnate Lord in his birth, it includes much more than this. It becomes a time when we reflect on the Lord's coming in its many dimensions: his historical coming in his birth, his eschatological coming at the end of time, his existential coming into our own present. The first of these, Christ's coming in the Incarnation, is not referred to in today's epistolary reading. It focuses instead, like the other epistolary readings for the First Sunday of Advent (Rom. 13:11-14; I Cor. 1:3-9), on the future "coming of our Lord Jesus" (verse 13). But the existential dimension is here as well, for the passage speaks of those things that are central to our appropriation of the Christ-event. It speaks of a God who can actually direct travel plans and bring them to fulfillment (verse 11), an apostle bound to his church by love (verse 12), a Lord who can so enrich Christian love that it reaches both inward and outward (verse 12). It also speaks of a Lord who makes our hearts firm and our lives holy and blameless in preparation for the Lord's coming (verse 13).

When Paul wrote these words, he had just a few months earlier established the Thessalonian church (cf. Acts 17:1-9). Much of the earlier part of the letter is spent recalling his founding visit and reflecting on his ministry among the people (cf. esp. 2:1-16). As one reads this epistle, it becomes clear that this young, fledgling church still occupies his thoughts and prayers. Even though he is now engaged in evangelistic activity in Corinth, his heart and mind still return to Thessalonica. He has tried to visit them but has been hindered from doing so (2:17-20). He recalls the success of the gospel among them, speaking of them as his "glory and joy" (2:20). He is obviously buoyed by the steadfastness of their faith in the face of persecution and resistance (2:13-16), but he is understandably anxious about their welfare. His anxiety is that of the minister who frets over new converts who have been left behind in a struggling mission church, knowing that their faith is fragile at best. Like a "gentle . . . nurse taking care of her children" (2:7), he is both thankful and joyful for them, but constantly prays that he may see them "face to face" so that he can shore up the gaps in their faith.

Here we are at the very center of the Lord's coming as it is understood existentially: the minister praying for the members of the church—thankful, joyful, triumphant, yet anxious to see them, concerned about their welfare, eager to teach them more and supply what is lacking, hoping that their love for one another will hold them together and that they will be presentable on the Day of the Lord.

In another sense as well, this passage illustrates the existential dimension of the Lord's coming. Here we see faith taking root—and taking shape. The Thessalonians have received the word of God not as a preacher's oral report, but "as what it really is, the word of God, which is at work in you believers" (2:13). God has come to them through the proclaimed Word, which Paul envisions here as still energizing them. God's presence remains a powerful force at work within their midst confirming them in their faith. And it is the community of faith bound to one another in love that becomes the locus of God's activity (verse 12). The apostle's heart is knit to theirs in love, and even in his absence his love for them grows rather than wanes. His hope is that their love for one another will increase even as his does for them, but their form of community is not to be narcissistic, turning in on itself and its own needs exclusively. Their love is to abound to "the whole human race" (JB; cf. Gal. 6:10). The church that genuinely experiences the coming of Christ into its own midst most fully embodies this presence when it extends its love beyond itself and lives for others. The church thus becomes a reenactment of the Christ-story—love for others.

However, the eschatological dimension is the most explicit motif in the passage. As is well known, the Second Coming of the Lord is a prominent concern in this epistle (cf. 2:19; 4:14-15; 5:2, 23; also II Thess. 1:7-10; 2:1, 8). The call for hearts "unblamable in holiness" is reminiscent of other early Christian teaching that insisted on sober preparation for the Advent of Christ (cf. 5:23; James 5:8). One exegetical point worth noticing is whether "all his saints" (verse 13) refers to Christians or angels (cf. Zech. 14:5). In either case, the thrust of Paul's remarks is clear: Christians are urged to prepare themselves for the final coming of the Lord.

As we have seen, even though today's passage is anchored in Paul's very personal reflections about the Thessalonian church, and in this sense is quite historically concrete, it enables us to think about the Lord's coming in both an eschatological and existential sense. For homiletical appropriation, it may be possible to explore the nature of Christian community as envisioned in this passage and the ways in which this best represents the type of preparation called for by the Advent Season. Or, alternatively one may explore the eschatological theme, reminding the church that past and future are interlocked in the Christ-event.

Luke 21:25-36

One can hardly imagine a more appropriate way to begin the Advent Season than to focus on texts that announce God's fulfilling the promise to bring justice, righteousness, and redemption. The means shall be through a righteous branch of David (Jeremiah); the coming of our Lord Jesus (Paul); the Son of man coming in a cloud (Luke). What may seem less appropriate, however, is the Gospel lection which proclaims the apocalyptic end of all things and the coming of the kingdom of God. Nothing is here of virgin and child, of shepherds and heavenly choirs, but rather the shaking of heaven and earth in perplexity, fear, and foreboding.

In each of the three cycles of the lectionary, Advent is begun with a Gospel reading from the apocalyptic discourse of Jesus. These texts impress upon the preacher and the whole church that the coming of the Lord includes much more than the Christmas story, that Advent is God's doing, apart from all human calculation or designing, and that Advent is of such significance, the entire cosmos reverberates with the signs and circumstances of these events.

Luke 21:25-36 is a portion of the larger unit, 21:5-38, which is itself set within 19:47–21:38, the teaching of Jesus in the temple. Whereas Matthew (24:1-3) and Mark (13:1-4) locate this apocalyptic discourse outside the temple on the Mount of Olives and address it to the disciples, Luke places it within the temple and addresses it to all the people (21:37-38). Our lection for today contains part of Jesus' answer to the twin questions of verse 7; When and with what signs will these things take place?

Luke's dependence on the Markan apocalypse (13:5-37) is quite evident. Within Luke 21:25-36 one notices, in addition to the expected rephrasing at points, the omission of Mark's verses 27 and 32 and the addition of Luke's own verse 28 and an entirely different ending to the discourse. The structure of Luke 21:25-36 is as follows:

Verses 25-28—the coming of the Son of man
29-31—the parable of the fig tree
32-33—the time of the coming of the Son of man
34-36—the ending to the discourse

If one places these four units within the whole discourse, Luke's sequencing of events seems rather clear. The followers of Jesus will have a time of witnessing (verse 13), in response to which there will be severe persecution, religious and political (verses 12-19). As a consequence Jerusalem will be destroyed before the eyes of the nations (verses 20-24). When the time of the nations has been fulfilled, the Son of man will come in a cloud with power and glory, attended by signs in the heavens (verses 25-28). This event will affect the whole earth and bring distress to all nations, but the faithful are to take heart and raise their heads: redemption is near. As surely as one can discern the approach of summer by the leafing of the fig tree, so these signs will announce that the kingdom of God is near (verses 29-31). And when? Within this generation, says Luke (verses 32-33). With this statement as to the time, Luke joins many other early Christians in the belief that they were living in the period between God's punishment of Jerusalem by the Gentiles (nations) and God's judgment of the nations by the Son of man whose appearing will bring redemption to the faithful.

Two additions by Luke to Mark's apocalypse deserve comment, especially in the Advent Season. The first is verse 28 which assures the followers of Christ that the final shaking of heaven and earth will not be for them an occasion for fear and distress. On the contrary, the day of judgment is the day of grace: "Look up and raise your heads, because your redemption is drawing near." The second addition, verses 34-36, concludes the discourse with a moral admonition. Grace does not mean an automatic exemption from the distress coming upon all peoples of the earth. Rather let this word about what will be have a sanctifying influence, producing a prayerful watchfulness and a freedom from indulgence and anxiety about things. The dulled and dissipated spirit is ensnared, not released, by the advent of God.

Second Sunday of Advent

Baruch 5:1-9 or Malachi 3:1-4; Psalm 126; Philippians 1:3-11; Luke 3:1-6

All the readings for this day focus upon the coming acts of God to save. The dominant mood is one of joyful expectation, but not without some reference to the dark background that precedes the coming salvation. Baruch 5:1-9 expresses promises to Jerusalem, and the calls for her to change from sorrow to joy. Though Malachi's messenger of the covenant brings good news to Jerusalem, there will also be a period of purifying judgment. Psalm 126 recalls the celebration when the Lord restored Zion and prays that those who sow in tears will reap shouts of joy. The epistolary reading is Paul's warm and joyful thanksgiving for the community at Philippi, looking toward the "day of Christ." Luke 3:1-6 reports the call of John the Baptist, characterizes his message as a baptism of repentance for the forgiveness of sins and cites the announcement of salvation from Isaiah 40:3-5.

Baruch 5:1-9

The Book of Baruch is one of the least known of the books of the Bible, and in fact there are those who dispute its standing as part of the Christian scriptures. Protestant Christians, following the lead of the Reformers, include it among the Apocrypha because it was not part of the Hebrew scriptures. Although no Hebrew text of the book has come to light, some of the work, at least, must have originated in Hebrew. The style in the first chapters is distinctly Hebraic, but that is less obvious in the concluding sections, including our reading for the day.

While the book purports to come from Jeremiah's scribe Baruch (see Jer. 32:12; 36:4; 45:1) at the time of the Babylonian conquests of Judah and Jerusalem, it must stem from a later period and from another unnamed person or persons. Among other sources, the work depends upon Isaiah 40–55 (ca. 539 B.C.) and Daniel 9 (167-64 B.C.). Consequently, it could be no earlier than the middle of the second century B.C. Some commentators date it to the time following the fall of Jerusalem to the Romans in A.D. 70, but that probably is too late. While not historically accurate, the assumption that the words are addressed to the defeated people of God, now scattered and exiled from the Holy City, is important for understanding the message of our lection.

The book as a whole, as most commentators have noticed, consists of two distinct parts, each with two sections. The first part (1:1–3:8) is in prose and contains an introduction (1:1-14) and Israel's confession of guilt (1:15–3:8). The second part (3:9–5:9) is in poetry, containing a poem in praise of God's wisdom (3:9–4:4) and announcements of salvation concerning the restoration of Jerusalem (4:5–5:9).

As part of a unit that begins in Baruch 4:30, the reading for the day is addressed to Jerusalem, understood both literally and metaphorically. It is on the one hand the actual holy place, the site of the temple, the home of the exiles. On the other hand, Jerusalem is personified, seen to be grieving like a widow for her sons, a lonely woman for her daughters (Bar. 4:16). She is told to remove her mourning garb and put on "the beauty of the glory from God" (5:1), to stand up and look toward the east to see her children gathered (5:5). As a bereaved woman she represents the suffering, defeated people of God, and her joy celebrates that of her returning children.

It is not surprising that the early church fathers attributed quotations from this book to the prophet Jeremiah. Although there are none of the usual messenger or oracle formulas ("thus says the Lord," "says the Lord"), the language of this chapter is prophetic both in form and content. It consists of a series of announcements of salvation. The pattern is an admonition or instruction to the Holy City followed by reasons (introduced by "for") to follow the admonition. Thus in 5:1-2 Jerusalem is to replace mourning garments with the symbols of God's righteousness, glory, and splendor "for"

(5:3-4) God will show the city's splendor everywhere and perpetually chant her name, "Peace of righteousness and glory of godliness." And in verse 5 Jerusalem is told to stand up and see her children returning "for" God is bringing them back (5:6), "for" God is preparing a safe and smooth way for their return (5:7-8), and "for" God will lead Israel "in the light of his glory" and with his mercy and righteousness (5:9).

The attentive reader will not miss the similarity of many of these words of salvation and assurance to those in Isaiah 40 and following. Compare 5:1-2 with Isaiah 61:3, 5:4 with Isaiah 60:14, 5:5 with Isaiah 49:18, and 5:7 with Isaiah 42:16 ff. In this respect as the Old Testament reading, it anticipates the citation of Isaiah 40:3-5 in the Gospel lection.

The message of the chapter is clear and unambiguous: a mourning and dispirited city and people will have cause for celebration because God is about to act to bring those people home. The God of mercy and righteousness will not leave his people scattered and in exile. It is possible that such a message, proclaimed and heard in the Season of Advent, can evoke hope and expectation in the hearts of those who wait for the coming of Jesus.

Malachi 3:1-4

"Malachi" probably is not a proper name but a title that comes from the passage before us, in which the Hebrew term means "my messenger." The book is thus anonymous, the words of an unnamed prophet or prophets of the postexilic period, following the return of the Judeans from Babylon. The existence of the second temple is taken for granted, and the regular offering of sacrifices there seems to have been resumed for some time. These facts indicate that the prophet was active after Haggai and Zechariah, who are concerned with the rebuilding of the temple about 520 B.C., but earlier than Ezra or Nehemiah, around 400 B.C. Malachi's understanding of correct sacrifices does not seem to be aware of the details of the law instituted by Ezra.

The book thus comes from the heart of the Persian period, perhaps the middle of the fifth century B.C. Judah and Jerusalem would have been under a "governor" (Mal. 1:8), doubtless appointed by the Persians. There is no evidence of external threats, and apart from a concern with intermarriage and criticism of neighboring Edom (Mal. 1:2-5), the book has little interest in affairs outside Judah.

The Book of Malachi gives us not a word about the prophet. That is not so surprising when we remember that as a rule Old Testament prophets give us remarkably little direct information about themselves. When they do speak of their backgrounds or experiences they do so in order to present the message of God, which is central. The person who stands behind this book is like earlier prophets in that he courageously speaks in the name of the Lord, and his words often concern the immediate future. However, many of his themes and interests are priestly, and he seems to have been identified with a particular priestly group, the Levites (Mal. 2:4-9), but not uncritically (Mal. 3:3).

There are some seven units in the book, each one in the form of a dialogue or disputation between the Lord, or the prophet on behalf of the Lord, and the group addressed. Sometimes the words of the opponents are quoted, thus indicating the problem addressed by the revelation. This pattern gives the book an argumentative character.

In our reading for the day, which in important respects stands at the center of the Book of Malachi's theology, the prophetic and the priestly dimensions come together. Malachi 3:1-4 includes most of the book's fourth unit (2:17–3:5), and must be understood in that context.

The disputation is addressed to those who have "wearied the Lord" (2:17) with particular words. They have said either that God delights in those who do evil, or asked where the God of justice could be found. The prophet's opponents are objecting to a real position, arguing—like Job—that it is not always the righteous who prosper, as Malachi 3:10-12 asserts. The problem is a particularly acute one for those who believe that there is or should be direct and immediate retribution or reward based on obedience to the law of God.

Our reading, then, is a response to the question of the justice of God. There will come a time, and soon, when justice will be established. First the Lord will send a messenger to prepare the way for his own appearance in the temple. It is not always easy here to distinguish between what the messenger is expected to do and what the Lord himself will do. The sequence of events, however, is transparent. The Lord will send a messenger, the messenger of the covenant, to prepare the way. The day of his coming—probably that of the messenger—will be a fearful one, for he will refine and purify "the sons of Levi," that is, the levitical priests (compare Isa. 6:5-7). They will then offer the right offerings, which will be pleasing to the Lord. Next (3:5), the Lord himself will come near for judgment, establishing justice by punishing the unrighteous, that is, everyone who "does evil" (2:17). The list of evildoers includes mainly those who oppress the weak (the hireling, the widow, the orphan, and the foreigner), but it also includes sorcerers, adulterers, and those who swear falsely.

Thus the prophet answers the question of the opponents, "Where is the God of justice?" (2:17). That God is coming, indeed, his messenger has already been sent. First there will be purification of worship, and then God will establish justice.

As an Advent lesson, this text articulates the hope and proclaims the good news that God will act to save. Its mood and tone, however, are not those of joyful expectation. Rather, some of the themes of the Gospel reading's account of John the Baptist are emphasized. Preparation for the coming of God includes responding to a call for repentance, or experiencing a time of purification. Furthermore, the good news of God's justice for the weak may entail judgment on the strong, and it is those who stand so near the center of worship—in this case the priests—who require purification.

Psalm 126

This psalm has been selected as a responsorial reading to Malachi 3:1-4 because of its connection in the history of interpretation with the return from exile. (Note the RSV marginal translation of verse 1: "When the Lord brought back those who returned to Zion.") At one time in the history of biblical interpretation, all of the "Psalms of Ascent" (or pilgrimage)—Psalms 120–134—were believed to have been sung by the exiles returning from Babylonia to Jerusalem. The note of anticipation, looking forward to redemption, which is found in the psalm also fits, like Malachi 3:1-4, the Advent theme.

The central content of the psalm revolves around the idea of the reversal of fortune. There is a twofold movement in the psalm. Verses 1-3 look back to an earlier time when God restored the fortunes or determined the destiny of Zion. Verses 4-6 look forward to the future. The first is confession—a declaration of what happened in terms of the human response—while the second is petitionary—a request for how things might be in the future.

The best theory concerning this psalm sees the imagery as reflecting the autumn festival in Israel which fell in the seventh Jewish month (our present late September—early October). This autumn festival of ingathering or tabernacles (see Exod. 23:16b) marked the movement from the old harvest year to the new agricultural year. Thus it was a Janus-type festival—looking back to the old (verses 1-3) and forward to the future (verses 4-6).

The fall festival was when, like our New Year, the fate and fortunes of the coming year were decreed. The worshipers here recall the past occasion as one of joy and celebration. (The theme of Christmas past.) The plea is that the future too shall be a time when conditions are good. The imagery of sowing and weeping followed by harvesting and shouting becomes understandable in light of the fact that planting in Palestine followed the fall festival when the autumn rainy season began anew in October.

Mythological and primitive concepts underlie the references to sowing with weeping, reaping with joy. The association of tears with sowing is based on several factors: tears symbolize rainfall; sowing involves death since the seed must "die" to appear as new grain growth; planting is a gamble and a risk; and the scattering of seeds resembles the shedding of tears. Such customs as weeping when sowing are found in many cultures around the world. Significant also is the idea of performing one type of action in the present so as to achieve the opposite at a later point in time. Deprivation in the present, the temporary suspension of gratification can be seen as the means to fuller realization in the future. Weep now and shout for joy later. Weeping puts us on the before side of Advent; shouts of joy alongside the shepherds in Bethlehem.

Philippians 1:3-11

Paul typically opens his letters with a prayer, usually of thanksgiving (Rom. 1:8-17; I Cor. 1:4-9; Col. 1:3-14; I Thess. 1:2-10; 2:13-16; 3:9-10; II Thess. 1:3-4; Philem. 4-7), sometimes of blessing (II Cor. 1:3-7; Eph. 1:3-23). It is important to remember that the letters were intended to be read before Christians assembled in house churches, and thus these opening prayers would have had a liturgical function. As one would expect, they are crafted with the hearers in mind, and they speak to the concrete situation of those addressed. Consequently, these opening prayers typically introduce motifs or themes that are later dealt with in the letter itself. In this sense, they serve as a table of contents for the rest of the letter.

This opening prayer of thanksgiving is no exception. As is well known, this letter was written partially in response to a generous gift from the Philippian church (4:14-18). Behind several phrases in the prayer we detect references to the generosity of the Philippians and their financial participation in Paul's ministry. Their "partnership in the gospel from the first day until now" (verse 5) had occurred not only because they had suffered, like Paul, for the sake of the gospel (1:29-30), but also because they had become financial partners with him (4:15). Their partnership with him existed at both a spiritual and financial level. The "good work" that God had started within them (verse 6) may in fact be a reference to this mission effort they had supported so loyally. What becomes clear throughout the prayer is that Paul regarded this church as full participants in his own ministry. They had become partakers "of grace" with Paul in his "imprisonment and in the defense and confirmation of the gospel" (verse 7). In one sense, the chains he had worn he had worn alone and his work of defending and establishing the gospel (cf. JB, verse 7) he had done alone. But in another,

26

perhaps even more real sense, he had done none of this alone. Rather, through their solidarity with him the Philippian church had shared in these activities, and in a real sense had participated in them with him (cf. 1:19).

It is this level of genuine partnership that existed between Paul and his supporting church that accounts for the intimate tone of this prayer. Every time he thought of them he became thankful. Every time he prayed for them, it was an occasion of joy. His bond with them is one of genuine affection: "You have a permanent place in my heart, and God knows how much I miss you all, loving you as Christ Jesus loves you" (verses 7b-8, JB). These are the affections generated by a long-standing relationship. Paul is not writing to a church he has only recently established, but to a church he has known for years. He has received their money (4:15-19), their emissary Epaphroditus (2:25-30), their prayers (1:19), and their concern (4:10,14).

This passage has been chosen for today's lection because of its twofold mention of the "day of Christ" (verses 6 and 10). The opening prayers of Paul's letters typically moved toward an eschatological climax. Early Christians, of course, expected the return of Christ in their lifetime. Paul speaks his sentiments, and theirs, when he later writes, "The Lord is at hand" (4:5; cf. 3:20). This provides the overarching perspective in which the prayer is cast. Paul sees the work of God begun within the Philippian church as reaching its fulfillment "at the day of Jesus Christ" (verse 6). In turn, it is his hope that they may be found "pure and blameless" at the day of Christ (verse 10). In both instances, Paul is insisting that they adopt the right perspective on the future, realizing first that any Christian understanding of the future must be defined with respect to Christ. It is no longer the "Day of the Lord" in the Old Testament sense, that is, one in which Yahweh would vindicate the cause of Israel. Rather, it is a future radically redefined by the Christ-event. Basic to this Christian understanding of the future is the realization that it is not fully realized yet. In fact, it is conceivable that some in the Philippian church, or perhaps outside opponents, had already laid claim to the future coming of Christ. One plausible reconstruction of the situation behind chapter 3 is that Paul is combating an overrealized eschatology by insisting that resurrection is still a future attainment. If so, his opening prayer reaffirms his insistence that our task is to live with an eye to the future, not as if we had already laid claim on it.

It is precisely this conviction that we have not yet realized fully the potential for Christian existence that prompts his prayer in their behalf toward the end of our passage. First, he prays that their love for one another will continue to increase (verse 9; cf. I Thess. 3:12). Later passages in the letter suggest that the Philippians still had something to learn about harmonious fellowship (2:1-13; 4:2-3). Second, he prays that their capacity for mutual commitment to one another will be reinforced "with knowledge and all discernment" (verse 9). His hope is that they would never stop improving their knowledge and deepening their perception (cf. verse 9, JB; cf. Rom. 15:14; Col. 1:9; Philem. 6). Third, he prays that a fellowship of love refined with discerning knowledge will give them the capacity to "approve what is excellent" (verse 10), or enable them "always [to] recognize what is best" (JB), which is "the gift of true discrimination" (NEB). The fellowship he envisions is both loving and discerning, informed by both the heart and the head. It is not insensitive but neither is it naïve. It is only through such tough-mindedness that they will emerge before the Last Day "pure and blameless." Fourth, he is convinced that out of such fellowship will spring "the fruits of righteousness which come through Jesus Christ" (verse 11; cf. Heb. 12:11; James 3:18; also Prov. 3:9; 11:30; Gal. 5:22).

Luke 3:1-6

On this second Sunday of Advent, all four writers of the Scripture texts look to the Day of the Lord, each having in mind an advent of God. Their understandings of the coming of the Lord differ but they are of one mind in the conviction that there is no advent without preparation. In that faith, the psalmist prays, the prophet looks to the coming of God's messenger who will purify Israel, the apostle ministers in anticipation, and the evangelist introduces John, the voice crying in the wilderness. John the son of Zechariah who prepares the way for Jesus is himself of unusual birth and a gift from God (Luke 1:5-25, 57-80), for Luke understands that not only the Lord's coming but also the preparation for that coming are the initiatives of a gracious God.

In beginning the Gospel with the ministry of John, Luke joins the other three evangelists. Even the Fourth Gospel, which opens with a hymn to the eternal Word (1:1-18), twice interrupts the hymn to comment about the Baptist (verses 6-8, 15) even though the narrative proper will begin with the witness of John's ministry (verse 19). However, the most elaborate introduction of John the Baptist is given by Luke who interweaves the accounts of the annunciations and of the births of John and Jesus. Having done that, Luke needs, at 3:1-6, only to identify him as the son of Zechariah (verse 2).

More important to Luke at this point is the placing in proper context the ministry of this obscure prophet from the hill country of Judea. Luke does so in two ways:

First, he provides the historical context. Multiple chronological indicators are listed (verses 1-2), the most precise of which is the fifteenth year of Tiberius Caesar, which would be sometime between A.D. 26 and A.D. 28, depending on method of calculation. The others in the list are political and religious rulers of lesser rank but whose positions enabled them to have more direct influence upon the careers of John and Jesus. Although unusually elaborate here, this method of beginning a chronicle of events was not uncommon for the time, and, for Luke, was probably patterned after the introduction to the books of Old Testament prophets (Jer. 1:1-3; Ezek. 1:1-3; Hos. 1:1; Isa. 1:1). Such detail is in keeping with Luke's own announced intention, after careful investigation, of writing an orderly account (1:1-4). Of more importance, this setting of the story in the Gospel in the larger religious and political arena is congenial to and expressive of Luke's theology. On its way from Jerusalem to Rome, as Luke unfolds the account in Acts, the Gospel will not only encounter the poor, lame, halt, and blind, but also the synagogue rulers, high priests, governors, kings, treasurers, city officials, leading women, philosophers of

Athens, captains of ships, imperial guards, and finally making its appeal to the emperor himself.

The second context Luke provides is that of salvation history, the tradition of God's dealing with the covenant community. John's ministry is the fulfillment of prophecy. Luke omits Mark's insertion of Malachi 3:1 into the Isaiah passage (Mark 1:2), reserving it until later (7:27), but he extends the quotation from Isaiah beyond Mark's use of only one verse (40:3). By citing Isaiah 40:3-5 Luke is able not only to testify to the universality of the gospel ("all flesh shall see the salvation of God"), but also to point out that God's embrace of all nations has been in the tradition all along.

After the manner of earlier prophetic calls, "the word of God came to John" (verse 2). In all the region about the Jordan John preached what Luke was soon to designate "the Gospel" (3:18). For this evangelist, the gospel is the gift of repentance and the forgiveness of sins, to Israel and to all nations (24:47). John's greatness lay in his making that announcement which was to be heard around the world.

Our Gospel for today begins, then, with a list of names and titles—how preachers hate lists!—but does it matter? Perhaps Luke was a history buff, but is it important to anyone else? The answer is yes. Luke, by setting the preparation for the advent of Jesus Christ in the context of world history and the universal purpose of God, says that the gospel belongs to all people. The gospel is not the church's possession to be subsequently carried to others. The gospel is for the world before it is ever uttered, by John, by Jesus, or by the church. This is God's gift to God's creation.

Third Sunday of Advent

Zephaniah 3:14-20; Isaiah 12:2-6; Philippians 4:4-9;
Luke 3:7-18

Preparation for Christmas continues in the readings for the day with a dominant mood of joyful expectation. Like the Old Testament lection for last week, Zephaniah 3:14-20 pictures a joyful Jerusalem, one that sees salvation on the horizon because God is in her midst. The responsorial psalm consists of songs of thanksgiving for Zion's deliverance. In the epistolary text Paul calls for his readers to rejoice in the Lord, who is at hand. The apocalyptic dimensions of the Lord's Advent are stressed in the Gospel as it summarizes the preaching of John the Baptist, concluding with the note that he "preached good news to the people" (Luke 3:18).

Zephaniah 3:14-20

According to the first verse of the book, Zephaniah was active during the reign of Josiah of Judah, that is, 640-609 B.C. It was the era of Assyrian hegemony over the small states in Syria and Palestine, including Judah, and was also the time of Josiah's revolt against Assyrian control and his reformation of religious practices (II Kings 22–23). The reform, generally associated with the Book of Deuteronomy, opposed pagan influence in Judah's religion and included the centralization of all worship in Jerusalem. Most of the Book of Zephaniah contains indictments of corrupt religious practices and announcements of judgment, even against the city of Jerusalem (3:1-13).

Our reading for the day thus stands in sharp contrast to most of the book in which it is located. Its message, style, and apparent historical situation are different. The concluding verse, for example, appears to assume that the people of God are scattered, are away from Jerusalem, and are now about to return. Consequently, this section, Zephaniah 3:14-20 probably was added to the book, either during the Babylonian Exile or the postexilic period. The community of faith that supplemented the book did not deny the validity of the previous announcements of disaster, but to the contrary they affirmed that Zephaniah was right. Yahweh had indeed punished the people, but now he is about to redeem them. Forgiveness follows judgment; celebration of salvation comes after separation and suffering.

Broadly speaking, the passage consists of two major parts of unequal length. The first part (verse 14) is a series of imperatives addressed to Jerusalem and calls for the Holy City to rejoice. The remainder of the passage is the second part (verses 15-20), which gives reasons for the celebration. A speaker in the prophetic mode first assures the addressee—Jerusalem and its inhabitants—concerning the past and the present: the Lord has removed the judgments, cast out her enemies, and is present with her, even joining the celebration and renewing his love for her (verses 15-17). The reasons for celebration continue as the speaker quotes the words of Yahweh (verses 18-20). These are promises concerning the future. In addition to reiterating some of the themes already introduced, the promises affirm that Yahweh will put an end to oppression, save the lame and the outcast, restore the people to their homeland, and restore both their reputation and their fortunes.

Several expressions and themes call for special comment. The translations "daughter of Zion" and "daughter of Jerusalem" (verse 14, RSV) are perhaps misleading. "Daughter Zion" or "Miss Zion" would more accurately convey the sense of the original, namely, the personification of the city as a young woman. The language in verse 15 echoes that of the Psalms of the enthronement of Yahweh as king (e.g., Ps. 47; 24:7-10; 68; 93; 97).

This text is also the last of the Old Testament readings for the Easter Vigil, on which occasion its joyful exuberance—both in mood and contents—appropriately anticipates the celebration of Easter. It is equally appropriate during Advent as the church looks to the birth of its Lord. Furthermore, the dual use of the passage stresses that the links between Christmas and Easter are eschatological. Both the birth and the resurrection of Jesus herald the coming of the messianic age, the establishment of the reign of God. The simple reading of this passage during Advent can contribute to the establishment of the mood and atmosphere of celebration called for by the occasion. But there is more. The church would do well to respond to these calls to Jerusalem, and for the reasons given: God reigns and will reign fully. The light of that future reign already begins to shine on our time and on our places. Because such a future is assured our lives can be lived as the celebration of hope.

Isaiah 12:2-6

The responsorial psalm is among that large number of hymns and other Old Testament cultic songs found outside the Psalms. One finds such songs frequently not only in the narrative books (e.g., Exod. 15:1-18, 21) but in the prophetic books as well (e.g., Amos 4:13; 5:8-9; 9:5-6). This fact, which should not be surprising, is due mainly to two factors. First, the authors of the books or the prophets would have been so steeped in the language of worship that they would have used such poetry where appropriate. Second, as the books subsequently were read in the context of worship psalms would have been added, as one finds in a modern publication of the lectionary texts with all the readings for the particular days printed in the order of their use.

The location of Isaiah 12 within the book is by no means accidental. Broadly speaking, it concludes the first major section of the work, chapters 1–12. For the most part the prophetic addresses and reports in this collection stem from the early period of the prophet's activity. Isaiah 13:1 clearly signals a new block of material, mainly oracles against foreign nations, different in terms of both form and content from the section concluded by Isaiah 12. More important for our understanding of the reading for the day is the fact that it directly follows a collection of prophecies concerning the Lord's saving acts for Jerusalem and Judah, acts that focus upon the descendants of David. These materials include 9:1-7 and 11:1-9, as well as 11:10-16, all of which herald the new age of peace and justice under "the shoot from the stump of Jesse" (11:1).

It is very unlikely that the prophet Isaiah wrote chapter 12. It was added as the sayings of the prophet were being collected and saved as a book. The chapter serves as a fitting response on the part of the community of faith to the reading of the promises of salvation. It is even possible that the juxtaposition of the hymn of thanksgiving with the word of God through the prophet reflects liturgical practice in the second temple, during the postexilic period.

Although the lection begins with verse 2, all of chapter 12 should be interpreted as a whole. It is not obvious whether the chapter contains a single song or two brief ones, along with liturgical instructions for their use. In any case, the chapter contains two distinct parts, verses 1-3 and 4-6. (Verse 3 is to be taken with what precedes, not—as the RSV divisions suggest—with what follows.) Each of the parts begins with the instructions, "You will say in that day." While it is not clear in English translation, the lines are different. In the original, verse 1*a* is second person singular and verse 4*a* is second person plural. Both are calls to give thanks, in verse 1 to an individual and in verse 4 to the community. The first section, then is a thanksgiving song of an individual, and the second is a communal hymn of thanksgiving and praise. As indicated in verse 1, the background of songs of thanksgiving is deliverance from trouble and the celebration of that deliverance.

The patterns and motifs of the chapter are familiar from the Psalter. Expressions of thanksgiving, trust, or praise are followed by their reasons, introduced by "for" (verses 1, 2, 5, 6). Confidence is expressed in the Lord as the individual's strength, song, and salvation (verse 2, using the language of the song of Moses, Exod. 15:2). Songs of thanksgiving are prayers, in which one calls to the Lord (verse 4). One sings for joy because the Holy One of Israel is both great and is among the worshipers (verse 6).

Three of the chapter's motifs call for particular attention in the Season of Advent. First, there is the emphasis upon the future and the hope for divine intervention in human events. The introductory phrases, "in that day" (verses 1, 4), make the songs of thanksgiving into promises: there will come a time when the people of God will experience salvation and will sing. Moreover, because the coming of that day is assured, even the present can be a time of joy. Second, because of its reference to Zion, the city of David, and its location in relation to chapter 11, the hope expressed here concerns the messianic age. Finally, though it is "the inhabitant of Zion" who sings for joy (verse 6), the message of hope is by no means for a single city or a small circle. Giving thanks to the Lord means making "known his deeds among the nations" (verse 4), proclaiming his name "in all the earth" (verse 5). Zion is the center, but when God is in its midst, the good news cannot be contained but must reach out to all the world.

Philippians 4:4-9

"Rejoice in the Lord always; again I will say, Rejoice!" These opening words from today's epistolary lection capture the essential mood of joy that characterizes the Third Sunday of Advent. This joyous note is reflected in the traditional designation of this day as "Gaudete Sunday," derived from the Latin "gaudete," the term for "rejoice" used in the Vulgate rendering of verse 4. The use of rose-colored vestments, or of a rose-colored candle in the Advent wreath, in connection with Advent 3 symbolizes the shift from penance to joy that occurs as we move toward the celebration of Christmas. We also find this theme of joy expressed in various liturgical texts used for this Sunday. For example, joy is the fundamental note struck in the words spoken in connection with the lighting of the third candle of the Advent wreath: "We light this candle as a symbol of joy. May the joyful promise of your presence, O God, make us rejoice in our hope of salvation. O come, O come Emmanuel!" A similar note is struck in the O Antiphon for Advent 3: "O come, thou Day-spring from on high; And cheer us by thy drawing nigh; Disperse the gloomy clouds of night; And death's dark shadow put to

35

flight." Cf. Don E. Saliers, *From Hope to Joy* (Nashville: Abingdon Press, 1984), pp. 52-53.

But what qualifies this reading as an Advent passage is Paul's declaration: "The Lord is at hand" (verse 5). The fundamental exegetical problem here with which the homilist will have to struggle is whether the statement is temporal or spatial. Ordinarily, it is understood eschatologically, and thus taken to mean, "The Lord is coming soon." This sense would conform to Paul's earlier remarks about "the day of Christ" (1:6, 10) and his eagerly awaiting the coming Savior (3:20-21), as well as other frequent New Testament references to an imminent Parousia (Rom. 13:12; I Cor. 16:22; Heb. 10:37 [Hab. 2:3]; James 5:8; I Pet. 4:7; Rev. 22:20). The language, however, is reminiscent of Psalm 145:18, "The Lord is near to all who call upon him, to all who call upon him in truth" (cf. also Ps. 119:151). If Paul is echoing the psalmist's sentiment, he may simply be reassuring the Philippians in the same sense: the Lord is always close by, especially to those who call upon him in anxious distress. What is striking is that, like the psalmist, Paul links his reassurance of the proximity of the Lord to an injunction to prayer. A similar connection is seen in Psalm 119:137-152, where the psalmist finds hope in being delivered from his enemies because the Lord is nearer to him than his enemies can ever get.

Given the prominence of the eschatological motif in Philippians, and in early Christian thought generally, a strong case can be made for the eschatological sense here. It may be, however, that Paul affirms the Lord's nearness in both senses. He may be combining the psalmist's reassurance of the Lord's existential nearness with early Christian expectation of the Lord's imminent return. If the eschatological sense is in view here, what is especially striking is the type of response Paul calls for. Rather than facing the future with gloom and despair, or even with penitence, we are called to rejoice at the prospect of the Lord's coming. These are words worth hearing—and proclaiming—since preaching on the Lord's coming can easily degenerate to shouts and threats. To be sure, Advent encompasses both threat and promise, but not threat alone.

Today's passage is instructive for the reassuring way it calls us to face both the present and the future. With a series of straightforward imperatives, it calls us to rejoice (cf. 1:4; 2:18; I Thess. 5:16), be tolerant and forbearing (cf. Tit. 3:2; James 5:8-9; Wisd. of Sol. 2:19), not to be anxious (Matt. 6:25-34; Luke 12:22-32; I Pet. 5:7), to be thankful yet bold in supplicating God (I Thess. 5:17-18; Col. 4:2; also Rom. 12:12; Eph. 6:18; Acts 2:42; I Tim. 2:1), to fill our minds with noble thoughts (II Pet. 1:5-8), and to hold fast to the tradition as we have learned and seen it in its most faithful witnesses (3:17; I Cor. 4:16-17; 11:1; Gal. 4:12; I Tim. 1:16; 4:12; Tit. 2:7; Heb. 13:7; I Pet. 5:3). Twice we are assured that if we proceed with our Christian commitment in this fashion rather than being filled with fits of frenzy, we will experience the peace of God even though it surpasses our capacity to understand (verses 7 and 9; cf. John 14:27; Col. 3:15; also Rom. 15:33; 16:20; I Cor. 14:33; II Cor. 13:11, I Thess. 5:23; II Thess. 3:16; Heb. 13:20).

"Rejoice! . . . The Lord is at hand!" In one breath Paul exclaims, "Rejoice!" and in another he affirms, "The Lord is at hand." Read in the context of Advent 3, these words remind us of that fundamentally optimistic strand that runs through the celebration of Advent: joy that the Lord has come, joyous expectation that the Lord will come.

Luke 3:7-18

Before we can celebrate Zephaniah's comforting word that God is "in your midst" and Paul's joyful announcement that "the Lord is at hand," we must first pass through the desert where an austere preacher of severe earnestness prepares the way for Christ's coming. John insists there is no other route to Advent. His message is a call to repentance with actions that demonstrate one's altered life. Since our Gospel this year is Luke, we can expect often to encounter one of his favorite words, "repentance." But repentance is also appropriate for Advent as we come clean and come empty to receive the gift of God.

Luke 3:7-18 continues the Gospel reading of last week and may be divided easily into three units. The first unit consists of verses 7-9, a general description of John's preaching.

These verses have no parallel in Mark, but are in Matthew 3:7-10 in almost precisely the same words except for the introductory descriptions of audiences. Apparently Matthew and Luke here follow a common source. Unlike Matthew, however, who addresses John's words to Pharisees and Sadducees, Luke says John's message was to the multitudes. In harsh and vivid terms, John portrays his listeners as fleeing from "the wrath to come" (Rom. 5:9; I Thess. 1:10), as snakes scurrying before a spreading fire. John's call is for a moment of truth, a call to abandon all devices used to maintain an illusion of innocence. "We have Abraham as our father," is neither a valid claim for exemption nor an acceptable excuse for failure. Life and deeds, not ancestry, count before the God whose ax is raised over the fruitless tree.

The second unit, verses 10-14, has no parallel in Matthew or Mark. These verses make it clear that John is not simply a loud evangelist whose screamings do little more than create fear and reduce a pathetic crowd to a pool of guilt. Three groups, the crowds, the tax collectors, and the soldiers, ask in turn, "What shall we do?" This, says Luke, is the same question asked by the crowds at Pentecost in response to Peter's preaching (Acts 2:37). The answers John gave to the seekers address the inequities and injustices of that society: food and clothing are to be shared with those who have none; taxes are not to be based on the insatiable greed of the powerful; and the military must stop victimizing the public by threat, intimidation, and blackmail. Just as Luke concluded the apocalyptic discourse of Jesus with a strong admonition (21:34-36), so here he makes it clear that a religion void of moral and ethical earnestness is exactly that, void.

The third unit, verses 15-18, has a briefer parallel in Mark 1:7-8, but again is closer to Matthew 3:11-12. However, only Luke introduces the question which, he said, was in the hearts of many, Is John the Christ? It is a concern that all the Gospel writers feel obliged to address at some point, but none more elaborately than Luke (1:5-80; 3:15-18; 9:18-22; Acts 18:24-28; 19:1-7) nor more directly than John (1:19-28; 1:29-37; 3:22-30; 5:33-36). Luke's response to the question here is twofold: Christ is mightier, before whom John is but an unworthy menial house servant, and their baptisms are of very different natures and purposes. John's baptism in water is a purging in that it is a baptism of repentance and forgiveness, but the one to come will baptize with the Holy Spirit and with fire (verse 16). Mark has only "with the Holy Spirit" and clearly has in mind the gift of the Holy Spirit which was the hallmark of early Christianity. Luke also understood the gift of the Holy Spirit as an identifying mark of the church (24:49; Acts 1:8; 2:38; 10:47, and others) and not of the Baptist movement (Acts 18:24-28; 19:1-7). However, here "Spirit and fire" can also mean "wind and fire" which were not only symbols for the Holy Spirit (Acts 2:1-4) but for judgment as well. In fact, the present context seems to give this meaning to the baptism of wind and fire: winnowing is an act of the wind to separate wheat and chaff, and the fate of chaff is the fire (verses 17-18).

Even with this understanding, however, one should not get preoccupied with the burning of chaff. The primary purpose is to save the grain. The listeners knew this (and still do) and hence were in great expectation; the preacher understood this (and still does) and hence the message was called "good news" (verse 18).

Fourth Sunday of Advent

Micah 5:2-5a (5:1-4a); Psalm 80:1-7; Hebrews 10:5-10; Luke 1:39-55

On the last Sunday before Christmas our expectations are heightened especially by the scene in the Gospel lection, as the two pregnant women, Elizabeth and Mary, marvel at the meaning of the birth of Mary's child. The stage is being set for the fulfillment of the ancient promises as Elizabeth blesses Mary for believing that the promise would come true (Luke 1:45), and Mary affirms that God is remembering what he said "to our fathers, to Abraham and his posterity for ever" (Luke 1:55). In this context, the Old Testament reading supplies one of the details of that promise, that the one who will be ruler in Israel will come from Bethlehem. The Psalm, the community's cry to the "Shepherd of Israel" for help in time of trouble, may be understood on this occasion as the prayer to which the coming of Jesus is the response. Hebrews 10:5-10 then indicates the purpose of the Incarnation.

Micah 5:2-5*a* (5:1-4*a*)

The prophet Micah was active in the eighth century B.C., a contemporary of Isaiah of Jerusalem, Amos, and Hosea. He was a Judean whose theological perspective closely paralleled that of Isaiah in his belief in the dynasty of David as God's means of care for the people and in the city of Jerusalem as God's holy place. His message stressed judgment upon the people because of social injustice, especially in high places (see Mic. 3:9-12).

On the other hand, the message of the *Book* of Micah is more complicated: God will indeed judge the people and punish them with military defeat and exile, but later, as an act of grace, the Lord will bring them back and establish a reign of perpetual peace, with its center in Jerusalem and its leader a king in the line of David. The most vivid statement of that promise is Micah 4:1-5, which is virtually identical to Isaiah 2:2-5. This message with salvation as the last word is the result of the history of the book's use and growth through the centuries after the time of the original prophet. Consequently, the book as we have it is the product of generations who heard the word of God in ever new circumstances.

It is not certain whether our reading for the day comes from the time of Micah or later. Because of the reference to the Assyrians in verses 5-6 one must keep open the possibility that the unit as a whole is from the eighth century. In that case the promise would be the prophetic response to the Assyrian invasions of Israel and Judah and the siege of Jerusalem. On the other hand, the announcement of coming salvation may stem from a time when there was little room for hope, the postexilic period in Judah. The slightly veiled promise of a Davidic ruler would then have been heard by people who no longer had their own king but lived under Persian rule.

Micah 5:2-5*a* (verses 1-4*a* in Hebrew) are best understood as part of the immediate unit, verses 1-6. The lectionary doubtless means by verse 5*a* only the first line of the verse, although it is not even a complete sentence. The unit follows a pattern familiar in the surrounding sections of the book, moving from a description of the present trouble to an announcement of salvation. The present trouble is character-ized as a siege of Jerusalem and the abuse of its ruler (verse 1). Salvation is coming first (2-4) through a new ruler who will care for the people "in the strength of the Lord" so that their security is assured. Second (5-6) peace will be established when "seven shepherds, and eight princes of men" are raised up to deliver the land from the Assyrian threat.

The heart of the promise is the expectation of a new "ruler in Jerusalem" from Bethlehem. Though the promise certainly is messianic—that is, of an anointed leader—there is no explicit reference to the promise to the dynasty of David, as in II Samuel 7. However, the new ruler, like David, comes from

Bethlehem (I Sam. 17:12). As in the stories of the elevation of David, we hear of the irony that the one who will be "great to the ends of the earth" (verse 4) comes from the one who is so little among even the clans of Judah (verse 2). The divine destiny of the anticipated ruler is expressed in the phrase "whose origin is from of old, from ancient days" (verse 2). The reference to the birth of the ruler—"when she who is in travail has brought forth"—echoes Isaiah 7:14. But before this one can come the people must be given up and then return—probably an allusion to the Exile and the return from Babylon.

It is the role of the new ruler which most closely expresses both the Old Testament understanding of the function of the Davidic kings and the New Testament hope at the time of the birth of Jesus. The one who comes is sent by God, rules in the Lord's strength, and fulfills God's purpose. That purpose is the care and feeding of the flock and the establishment of peace to the ends of the earth. Just as the kings were seen as God's means of care for the people, so Matthew 2:6 can apply this passage to the birth of Jesus.

Psalm 80:1-7

Psalm 80 is a community lament composed for use when the people had suffered humiliation, probably at the hands of a foreign enemy. As such, it is a request for revival, renewal, restoration.

In the psalm, two images are used for the Divine and simultaneously two images for the people. In verses 1-2, God is depicted as shepherd; in verses 8-18 as a vine grower. Israel is thus his sheep and his vineyard. The two professions, shepherding and viticulturist, require of the shepherd and vineyard keeper great concern and tender care. The shepherd must direct his flock, look for its pasture, defend it from its predators, care for its injured and sick members, insure the succor and nurture of its young, and search for and return its wayward members. The vineyard keeper must prune his vines in season, fertilize his plants, weed his fields, and protect his crops from marauders and plunderers.

This psalm accuses God of failure on both accounts. As a shepherd he has not cared for his sheep. As a vineyard keeper he has functioned foolishly so that the vineyard is left without protection, to be used as public property and a haven for wild beasts. The appeal to God throughout the psalm requests a favorable response in which the troubled people would be redeemed and God would show himself a concerned shepherd and a compotent viticulturist. That is, the psalm is a supplication for a return to normal in the divine-Israel relationship.

Two expressions in verses 1-7 need elucidation for the average reader. The description of God as "Thou who art enthroned upon the cherubim" (verse 1) draws upon the imagery of early Israelite warfare. The ark was originally conceived as a movable throne upon with the Deity sat. The presence of the ark in battle represented the presence of the Divine. The cherubim were mythological flying guardian figures which were artistically represented on the ark (for this view of the ark, see the story in I Sam. 4). (Another interpretation of the ark, which had probably disappeared before much of the Old Testament was written, saw it as a container for the law; see Deut. 10:1-5.) The reference to Yahweh as the one enthroned on the cherubim was a way of recalling the times of bygone warfare and better days and a means of reminding the Deity of his militancy, now neglected. "To let the face shine" was a metaphorical way of saying "to show favor" or "to be favorably deposed toward." So the refrain in verses 3, 7, and 19 contains parallel requests: "restore us" and "let thy face shine."

How may this psalm be related to Advent? First of all, its sentiments lie on the before, the pre-side of Advent. The people described their conditions as desperate: God is angry with their prayers (verse 4), tears are their constant companion (verse 5), and they are the butt of their enemies' jokes (verse 6). The personal, interpersonal, and divine-personal relationships are all askew. They had yet to take the road to Bethlehem. Second, they nonetheless look forward with pleas for redemption and restoration, and hope and expectation are the hallmarks of Advent.

Hebrews 10:5-10

Unlike the three previous epistolary readings which spoke of Christ's Second Coming, today's epistolary reading, with its opening phrase, "when Christ came into the world" (verse 5), shifts the emphasis to his first coming. The focus is not so much on his birth per se as it is on his coming into the world that is seen as a single event. The phrase has a Johannine ring to it (cf. John 1:9; 6:14; 11:27; 12:46; 16:28; 18:37).

Our passage is striking for the way in which the words of Psalm 40:6-8 are attributed to Christ himself. They are introduced here as words that "he said." In what sense he said them remains unclear. It is possible that during his ministry Jesus quoted these words from the psalmist and interpreted his own mission in light of them. Yet nowhere in the Gospel tradition do we find Jesus quoting Psalm 40, even though he does share the prophetic conviction expressed in our passage that genuine obedience of the heart is more valuable than offering sacrifices (Matt. 9:13; 12:7; cf. I Sam. 15:22; Isa. 1:11; Hos. 6:6; Amos 5:21-24; Ps. 50:7-11; 51:16-17; Prov. 15:8). The phrase, "I have come to do thy will, O God" (verse 7), is strongly reminiscent of the Gospel of John (4:34; 5:30; 6:38-39), but it also reminds us of Jesus' words in Gethsemane (Mark 14:36 and parallels).

In at least two senses, then, does Psalm 40:6-8 "speak for" Christ. First, it expresses Christ's conviction that a life obedient to the will of God is fundamentally more pleasing to God than offering various types of sacrificial offerings. Second, it defines the purpose of Christ's coming specifically in terms of doing the will of God.

An additional connection between Psalm 40 and the work of Christ, as understood by the author of Hebrews, is found in the phrase "a body hast thou prepared for me" (verse 5). This is the wording found in the Greek version of Psalm 40. The Hebrew text reads instead, "thou hast given me an open ear," or literally "ears thou hast dug for me." In the context, the sense of the latter is clear. God has given the psalmist open ears through which to hear, and consequently do, the will of God, and this God prefers to the offering of sacrifices.

In the Greek version, however, the meaning shifts slightly, probably by extending one part of the body to the whole. The sense is still clear: "In contrast to sacrificial offerings, you have given me a body, that is, my whole life, to offer as a sacrifice." Obviously, the Greek version lent itself to Christian interpretation, given the author's emphasis on the "offering of the body of Jesus Christ once for all" (verse 10; also 7:27). For his purposes, our author is able to use Psalm 40 to show that the single offering of the body of Jesus far surpasses the multiple offerings of animal sacrifices that were offered "according to the law" (verse 8). More important, it provides Scriptural basis for showing that a single sacrifice of a body duly prepared by God and thoroughly committed to doing God's will represents the truest fulfillment of God's original intention. Thus, God "abolishes the first in order to establish the second" (verse 9).

In its liturgical setting, today's epistolary passage is significant not only because of its explicit use of incarnational language, but because it links the Incarnation with the atoning death of Christ. If the words of the Magnificat in today's Gospel reading focus our attention on Christ's birth, the epistolary reading carries us forward to Christ's death. As we all know, we are scarcely able to celebrate one moment in the life of Christ in isolation from the rest of his life. We know how the story ends. And so did the Gospel writers. After all, they wrote the Gospels from the Passion backward. It was the ending that enabled them to make sense of the beginning. As our text states, it was the atoning death of Christ through which we were sanctified (verse 10; cf. 10:14, 29; 13:12; also I Thess. 4:3; Eph. 5:2). And yet, his death provides us the vantage point from which to view the work of Christ in both directions—backward to his birth and forward to his coming again. In this respect, our text extends our reflections to include the whole sweep of the Paschal Mystery. (Cf. *From Ashes to Fire* [Nashville: Abingdon Press, 1979], pp. 11-27.)

A final word about the limits of the passage. Beginning the passage with the word "consequently" (verse 5, RSV), may seem too abrupt to some. One solution is that adopted for Annunciation (March 25), where the same epistolary reading is used: start the reading with verse 4, which helps establish the context and provide a slightly smoother opening.

Luke 1:39-55

If there are Sundays when the church senses that the Scripture readings are distant from one another, today is not one of them. Micah 5 anticipates the birth of a great ruler in the small village of Bethlehem; Hebrews 10 explores the meaning of Christ coming into the world; and Luke 1 helps us, through Mary's joy and excitement, to stand expectantly at hope's window. Even today's Psalm (80), resonates with Bethlehem, David, and the Christ in its address to God as shepherd of Israel.

If there are Sundays when the church senses the Scripture readings are distant from the life and mood of the congregation, today is not one of them. As music and song fill the Advent Season, so has Luke chosen to sing rather than explain or prove or exhort our Gospel lection. That the story has been cast as song reminds us of the importance of the nonsemantic quality of language and of the affective force of its form.

Luke 1–2, while of a piece in images and themes with the remainder of the Gospel, has its own structure and focus. The two largest blocks of material announce the promised births of John and Jesus (1:5-38) and narrate the birth stories themselves (1:57–2:20). These two large units are joined by the moving account of the mother of John being visited by the mother of Jesus (1:39-56). This small story of Mary's visit to the Judean hill country home of Elizabeth states in its own way the twin themes of the narratives surrounding it: prenatal and natal signs point to the greatness of both John and Jesus, but the signs are equally clear that Jesus is the greater of the two.

Our Gospel lection, Luke 1:39-55, consists of two parts: the first being Elizabeth's song with a brief narrative introduction (verses 39-45) and the second, Mary's song, commonly called the "Magnificat," so named because Magnificat is the first word of the song in the Vulgate (verses 46-55). The narrative introduction to Elizabeth's song (verses 39-41) locates the scene in an unnamed city in the Judean hills, tells of Mary greeting her kinswoman (verse 36) Elizabeth, and of the babe in Elizabeth's womb leaping at the sound of the voice of Mary, "mother of my Lord" (verse 43). Luke is here undoubtedly recalling both a historical reference and a theological point. The historical reference is to Rebecca in whose womb Esau and Jacob struggled, the message being, as in Elizabeth's case, "the older shall serve the younger" (Gen. 25:21-23). The theological point is that prenatal activity, preceding as it does all works or merit, accents the sovereign will and purpose of God. The content of Elizabeth's song is a eulogizing of Mary, pronouncing upon her the blessing of God. This blessing of Mary is not mere sentiment or a burst of emotion as Luke later records from "a woman in the crowd" (11:27-28). Here Elizabeth is inspired by the Holy Spirit and blesses Mary on two grounds: she has been chosen to be the mother of the Lord and she believed and accepted the word spoken to her from God (verses 26-38).

The second part of our lection, Mary's song, praises God for the favor bestowed upon a handmaiden of low estate (verses 46-50), and then proclaims the triumph of God's purposes for all people everywhere (verses 51-55). While the Magnificat is a mosaic of biblical texts, it draws primarily upon Hannah's song in I Samuel 2:1-10. The preacher would do well to read again that moving story of God's gift of Samuel to Hannah and Hannah's gift of Samuel to God. In movement, Mary's song makes an easy transition from the remarkable act of God to and through Mary to the remarkable act of God by which all the oppressed, poor, and hungry of the world will be blessed. This triumph of God's favor is presented in the form of an eschatological reversal in which the powerful and rich will exchange places with the powerless and poor. And so confident is the singer's faith that God's justice and grace will prevail that the expression of hope is cast in the past tense. Mary sings as though what *shall* be is already true. In this trust, God's servants continue to sing.

Christmas, First Proper (Christmas Eve/Day)

Isaiah 9:2-7; Psalm 96; Titus 2:11-14; Luke 2:1-20

Now the day has arrived, the one long-expected both in ancient times and in our own. And for its celebration communities of faith over the ages have bequeathed to us these texts to hear, to ponder, and to sing. The Gospel lection tells the story of the birth of Jesus, set in real history and yet full of transcendent meaning. The reading from Isaiah expresses the promise that this birth fulfills, and the responsorial psalm gives us a new song to sing, a song full of praise to the Lord who reigns. The epistolary text draws our attention to the purpose of this birth, both in God's design and in our own lives.

Isaiah 9:2-7

If there were any doubt that ancient texts could legitimately have diverse meanings, texts such as Isaiah 9:2-7 should lay those doubts to rest. In the eighth century B.C. the words were uttered about a specific king in Judah, subsequently applied to other kings, and even later to an expected Messiah. The early church heard that promise and saw it fulfilled in Jesus. Christians at worship will hear the words as proclamation of the birth of Jesus. All that is as it should be, for this ancient song helps us understand the meaning of Christmas. One of our struggles as preachers faced with such texts is to proclaim the Christian meaning without thereby either ignoring or obscuring the ancient Israelite contribution itself.

In terms of its literary context, Isaiah 9:2-7 is the final unit of a collection of traditions that began in Isaiah 6:1. Most of the traditions are reports of prophetic activity, many speak of symbolic actions such as births and the names of children, and most concern the events during and immediately following the Syro-Ephramitic war of about 734 B.C. (see Isa. 7:1-2; II Kings 16:5-9). Most important here is the historical and geographical notation in Isaiah 9:1, which interprets our text as a promise of salvation concerning a particular time and place.

Although our reading comes from a prophet and in some respects is like a prophetic announcement, its basic structure more closely resembles a hymn of thanksgiving. It is a lyric poem consisting of two major parts: verses 2-3 give a poetic account of release and celebration, and verses 4-7 present the three reasons for that celebration, each introduced by "for." The reasons for celebration are the release from an oppressor (verse 4), the destruction of the gear of battle (verse 5), and the birth of a child (verses 6-7). Although the reasons are remarkable and unusual, this pattern is common in songs of thanksgiving (see Pss. 18:5-20; 32:3-5). Moreover, as in such songs, at least some of the words (verses 3-4) are in the form of prayer, addressed directly *to* God, and the "rejoicing" is a cultic celebration.

One should not miss the fact that most of the verbs in the song are either past or present tense; that is, most of the events are seen either to have happened already or they are happening even as the prophet sings. The people "have seen" the great light, God has multiplied the nation and increased its joy, and broken the rod of the oppressor. And most dramatically: "A child is born . . . a son is given." It is the events that have occurred and are occurring that give rise to the future promises that the government will be on the shoulders of this child, and that justice and righteousness will reign forever.

In terms of its meaning and function in the original historical context, two major alternatives have presented themselves. On the one hand, many commentators have seen here a song for the coronation of a new king, most likely Hezekiah, or celebration of the anniversary of his enthronement. In this view the royal names of verse 6 are seen as parallels to the "great names" or throne names given the Egyptian pharaoh when he ascended to the throne. The

49

expressions in verse 6*a*, "to us a child is born, to us a son is given," are taken as the adoption formula in the enthronement ritual, as in Psalms 2 and 89. On the other hand, it is more likely that the song originated to celebrate the birth of a new crown prince in Jerusalem. The words of verse 5*a* are spoken by the people—not by Yahweh—as a birth announcement (see Jer. 20:15; Job 3:3). In short, the birth and the celebration of it are seen by the prophet as signs of salvation, that the Lord will fulfill the ancient promises.

So that is a central theme for the preacher of this text: the birth and its celebration as signs of hope. But there are other important matters as well. This passage speaks above all of the nature of the Messiah's reign as one of perpetual peace, founded on justice and righteousness, one that will bring an end to the dark, harsh, loud, and bloody martial alternative (verses 2-5). In Isaiah's view, God's will for justice, righteousness, and peace is made flesh in the weakest of human creatures, a little baby.

Psalm 96

The three psalms selected for the Christmas propers all reflect common themes—the triumph and reign of God as king and judge. These like other so-called enthronement psalms (such as 47, 93, and 99) appear to have been originally used in the full festival that coincided with the beginning of the new agricultural year and thus with the New Year season. Part of the festival seems to have emphasized God's re-creation of the world and the reestablishment of world order. Such themes are appropriate for Christmas as the time when God began the reestablishment of his rule.

Psalm 96 falls in two halves each with introductory section (verses 1-3, 7-9) and main body (4-6, 10-13). This does not suggest, however, that the work is made up of two independent compositions; it simply suggests the artistry of the poet. The two introits call upon the whole earth and all its people to acknowledge and praise God.

The first main section (verses 4-6) praises the incomparability of Yahweh, who stands without peer in the universe. Of all the gods, only Yahweh is to be feared. Other gods are merely idols but Yahweh is the creator of the heavens. (On the gods of other nations and a parody on idols, see Isa. 40:18-20; 44:9-22.) His creatorship and the world as his creation testify to the fact that Yahweh, the God of Israel, is the only divine power with which people must deal.

Verse 10a seems to contain a shout of the fall festival which is best translated, "Yahweh has become king" (the RSV reads "the lord reigns"). As such, it is the proclamation of the gospel, the Good News, that the universe is and remains under divine control.

Divine dominion and divine judgment are depicted as the consequence of God's rule (in verse 10b-13). The dominion is affirmed in the assertion that the world is established and shall never be moved. Such an affirmation gives expression to the belief that the world has a security about it and that one can dwell and live in the world in confidence. Stability and with it predictability are implied by the stress on the establishment and immovability of the world and existence.

Judgment is, however, seen as an aspect of the Divine's relationship to the world. Like the kings in the ancient oriental world, so also Yahweh was viewed as a supreme judge. In this psalm, judgment is seen as a source of and reason for joy. The rationale for this is to be found in what is said about divine judgment. God is said to judge with equity (verse 10c), with righteousness (verse 13a), and with his truth (verse 13b). Such divine judgment may be seen as standing over against or far surpassing human judgment with its inequities, favoritisms, and partial truth.

The whole of the natural order—that is, all the established creation—rejoice and greet the coming of the king in judgment—the heavens, the earth, the sea, the field (cultivated land), the forest (the uncultivated land).

In the coming of God, the world can rejoice and in his judgment find joy. The appropriate response is to bring an offering—make a gift—and to worship (verses 8-9).

Titus 2:11-14

If Christmas is a time for the celebration of faith, it is also a time for the affirmation of faith. This epistolary text, traditionally read at Christmas, presents us with such a bold affirmation of faith. It begins with the emphatic declaration: "For the grace of God has appeared for the salvation of all men" (verse 11). The reference point is a definite moment in the past, as seen in the use of the aorist tense ("appeared"). The chief exegetical question is whether the birth and nativity of Christ are the locus of the "appearing" or whether his whole life is telescoped into a single event. Even if it is the latter, when read in the context of a Christmas service these words will naturally remind us of the very dawn of the grace of God as it was seen and experienced in the birth of Christ.

Wrapped in this bold faith-claim is one of the central elements of the Christmas faith that celebrates divine grace manifested in human form: God's grace openly revealed. Although this passage does not explicitly link the manifestation of God's grace with the person of Jesus, it is a central Christian conviction to do so. Almost invariably New Testament writers see Jesus Christ as the locus of God's grace (cf. John 1:14-17; I Cor. 1:4; II Tim. 1:9-10). By participating in time and history, Christ entered the realm of the visible and knowable, as suggested by the word "appearing," which has the connotation of "showing forth." It was an event in the public domain, out in the open for all to witness. Another way of stressing this is in terms of "the revelation of the mystery which was kept secret for long ages but is now disclosed" (Rom. 16:25).

Since this text is read alongside Luke's account of the birth of Jesus, it is worth noting that Luke's birth and infancy narrative dramatically highlight God's revelation in Christ as a publicly displayed event. Numerous characters cross the stage of Luke's account: Elizabeth and Zechariah, Mary and Joseph, angels named and unnamed, shepherds, Anna and Simeon, teachers in the temple. In various ways, they all witness the "appearance of God's grace." His account is punctuated with announcements, revelations, prayers, songs, and prophecies—all serving as arrows pointing to this central event. His narrative is so carefully and thoughtfully constructed that both our audial and visual senses are activated. We would have to be both deaf and blind not to see God's grace appearing before us.

There is another central feature of the opening words of today's text: salvation for everyone (cf. I Tim. 2:4; 4:10). This, too, echoes Luke's birth and infancy story, which speaks frequently of salvation promised by God and realized in Christ (Luke 1:47, 69, 71, 77; 2:11, 30). Luke's account also stresses from the very outset that God's salvation will be universal in scope, serving as "a light for revelation to the Gentiles, and for glory to thy people Israel" (2:32; cf. 3:6).

Both of these ideas—the revelation of God's grace and universal salvation—are captured especially well by the NEB rendering of verse 11: "For the grace of God has dawned upon the world with healing for all mankind." (Even greater universality would be achieved by rendering the last phrase as "for all humankind.") With the metaphor of "dawning," the NEB translators have opened up interesting possibilities for interpretation. It anticipates the later reference to the future appearing of the "glory [or splendor] of our great God and Savior Jesus Christ" (verse 13). One could interpret our passage as encompassing the whole sweep of salvation-history from the dawning of God's revelation in the Incarnation to its even more splendid manifestation radiated in the Second Coming. This imagery of light shining in darkness could be reinforced even further by examining crucial passages in Paul and John (cf. II Cor. 4:4-6; John 1:1-18). The Christian view of time and history envisioned in our passage runs not from dawn to dusk, but from dawn to even more brilliant splendor.

We have selected only two motifs from the passage that might be pursued homiletically or devotionally. Obviously, there is much more embedded in this unusually rich text. One of the most conspicuous strands in the text are the ethical demands required by the appearance of God's grace. Clearly, this text sees a direct link between the Incarnation and the moral life, which is etched in both negative and positive terms. Typical of the Pastoral Epistles, there is unabashed praise of "good deeds" (Tit. 3:8, 14; cf. Heb. 10:24; I Pet. 3:13). Also, as the text unfolds, it moves from Christ's first coming to his Second Coming, speaking of the latter as our "blessed hope" (verse 13). Here, again, we see the two central themes of Advent combined in a single text. Finally, the text speaks of the redemptive work of Christ "who gave himself for us" (cf. Matt. 20:28 and parallels; Rom. 3:26; II Cor. 5:15; Gal. 1:4; 2:20; Eph. 5:2, 25; I Tim. 2:6; I Pet. 1:18; also Ps. 130:8), and in doing so formed "for himself a people of his own" (Exod. 4:23; 19:5-6; Deut. 7:6; 14:2; 32:9; Ezek. 37:23).

Luke 2:1-20

The Christmas lections are the same each year, but this is no reason for the preacher to scurry about for something new or different as a pulpit offering. The texts for this day are rich enough for a lifetime of preaching without final closure as though nothing more need be said. Luke says that when the shepherds went to Bethlehem, their story created wondering and pondering (2:17-19). The preacher who lives between those two words has grasped the size of the message and will never lack for a word to say. More importantly, the use of the same texts each year reminds us of the importance of tradition in the Christian community. The church knows the Christmas story, and hearing it again confirms and identifies them as believers who are continually receiving and being shaped by the gift of God's Christ.

All the lections for today join strikingly different images in expressing the act of God's salvation. Isaiah places a newborn child on the royal throne of David; the psalmist offers a new song to God voiced by both nature and nations; the Epistle to Titus speaks both of Christ's having come and of his future coming; and Luke understands both secular and sacred events as serving the purposes of God. In his now familiar pattern of alternating stories about John the Baptist and Jesus, Luke follows the account of John's birth (1:57-58) and the inspired declaration of John's significance (1:59-80) with the account of Jesus' birth (2:1-7) and the angels' revelation of Jesus' meaning for "all the people" (2:8-20).

The record of Jesus' birth (verses 1-7) is straightforward, without hint of miracle or unusual incident. It is told as a historian would relate it, citing date, place, and circumstance. It answers the most natural question, How is it that

Jesus of *Nazareth* was born in Bethlehem, David's city? To say that Luke writes as a historian here is not to say that extrabiblical sources confirm his account. Luke began by placing these events in the days of King Herod (1:5) and now refers to a census at a time when Judea was under the rule of a Syrian governor. Archelaus, who ruled in Judea upon the death of his father Herod, was deposed in A.D. 6 and Judea was placed under Roman procurators and the land again considered by Rome as a part of Syria. Luke's chronology and the census referred to in 2:1-2 do not fit in the history to which we have other access. The commentaries argue the issues involved. The point beyond any argument, however, is Luke's conviction that governments, emperors, and laws serve the purposes of God even though those involved may not know it. In this he agrees with Isaiah 45:1. Caesar Augustus is an instrument of God's will. In Luke's theology, there does not have to be a miracle, a voice from heaven, or a supernatural event for God to be at work. God works miracles, to be sure, but God works without them, too.

Verses 8-20 provide the commentary upon the significance of Jesus' birth, an angel and a multitude of the heavenly host being the messengers. It was customary in the Roman Empire for poets and orators to declare the benefits of peace and prosperity attendant upon an emperor's birth. In that pattern the Good News of joy for everyone, the praise of God and the promise of peace on earth is here proclaimed upon the birth, not of an emperor, but of him called Savior, Christ, and Lord (verse 11). And not in palace halls but in the fields, to poor and unregarded shepherds, the news first comes. In fact, it is from the shepherds that Mary and Joseph hear of angels visitant and heavenly song. These two, busy with the chores of childbirth under most difficult circumstances, do not themselves experience heaven's visit, but hear of it from the shepherds. How unusual! But theirs is the baby, and that is enough. As a matter of fact, the sign granted to the startled shepherds is not the appearace of a heavenly choir, but the baby in the manger (verse 12). Without the Christ Child, there is no song, no reason for the heavenly host.

That shepherds figure so prominently in the story is not surprising. They belong not only in the record about the son of David who was himself called from the sheepfold to rule Israel (II Sam. 7:8), but also in Luke's guest list for the kingdom of God: the poor, the maimed, the blind, the lame (14:13, 21).

Christmas, Second Proper (Additional Lessons for Christmas Day)

Isaiah 62:6-7, 10-12; Psalm 97; Titus 3:4-7; Luke 2:8-20

All the texts for this occasion proclaim the unqualified good news that God reigns in graceful power. In the Old Testament reading the Lord announces Jerusalem's salvation, vindication, and redemption. The responsorial psalm, describing the awesome appearance of the Lord, is a hymn celebrating the kingship of God. As in the previous reading from Titus, the epistolary text points to God's purpose in the Incarnation, our justification by grace. The Gospel lection repeats the second part of the first reading for Christmas, concentrating attention on the response of the shepherds, the angels, and Mary to the birth itself.

Isaiah 62:6-7, 10-12

Our Old Testament reading is part of the Book of Isaiah (56–66) generally attributed to Third Isaiah. While individual prophets stand behind the literature in Isaiah 1–39 and 40–55, it is unlikely that such is the case with regard to 56–66. Rather, the chapters are sufficiently diverse to indicate that they come from a prophetic group or "school," active in the postexilic period (ca. 538–515 B.C.), that held Isaiah and Second Isaiah in the highest regard. The historical situation is thus the city of Jerusalem after the return from Exile, when Judah lived under the Persian Empire.

The identity of the various parties—speakers, addressees, persons mentioned—is not always clear. Who speaks in verses 6-7—God, the prophet, or someone else—and who is addressed? In view of the opening verses of the chapter and the fact that the Lord is mentioned in the third person, the speaker most likely is the prophet, calling upon other persons—perhaps other prophets—to be "watchmen" for the city. Likewise in verses 10-12 it is the prophet who calls for others to prepare the way, and who announces the Lord's good news of salvation. Most important of all, who are the "people" and the "peoples" of verse 10, Judeans returning from Exile, or the nations of the world? Most commentators see here only Judeans, but the minority view is probably the correct one: The prophet proclaims that God's "ensign" will be lifted over all the peoples of the earth, and they will—as in Isaiah 2:1-4—see Jerusalem as the center of the divine reign. That is then one of the central elements of this passage, the good news to all peoples.

While there is some doubt about the identity of the parties in verses 6-7, there is no question about their roles. The prophet fulfills the divine charge to set watchmen for the city. Watchmen, or "sentries," ordinarily look out for danger and warn the inhabitants of its approach. The imagery as applied to prophets is well-known from Ezekiel, for whom it is a matter of life and death to sound the warning (Ezek. 3:16-21; 33:7-9). But these sentries are different. They are to neither rest nor be silent, not in order to keep the city alert but, remarkably, to give God no rest. They are thus intercessors on behalf of the people, to, in effect, pray without ceasing until the Lord "establishes Jerusalem and makes it a praise in the earth."

Such an idea—of giving God no rest until the prayer is answered—may appear shocking to our modern ears, or at the very least not properly deferential. However, it is not at all unusual in the Old Testament, especially in songs of lament or complaint. In such prayers in the Psalter the individual or group in trouble may confess its sins or even its innocence (Ps. 17), imploring God to answer, to hear, to respond, to act. The worshipers in ancient Israel did not conceal even their anger from God.

In addition to the use of motifs from the Psalms of lament, there are other ritual or liturgical allusions in these verses. The imagery of a "highway" for the people (verse 10) has been taken over from Second Isaiah, for whom it meant the way through the desert from Babylon to Jerusalem. Here, however, it is an allusion to a procession from outside the city to the temple (compare "courts of my sanctuary," verse 9). Moreover, Zion, the site of the temple, is a focal point of the entire chapter.

The chapter, and with it a section that began in Isaiah 60:1, concludes on a powerful note. The prophet seems almost to have looked through older traditions with a concordance to find the right names to give the people when God comes to them. New names indicate new status, or standing before God. These people—either Judeans or all peoples, see above—shall be called "the holy people" (Exod. 19:6; Isa. 61:6), "the redeemed of the Lord" (Isa. 35:9-10), "sought out," and "not forsaken." Now the ones addressed by such titles know who they are.

Psalm 97

As in Psalm 96, the kingship of God and divine judgment are the focal concerns of this psalm. Like other enthronement psalms (see Ps. 93), this one opens with the affirmation, "Yahweh reigns," or perhaps better, "Yahweh has become king." It thus represents part of the autumn ritual in ancient Jerusalem when Yahweh's rule as king was annually celebrated.

The three stanzas into which the RSV divides the psalm can provide a means into the hymn. In the first stanza (verses 1-5), the coming of God as king is described. The metaphorical imagery used in the psalm has many parallels to other biblical texts. For example, its references to fire, smoke, and lightning recall the account of Yahweh's appearance on Mt. Sinai in Exodus 19:16-18 and Deuteronomy 4:11; 5:22. The usage of thunderstorm imagery is reminiscent of Psalm 29. The same type of imagery could also be used in ancient Israel when the prophets spoke of the coming day and visitation of God (see Joel 2:1-2; Zeph. 1:14-16).

The God who comes is one who dwells in clouds and darkness (verse 2). This presentation of the Deity as one who dwells in darkness (see I Kings 8:12) has given rise to speaking of the Deity as the *Deus Absconditus* (the Hidden God). This psalm, like Advent and Christ, proclaims the self-revelation of the hidden God. Just as clouds and darkness are associated with the Divine, so also are righteousness and justice. The one revealed is thus not a god capricious but one upon whom people can rely. As justice and righteousness are the foundation of his throne, so proper order and right conditions should be the product of his appearance. One could argue that the text implies that social transformation attends his coming. The focus, however, in verses 1-5 is a stress on the events occurring in the natural realm: fire destroying divine opponents, lightning causing the world to tremble, and mountains melting like wax. (All such descriptions were understood metaphorically; probably no ancient Hebrew really believed that mountains melted like wax!)

The second stanza (verses 6-9) speaks of the reordering of life or the reaction of humans to the coming of God as king. The negative consequence involves the submission of the gods and the shame of those who worship idols. The positive consequence is the rejoicing of Zion and the other Judean towns (the daughters of Judah). One can see in this depiction the recurring motif that might be called the "reversal of fate." Judah and Jerusalem, the worshipers of the true god, that had suffered from foreign oppressers and the worshipers of idols, would find their condition reversed.

One should note that there is a certain assurance or smugness about this portion of the psalm. The judgments of God (verse 8c) are assumed to result in the salvation and blessing of Zion. This would suggest that this psalm derives from the official cult and from worship that gave expression to Judah's confidence in its divine protection. Judgment would be her source of joy.

The third stanza (verses 10-12) infuses a moral coloration to the psalm and moderates the self-assurance of verses 6-9. These verses may be seen as the explication of the identity of those who can rejoice at the judgment of the king: those who hate evil, the saints or loyal servants, the righteous, and those upright in heart. For such, the coming of God is always good news; the visit of the king is a time to rejoice and give thanks.

Titus 3:4-7

It is easy to see why this passage has earned a place in the Christmas service. Within a few short verses, the whole drama of salvation-history is unfolded. The text begins by referring to the dawning of God's kindness in the world and ends with the faithful looking forward to eternal life. In the very heart of the passage, we are reminded that "God saved us" (verse 5), which is, after all, what brings us to celebrate Christmas. Just as the Lukan birth story reminds us that Christ is our Savior (Luke 2:11), so does this passage prompt us to recall the saving work of God and Christ (verses 4 and 6).

Before looking at certain features of the text, we should consider whether this is the best way to delimit the text. On the front-end, the preacher should decide whether the thought actually begins in verse 3 (RSV; cf. NEB) or verse 4 (JB). If verse 3 is included in the text, it sharpens the contrast between what we once were and what we now are. On the tail-end, a good case can be made for concluding the text with verse 8a: "The saying is sure" (RSV). The summarizing force of this verse is more clearly brought out in NEB: "These are words you may trust" (also JB).

It is also worth noting that in the latest edition of the Greek New Testament (Nestle-Aland, 26th ed.), verses 4-7 are treated as a self-contained unit and are printed strophic-ally—a recognition that this text might embody an ancient baptismal liturgy. This would explain the grand sweep of the text, since a baptismal setting would provide the appropriate context for rehearsing in summary form the work of God from the first appearance of God's kindness to our inheritance of eternal life. It would also account for the prominence of certain motifs, such as the "washing of regeneration and renewal in the Holy Spirit."

Given the liturgical context in which the lection is read, it is certainly defensible to begin with verse 4, since this keeps the saving work of God at the center of our attention. But, a good case can be made for concluding the lection emphatically with verse 8a. Christmas is a time for us to be reminded that "this is doctrine that you can rely on" (JB).

Even though the text is not a nativity text in the sense that it mentions the birth of Christ, it does recall themes we celebrate at Christmas.

First, the appearance of *the goodness and loving kindess of God our Savior*" (verse 4). The phrase echoes the Old Testament (Ps. 31:19; cf. Wisd. of Sol. 1:6) as well as Paul's emphasis on God's kindness (Rom. 2:4; 11:22; cf. Eph. 2:7), but the word rendered "loving kindness" in RSV is actually *philanthropia*, which might be rendered more correctly as "love for humanity." Thus, the text actually speaks of the appearance, or revealing, of God's kindness and love for humanity. Both are directed toward our salvation, since they emanate from "God our Savior" (cf. I Tim. 1:1; 2:3; 4:10; Tit. 1:3; 2:10). In this respect, the epistolary lection echoes a central theme of the Lukan birth story: it is God who is to be glorified and praised for beginning the work of salvation in a manger (Luke 2:14, 20).

Second, *salvation by grace* (verse 5). Just as Israel was reminded that it was not their own righteousness that enabled them to possess the land (Deut. 9:5), so are we reminded that we are not saved by our own doing, even by our own righteous doing (cf. Eph. 2:8-9; II Tim. 1:9). The voice we hear is Paul's: our salvation comes as a display of God's mercy and grace (Rom. 3:24; 5:1). Also Pauline is the notion of "washing" (I Cor. 6:11; cf. Eph. 5:26; Heb. 10:22; II Pet. 1:9), even if the metaphor of rebirth is not (cf. John 3:5; I Pet. 1:3). Through salvation comes "renewal in the Holy Spirit," or perhaps "the renewing power of the Holy Spirit" (Rom. 12:2; II Cor. 5:17; Col. 3:10).

Third, *Jesus Christ our Savior* (verse 6). It is worth noticing here that our text envisions Jesus as the one through whom the Holy Spirit is mediated to us (cf. John 15:26). Obviously, Jesus as "Savior" connects this text with the Lukan birth story (cf. Luke 2:11; also Phil. 3:20; II Tim. 1:10; Tit. 1:4; 2:11, 13; II Pet. 1:11).

Fourth, ourselves as *"heirs looking forward to inheriting eternal life"* (verse 7, JB). As much as our minds return to

Bethlehem in the celebration of Christmas, we nevertheless find ourselves looking forward and living "in hope." It was, after all, an atmosphere of hopeful anticipation in which the nativity of Jesus occurred, and his birth directs us to the God who brings the future into the present each time we celebrate his birth.

Once we begin to grasp the fullness of the claims made in this text, our faith begins to be affirmed and reaffirmed. Our confidence grows that this is a "sure saying," and we can exhort our congregations as we read and celebrate the Christmas story, either in narrative form from Luke, or in the form of a baptismal liturgy from Titus: "These are words you may trust" (verse 8a).

Luke 2:8-20

Luke's account of Jesus' birth lends itself easily and naturally to treatment in two worship services for the church planning a second gathering. Luke 2:1-7 is the story of the birth and verses 8-20 concern the annunciation of the birth to the shepherds. Even through the entirety of 2:1-20 was the Gospel lection for Christmas, such a division would not violate the text since it would follow Luke's own method of presenting the narrative. If these additional lessons are being used, the preacher may wish to review the comments made on this lection for Christmas Eve/Day. Here it may prove helpful to focus upon several observations on the text which were offered only scarcely, if at all, in the commentary on Luke 2:1-20.

First, since Luke is our Gospel for this year, the preacher can learn from these opening stories and share with the parishioners Luke's characteristic way of appropriating tradition. While this Evangelist sometimes quotes directly from the Old Testament, especially when presenting Jesus involved in controversy (6:3-5; 19:45-46; 20:41-44), a major use of the Scriptures is by allusion; that is, by using them indirectly and informally in the very texture of his own story. Jesus' life does not for Luke simply fulfill prophecy in a wooden or legalistic sense as though he were, as in the manner of Matthew, arguing his point. Rather many threads from the Old Testament are woven into Luke's account, enriching rather than "proving" it. For example, Isaiah 1:3, Jeremiah 14:8, and Micah 5:2 nourish 2:1-20.

Second, our text offers early evidence for Luke's special concern for the poor and oppressed of the earth. Mary is a lowly handmaiden, Jesus is born in a stable, and shepherds are the first to know and to come to the manger. This focus is present throughout the Gospel. However, Luke does not allow this concern to sink into a sentimentality cast against a backdrop of bitterness and cynicism toward the non-poor. In other words, Luke does not get trapped in a reverse prejudice which excludes some in the passion to include others. For this Evangelist, the Gospel was inclusive: "I bring you good news of a great joy which will come to all the people" (verse 10). "All the people" included persons of position and means (8:1-3; Acts 8:27; 16:14-15; 17:12). Such a spirit can serve no less vigorously the needs of the poor.

Third, the text of the song of the heavenly host (verse 14) deserves careful attention. They sing of peace, that wholeness of life God grants to persons and societies through a balancing of all the forces in creation which influence our lives. This eschatological hope (Isa. 9:6; Zech. 9:9-10) is to be fulfilled in Jesus. But the offer of peace carries with it a condition: peace will be among those of goodwill, those with whom God is pleased (RSV), or those on whom God's favor rests (NEB). Although some ancient manuscripts read "peace, goodwill among men," this is clearly a modification of the text. There is a tension in Christian theology between the doctrine of unconditional grace and the demand for moral and ethical earnestness. Luke is not exempt from the tension. He proclaims God to be "kind to the ungrateful and selfish" (6:35) and yet more than any other New Testament writer, Luke issues the call to repentance (13:1-5; 15:7, 10; 16:30; 17:3; 24:47; Acts 2:38; 3:19, and many more). The preacher will want to avoid a simplistic flattening out of this paradox.

Finally, the appearance of an angel as the bearer of God's word should prompt reflection upon our own understandings of how God's way may be known among us. Luke has spoken of the influence of the Holy Spirit (1:41; 1:67) and of visiting angels (1:11; 1:26; 2:10). We are no less persuaded that God is available to us and at work among us, but what is our clearest way of understanding and expressing that conviction?

Christmas, Third Proper (Additional Lessons for Christmas Day)

Isaiah 52:7-10; Psalm 98; Hebrews 1:1-12; John 1:1-14

These four readings for Christmas are among the best known texts of the Bible. Taken together, they announce and celebrate the good news of the coming of Jesus and interpret the meaning of the Incarnation. Isaiah 52:7-10 calls for celebration because God reigns, has comforted his people and redeemed Jerusalem. Psalm 98, as a hymn in praise of the kingship of God, is a fitting response. Both the epistolary and the Gospel lections set the coming of Jesus into its historical and cosmic context and stress that it is the Incarnation of the Son of God.

Isaiah 52:7-10

Although spoken by a prophet, and resembling a prophetic announcement in some ways, Isaiah 52:7-10 is best understood as a hymn, a pilgrim victory song. The lines are soaring and lyrical, and their poetry best grasped when sung. When Second Isaiah composed the passage in Babylon in approximately 539 B.C., he would have expected the people to sing along with him as they returned home to Jerusalem. In fact, the future release and return were so certain that they could already be spoken of as present events. As the text is now located in the Book of Isaiah, it seems to function as a responsorial psalm to the message of good news of the immediately preceding chapters.

In terms of content, these four verses reflect most of the basic themes in the message of Second Isaiah. There is the

66

announcement of the good news of salvation to Israel, in the concrete and specific form of their release from Babylon and return to Jerusalem. That salvation is an act of the one God who is over all the world, and it is motivated by pure grace. This text does not focus upon the release itself but upon the occasion when the news of that release is proclaimed. The most fundamental response the prophet calls for is the celebration of and participation in that good news. Elsewhere he indicates that Israel is being released in order to be a "light to the nations" (Isa. 42:6). Here God's purpose also includes "all the nations . . . all the ends of the earth" who shall see God's salvation. As the prophet indicates over and over again, there is but one God, and thus one God for all peoples.

Consider the various parties in this brief passage, any one of whom could be the focus of homiletical reflection. There is the prophet himself, who introduces all the other speakers and addressees. Then there is the one "who brings good tidings." That long phrase renders a single Hebrew word, better translated "herald" (NEB). Next is Zion, to whom the good news is given. Throughout the passage, Zion and Jerusalem mean both the actual city and the site of the temple, and also the people who live there. Next "your watchmen" join in the song of good news. These would be the sentries on the walls of the city. Then even the "waste places of Jerusalem" sing. Many take this as a reference to the desolated areas in and around the city, but it is likely that the expression has become in Second Isaiah a metaphor for the Judeans now in Babylonian captivity. The next stage is the reference to the Lord's people, whom he has comforted. Finally, the eyes of "all the nations . . . the ends of the earth" recognize what has happened. The movement is from a single voice announcing good news to its universal recognition.

The central figure, however, is the one who neither speaks nor is addressed, but whose activity is the good news, the God of Israel. All of the subject matter of the proclamation, all of the reasons for celebration are the actions of God. The first proclamation encompasses all the rest: "Your God reigns" (verse 7). The prophet has the herald announcing—in language from the enthronement hymns—that a new era is now breaking in, an era in which the Lord rules. As it is then spelled out, it is clear that this rule is not simply abstract or only spiritual. First, the sign of that reign is "the return of the Lord to Zion" (verse 8). Some had doubtless considered the Exile to be the departure of God from his people. For them, the era of the absence of God is over. Ezekiel speaks even more directly of the departure of the presence of God from Jerusalem during the Exile (Ezek. 11:22-25; 43:1-7). Second, the reign of God is being established as he comforts and redeems the people (verse 9), that is, brings the captives home. Finally, this reign is revealed ("The Lord has bared his holy arm," verse 10) to all peoples.

This passage pictures those who proclaim or hear the good news, not the scene of the actual release from captivity. It thus parallels our own situation: at a distance from the saving events we hear the good news and then proclaim it to others. Moreover, Second Isaiah's good news corresponds in its most important respects to the good news of the coming of Jesus. Both what the prophet saw and the early church proclaimed was an eschatological event and a new age. It is in comforting and redeeming that the Lord comes to establish the divine reign, to the ends of the earth. The Christmas message is this, "Your God reigns." The God who reigned in setting the captives free is the one whose Incarnation we celebrate today.

Psalm 98

Psalm 98, like Psalms 96 and 98, proclaims the enthronement and kingship of God. Various motifs are found in all these psalms: Yahweh as king, the judgment of the world, the stabilization of the created world, and the universal rule of God. As a hymn, the psalm is celebrative, oriented to confessional praise, and speaks about, rather than to, the Deity.

Verses 1-3 call upon the people to sing to Yahweh a new song to celebrate his victory. What victory is the text concerned with? Different answers have been given to this question: (1) the redemption from Egypt, (2) the return of the

Jews from exile, (3) some victory in warfare, (4) the creation of the world, or (5) the annual celebration of God's creation of the world. The latter seems the most likely possibility. Such an interpretation assumes that every year at the fall feast of tabernacles, the people led by the king celebrated Yahweh's rule as king over history, the nations, and creation. Since this was the time of the new year, the festival celebrated the creation of the world, and it was assumed that Yahweh re-created the world and reestablished the orders of creation at this time. (If the idea that God annually created the world sounds unusual, we should compare it with the fact that we sing every Christmas that Christ was born today!) As creator, he thus ruled as king and judge over the whole of creation. The victory would thus be God's triumph over chaos or disorder and his establishment of cosmos or order in the universe. In many ancient cultures, it was assumed that the creation of order involved the victory of the creator god over the powers of disorder and chaos (see Ps. 89:9-10). Every year, order had to be reestablished, the hostile powers subdued, and a new beginning made. What God did in his victory is related both to Israel and to the nations (the Gentiles) and thus has a universal quality about it.

Verses 4-6 call for the whole earth to praise and sing to Yahweh, with various musical instruments, because Yahweh is the universal king. Interpreters of the Bible used to assume that the idea that God ruled over the whole world developed later in Israel. One can assume, however, that this was a very old idea and that God's kingship was celebrated in the Jerusalem temple from the time of Solomon. It is true that Yahweh did not actually rule over the whole world, that is, his worshipers were not universal nor did his people rule the whole world. This did not prevent this fact from being proclaimed in the cult. In a sense, one might say that such proclamations were "predictions" or yet to be realized in fact.

The final verses of the psalm (7-9) talk about the roaring of the sea and the world, floods clapping their hands and hills singing for joy before Yahweh. Here we are obviously in the realm of metaphorical speech. But it is speech that is right at home in the talk about creation of the world. Thus it is a call for the natural and human world to accept the fact that

Yahweh is judge, that is, that Yahweh establishes and upholds order in the world of the universe.

The problem of the particular (the elect, the chosen, the people of God, the Jews) versus the universal (the outsiders, the non-elect, the Gentiles) in religion has always plagued believers. The early church had to struggle with universalization of its faith and the inclusion of Gentiles. Such psalms as 98 demonstrate that the Old Testament itself already had strong universal interests and inclinations incorporated within its pages—a universalism that dares to challenge any totally exclusivistic reading of the work of God in the world.

The call to praise and sing in this psalm suggests that ancient Israel realized that certain times and ideas are best celebrated in joyful sound and song. The Christmas Season should itself be seen as such a time—a time for carolling more than a time for preaching. A season of the heart more than the head; a time for those sentiments awaken by song and celebration rather than by syllogism and cogitation.

Hebrews 1:1-12

This epistolary lection consists of two parts: (1) the prologue (verses 1-4), and (2) the scriptural argument for Christ's superiority to angels (verses 5-12). The thought-unit actually runs through verse 14, but concluding with verse 12 gives the lection an emphatic ending.

Set in the liturgical setting of Christmas, this text commends itself as an elevated meditation on Christ. The sheer richness and variety of traditions and images that cluster here suggest an advanced level of christological reflection, if not in time at least in thought. It looks as though the author has thought long and hard about Christ both as person and event. But besides ransacking his mind for appropriate images with which to capture the significance of the Christ-event, the author has also perused the Old Testament. There he has found a string of passages that attest the preeminence of Christ, especially as a heavenly being far superior to angels.

For him, Christ is the hinge of history, standing between two eras. At one time God's revelation occurred in many forms and was spoken through many persons. But now, these many voices and sounds of God's revelation have become fused into a single voice. No longer is God's word delivered in scattered and fragmented ways. It comes to us in and through one figure: Jesus Christ. Our text thus draws a sharp line between then and now, between the way it was and the way it is. It directs our attention to "the last days" (verse 2), the eschatological age where a new realm has set in. At Christmas, our minds are positioned at the borderline between B.C., and A.D., and here we celebrate the birth of Christ as the event that "turned the ages." The author of Hebrews, no less than the Gospel writers, looks back on the course of history and sees that with the coming of Christ history turned a corner.

If we think of this meditation on Christ as a suitable Christmas text, we should consider some of the separate claims being made here.

First, Christ as *the Son who has been appointed heir of all things*. To be a son is to be an heir (cf. Matt. 21:38; Gal. 4:7), but here the legacy is "all things." This echoes the sentiments of Psalm 2, the royal psalm that speaks of the crowning of the king as God's son and God's promise to make the nations his heritage and the ends of the earth his possession (Ps. 2:7-8). In similar fashion, God's legacy to Christ is universal dominion of all things.

Second, Christ as *the agent of creation*. As the prologue of John's Gospel asserts in today's Gospel reading (John 1:3), the creation of the world cannot be thought of apart from Christ. The more early Christians began to think of the preexistence of Christ, the more they regarded him as active agent and divine assistant in the creation of the world (I Cor. 8:6; Col. 1:16; cf. Rev. 3:14). Here we see Christ supplanting Wisdom who, in the Jewish wisdom tradition, was seen as the One through whom God created the world (Wis. of Sol. 9:1).

Third, Christ as the *sustainer of the universe by his powerful word*. Closely related to our confession of Christ as creator is the conviction that through him the universe is upheld, or stays on its course. It should be noted that the means of sustenance is his "word of power," or his divine command

(JB). This doubtless presupposes the ancients' understanding of divine utterances as dynamic forces capable of holding the world together. In a slightly different vein, Christ is confessed in the Colossian hymn as the One "in whom all things hold together," a sort of cosmic glue as it were (Col. 1:17). The important point here is that just as the author cannot conceive the creation of the world apart from Christ, neither can he conceive the ongoing of the world, heaven and earth alike, apart from Christ.

Fourth, Christ as *a reflection of the glory of God*. Reflection here is not thought of in the sense of a shadow, but rather as a shaft of light emanating from a dazzlingly brilliant source. In fact, the term "glory" is best understood as "brilliance" or "splendor." The image of light is fundamental to understanding the term. Most likely, the story of God's revelation to Moses at Sinai informs the image (cf. Exod, 24:16; cf. II Cor. 3:4; also 4:4). Again, the role assigned to Wisdom in the Jewish wisdom tradition appears to be transferred here to Christ (cf. Wisd. of Sol. 7:25).

Fifth, Christ as *the very stamp of his nature,* or "the perfect copy of God's nature" (JB). Once again, Alexandrian philosophical traditions supply the metaphor, as our text insists that Christ is an exact replica of God's innermost nature, or substance (cf. Col. 1:15; also John 14:9). The ancients debated whether the imprint of a seal on wax could ever be as pristine and original as the seal itself, but this is not the thought in view here. Rather, the claim being made is that Christ in every sense bears the very stamp of God's own nature.

Sixth, Christ as *the exalted high priest who has made purification for sins*. Unlike the other images that tend to be abstract, this one is quite personal, recalling the person of the high priest. Being seated at the right hand of God was one of the ways Christians pictured the exalted Christ after his resurrection (Heb. 8:1, 10:12; 12:2). The language is provided by Psalm 110:1. Christ as the high priest who officiates "once for all" in behalf of us is, of course, a prominent theme in the epistle (cf. Heb. 9:14, 26).

Any one of these christological claims is staggering enough in its own right, but the power of this passage stems from the fact that so many such claims are clustered together. Little wonder that Christ is said to be superior to angels! In no sense is he just another heavenly being, some angel, even an archangel, whom God has chosen from the heavenly hosts. He is rather in another category altogether. He is *the* Son of God, with all that entails.

John 1:1-14

The preacher must not allow the fact that John 1:1-14 is offered as a second additional Gospel for Christmas to be taken as a value judgment on the significance of this lection for the season. On the contrary, because of its theological depth, its christological assertions, and its importance in the history of Christian faith, John 1:1-14 is strongly urged upon the preacher for use at Christmas. This Gospel reading and today's epistle, Hebrews 1:1-12, offer similar ways of expressing the central role of Christ in God's creating and redeeming relation to the world.

The prologue to John's Gospel is not, to be sure, as easily and warmly embraced by the church as is Luke's story of the Nativity. However, upon reflection, their similarities are striking. Both are hymnic, a fact which is in itself worth pondering. Why are so many of the great affirmations of the faith, biblical and otherwise, in the form of psalms and hymns? In both John and Luke, the event of Christ is of cosmic significance. In Luke the Christ lies in a manger; in John the Christ comes in the flesh. Luke's Christ is born in a stable; John's Christ "pitches his tent" (dwells) among us. But having said that, we need now to focus entirely on John.

With the exception of verses 6-8, which are both in subject matter and literary form clearly an insertion for polemic purposes against the followers of John the Baptist, the text before us is poetic. It moves in a kind of parallelism in which the final significant noun in one clause becomes the subject in the next. The central subject throughout is the Logos, the eternal Word. Judaism held that God created the world through speech or word (Gen. 1:3, 6, 9, 14, 20, 24, 26; Ps. 33:6-9), and hence it is no accident that John 1:1 repeats a portion of Genesis 1:1. So important was "word" in

Judaism's understanding of God's way of dealing with the world that sometimes writers referred to God's Word (also called Wisdom) not only as an entity distinct from God and doing God's work, but also as a personification, as a separate being (Prov. 8:22-31; Sir. 24). It is this expression of God's creating, sustaining, and reconciling power which became flesh, became incarnate in Jesus Christ (verse 14).

There is nothing in this text which undermines monotheism; God remains the subject of the New Testament as well as the Old. The Word was "with" God (verse 1), "in the bosom of" God (verse 18), and what God was, the Word was (verse 1). However, in verse 1, the absence of the definite article (in the Greek) before "God" in the expression "the Word was God" was the usual way in which that language expressed quality of being rather than identity of being. In other words, heaven was not emptied when the Word became flesh and Jesus did not pray to himself. Even the high Christology of John will not let us forget God in this season of centering attention on the Christ. John insists that we believe in Christ as the one whom God has sent to us (17:4).

So deep and rich in thought are these verses and so necessarily confined is a single sermon that it might be helpful to break the passage into smaller units.

Verses 1-2 present the nature of the Word in relation to God.

Verses 3-5 speak of the work of the Word in creation and in the continued life and light of the whole world. These verses forever forbid a view of the creation as being by nature evil.

(Verses 6-8, a prose insertion into the poem, refer to John the Baptist and deny that he was the Christ.)

Verses 9-11 turn the reader's attention from all creation to the world of humankind. That the Word wanted to dwell among the people of the earth but was rejected draws upon the beautiful and helpful account of Wisdom's effort to come to earth in Ecclesiasticus (Sirach) 24.

Verses 12-13 tells us that the Word's attempts to love and redeem the world will not be thwarted. The power to become God's children is continually granted to all who believe. (Note: even though a few later versions changed the plural "who were born" of verse 13 to a singular, "who was born," in order to give John a virgin birth story, the text is clear: the reference is to believers being born of God.)

Verse 14 gives us the Christmas story. In whatever way and time the eternal Word came to the world, only to have the door slammed in unbelief, it is now clear a new and marvelous move has been made. The Word has come in flesh to live among us and to make God known to us. This is John's way of telling Luke's manger story and affirming Matthew's Emmanuel, God with us (Matt. 1:23).

First Sunday After Christmas

I Samuel 2:18-20, 26 or *Ecclesiasticus 3:3-7, 14-17; Psalm 111;*
Colossians 3:12-17; Luke 2:41-52

The First Sunday After Christmas is traditionally associated with the childhood and family of Jesus. The Lucan
account of the boy Jesus with his parents in Jerusalem at the
time of Passover sets that theme. The reading from I Samuel 2
is the story of another precocious boy, Samuel, and it
includes the lines quoted in the Gospel lection. The other
readings for the day call attention to those virtues especially
important in family life. Psalm 111 is a hymn of praise that
emphasizes the importance of piety. Ecclesiasticus 3:3-7,
14-17 is a virtual commentary and sermon on the commandment, "Honor your father and your mother," and the
passage from Colossians provides a catalog of Christian
virtues.

I Samuel 2:18-20, 26

We may better understand the story of the young Samuel
by locating it in its literary context. Two themes are
intertwined in the first three chapters of First Samuel, the fall
of the priestly house of Eli and the divine election of Samuel.
Two episodes in the Samuel story precede the reading for the
day, the account of his birth to Hannah in her old age, and the
report of his consecration to serve the Lord, thus fulfilling
Hannah's vow. The song of Hannah (I Sam. 2:1-10) is
presented as part of the service of dedication. Most likely
I Samuel 2:26 originally followed 2:18-20, as our lection has it,
but was separated from the earlier verses by the insertion of
the account of the sons of the old priest Eli (2:22-25). Thus
Samuel, young but faithful and maturing, stands in sharp

contrast to the corrupt priests who would logically expect to succeed their father.

The atmosphere of the story is archaic and cultic. Its setting is the sanctuary at Shiloh, the home of the ark of the covenant and probably the major center for worship among the tribes of Israel. Samuel himself slept near the ark, in or very close to the holy place (I Sam. 3:3). When the old priest Eli gives his blessing to Elkanah and Hannah we know that the words will be powerful and effective, as indeed they are (verses 20-21). From the time that he came to Shiloh Samuel carried out priestly functions; we are expressly told more than once that he "ministered before the Lord" (I Sam. 2:11, 18; 3:1). The "linen ephod" and perhaps also the "little robe" would have been priestly garb.

The little boy Samuel is a child of destiny. As the contrasts between him and the sons of Eli already indicate, he and not they will succeed their venerable father as chief priest in Israel. The mantle of prophecy will also fall upon him, for he will hear the call of God and throughout his lifetime will communicate the word of the Lord to the people. Moreover, as political leader he will be the bridge between the era of the judges and that of the kings, anointing both Saul and David. There had not been one like him in Israel since the time of Moses.

So it even children of destiny have parents. The emphasis here is, of course, upon his mother Hannah. Although she had "loaned him" to the Lord (I Sam. 1:28; 2:20), in fulfillment of her vow, she continued to be his mother. One cannot help being touched by the account of the mother who sees her young son but rarely, and each year bringing him "a little robe." He is, after all, a growing boy, and last year's robe will soon be too short.

So it is a story of growth and development, and of preparation for destiny. That growth takes place, so this account suggests, in the context of both family and worshiping community. The piety of the family—their regular pilgrimage for the sacrifice—is noted in a matter-of-fact tone as only normal. But especially important was a mother willing to gain her son by giving him up. Thus the boy "continued to grow both in stature and in favor with the Lord and with men" (verse 26).

Ecclesiasticus 3:3-7, 14-17

Since readings from the book of Ecclesiasticus appear so infrequently in the lectionary, some introductory remarks concerning the work may be useful at this point. The other name for the book, The Wisdom of Jesus ben Sirach or simply Sirach, indicates the author. Jesus ben Sirach was a Jewish scribe and teacher who conducted a school in Jerusalem in the second century B.C. He wrote the book that bears his name ca. 180 B.C., during the Hellenistic period and before military conflict had broken out between the Maccabees and the Seleucids. The book was written both to pass on the teacher's wisdom to later generations and to present the Jewish faith as reasonable in a Greek context. The book has come down to us through the Christian canon, and primarily because it was translated into Greek (ca. 132 B.C. in Alexandria) by the author's grandson (see the Prologue).

The book of Ecclesiasticus and its author stand near the end of a long tradition that reaches back at least to the time of Solomon. The work is wisdom literature, the type of material that was either created or collected by Israel's "wise men," teachers, and scribes. Such literature includes collections of individual sayings and proverbs (as in Prov. 10–30), collections of poems (as in Prov. 1–9), and longer compositions (such as Job, Ecclesiastes, and the Wisdom of Solomon). The book of Ecclesiasticus is a composition, but while material is arranged topically, its overall plan is difficult to discern.

The thought of wisdom literature is distinctive in the Old Testament in its reliance on understanding based on experience and traditions of such experience. It is practical, prudent, often occupied with the best advice for success in the world, and tends to support the status quo. Nonetheless, like the prophetic tradition, it is concerned with justice, and like the priestly perspective it respects the law and worship. In later wisdom literature the perceived tension between revelation and rational understanding is resolved through the affirmation that "the fear of the Lord [that is, genuine piety] is the beginning of knowledge" (Prov. 1:7), and the recognition that wisdom is a divine attribute and divine gift to human beings. A persistent assumption of the wisdom literature, visible also in the passage before us, is the view that there is a direct relationship between righteousness and rewards, unrighteousness and punishment.

Our reading is part of a distinct section in the book (3:1-16) concerning respect for one's parents. Verse 17 is the opening of a new unit on the virtues and rewards of humility. The passage is a virtual commentary and sermon on the commandment, "Honor your father and your mother" (Exod. 20:12; Deut. 5:16). It begins with a typical address, as a father addressing children (3:1; see also 3:17), but the more likely setting for such expressions was the school, with the teacher addressing the students. The address consists of a series of admonishing and exhorting sayings. They are indirect in the sense that they are not entirely in the second person, to the addressee. However, their clear goal is to motivate and affect the attitudes and behavior of the listeners or readers. The rhetorical technique is to draw the connections between the desired behavior and rewards, between wrong actions and punishment.

The point of the passage is quite clear: Children should honor their parents, both their fathers and mothers. Verse 2 explains the injunction theologically by indicating that the place of parents was established by God. One is thus to "honor" the father and "glorify" the mother (verse 3), serve one's parents as masters (verse 7), show kindness to one's father (verse 14), and neither forsake one's father nor anger one's mother (verse 16). The rewards of obedience include long life, honor from one's own children, and, most remarkably, atonement for (verse 3) and credit against (verses 14-15) sin. That is, good deeds may cancel out bad ones, and obedience functions like sacrifices (Ecclus. 35:1). Moreover, one who does not follow the commandment stands under the divine curse (verse 16).

The theology of this text presents the preacher with a challenge. On the one hand, no one would dispute the point that children should be encouraged in the strongest possible terms to honor their parents, or the theological foundation that such a relationship is part of the divine order. On the other hand, the general view that rewards will follow and the specific point that obedience atones for or cancels out sin must be approached with caution. Our own experience confirms that the righteous also suffer (Job) and that the race is not always to the swift (Ecclesiastes). Furthermore, it stands at the heart of the gospel that atonement for sin finally comes from God alone. Consequently, we must look more deeply for the motivations of the command to honor one's father and one's mother, for example, that we are able to love because they first loved us.

Psalm 111

This psalm is fundamentally a psalm of thanksgiving. If one omits the opening hallelujah ("Praise the Lord"), which occurs frequently in this section of the Psalter (see Pss. 111:1; 112:1; 113:1, 9), then the psalm begins with an assertion about offering thanks to God. The "I" in the first verse suggests that the psalm was composed to be spoken by an individual as part of giving testimony before the congregation (verse 1c).

The psalm is an alphabetic poem or what is called an acrostic. Each of its twenty-two short lines (again omitting the opening hallelujah) begins with a consecutive letter of the Hebrew alphabet. The poem then works its way through the alphabet from "A to Z."

This psalm reflects a safe and secure attitude toward the world and life. One who has embraced the world with affection and in that embrace found succor would be at home in the sentiments of this psalm. Verses 2-10 are actually a hymn in praise of God and his works. The thoughts in the psalm give the impression that the world and God's activity are trustworthy and that life lived on the basis of such expectations will itself be calm and successful.

Generally, a thanksgiving psalm looks back on some calamity or catastrophe from which the one offering thanks has been rescued. This trouble in life was averted by the intervention of God and the worshiper now acknowledges the depth of the trouble, the narrowness of escape, and yet delights in divine redemption. This psalm, however, does not show this pattern and acknowledges no faith or existence threatening predicament in the past. Thus, the thanksgiving is basically an expression of appreciation for and a proclamation of the constancy of God and the goodness of life.

Throughout the psalm, there is an emphasis on the eternity of certain things established and qualities possessed by the Deity. Five times, some form of "forever" punctuates the thought of the psalms.

1. In 3b, God's righteousness or perhaps his righteous actions (noted in verses 2-3a) are said to endure forever.

2. In verse 5b, God is declared to be forever mindful of his covenant or his obligation. His mindfulness of the covenant is perhaps illustrated in verses 4-5a.

3. His works manifested in the giving of the land (verse 6) and his precepts are established for ever and ever (verse 8a) having been done (both works and precepts) in faithfulness and uprightness (verse 8b). Or in a more narrow sense, the precepts of God are established forever, to be performed faithfully and uprightly (so the understanding reflected in the RSV).

4. Verse 9b declares that God has commanded his covenant forever. In the Old Testament, this is an unusual way of talking about God making the covenant. The usual expression is to speak of cutting a covenant. The commanding of his covenant could refer to God's imposition of a covenant obligation on Israel, that is, the giving of the law as the people's way of responding to the divine redemption.

5. Finally, praise of God is said to last eternally (verse 10c). Praise of God flows from the fear of God or the obedience to his will which is what fear of God seems to denote (verse 10ab).

As part of the Christmas Season, Psalm 111 might be seen as affirming the eternal fidelity of God and the positive assessment of existence, conditions that the Incarnation demonstrates and proclaims.

Colossians 3:12-17

Properly observed, Christmas sets us thinking about the difference Christ's coming has made in our own lives. Not only does it enrich and reorient our personal commitment, but as a celebration in which the entire church participates it deepens our fellowship with one another. Today's epistolary text, read the first Sunday after Christmas, addresses us at both the personal and corporate level. Even though our text is a miscellany of instructions and admonitions, it calls for a quality of life together that mutually edifies and enriches our fellowship with one another. Throughout the text, we are called to be a community of faith living responsibly before one another and genuinely sensitive to one another's needs.

Any division of the passage is somewhat arbitrary, but there appears to be a break with verse 16, where the instructions more directly relate to worship. Thus, we may divide the text in two parts. In verses 12-15, we are given a profile of the new life that is ours in Christ. In verses 16-17, we are told how our worship may be enriched.

A profile of the new life in Christ (verses 12-15). This positive portrait provides the counterpart to the preceding section that sketches the negative portrait of the life we left behind (3:5-11). Several features are worth noting.

1. It is God's action that provides us our new status. We are addressed as "God's chosen ones, holy and beloved" (verse 12). God took the initiative in calling us. Like Israel, we are God's elect (Rom. 8:33; 9:11; 11:5, 7, 28; I Cor. 1:27, 28; I Thess. 1:4; I Pet. 2:9). Consequently, we share God's holy character; we are "God's own" (NEB). But this was not a cold, impersonal summons. It was rather an expression of God's own love. As God's beloved, we are the objects of God's love (cf. Eph. 5:1). As was the case with Israel, election is a concrete manifestation of divine love (Hos. 11:1).

2. Given our new status, we are to be clothed with a new character. We are called to wear a new wardrobe. The charge to "put on" certain virtues is literally a charge to don new clothing (cf. JB, NEB). Again, this metaphor is the flip side of earlier instructions to put away, or strip off, an old form of behavior (3:8-9). Several virtues are singled out: compassion, kindness, lowliness, meekness, patience, forbearance, and a forgiving spirit (cf. Eph. 4:31-32). The first four are aptly paraphrased by C. F. D. Moule: "ready sympathy, a generous spirit, a humble disposition, willingness to make concessions."

These are the qualities of life that make for genuine community, yet our text recognizes that even among God's chosen there will arise disputes and complaints. In words reminiscent of Jesus himself, we are urged to be forbearing and willing to forgive (Matt. 6:14; 18:21-35; cf. also II Cor. 2:7; Eph. 4:32). Nor are we asked to muster the power to forgive from within ourselves, but our willingness to forgive should be based in the prior action of the Lord himself who has generously forgiven us (verse 13).

That which binds all the others together, indeed which makes them possible, is love (cf. Rom. 13:8-10; I Cor. 13:13; 14:1). If the clothing metaphor is continued here, we are actually being instructed to put on love as the final article of clothing, the overcoat as it were that keeps all the other pieces in place. Or, another possibility is that love is envisioned as the belt that secures all the other garments. In any case, our capacity to love is seen as a response to God's own love for us (verse 12).

3. The peace of Christ should be the ruling force within us. The word for "rule" in verse 15 may be more literally rendered "umpire." Hence, "let Christ's peace be arbiter in your hearts" (NEB). It is presupposed that first we have been called into the one body of Christ, and as such share a common life (Rom. 12:5; Eph. 1:23; 2:16; 4:4). Here, we might recall the song of the heavenly host proclaiming "peace on earth" (Luke 2:14). With Christ as the bearer of this peace within our midst, we have a means of resolving, or umpiring, disputes and conflicts, and thus becoming the place where God's *shalom* receives concrete manifestation.

The character of Christian worship (verses 16-17). This is by no means a complete catalog of Christian worship, but several important elements are mentioned.

1. "Let the message of Christ, in all its richness, find a home with you" (JB). As the church, we are charged to allow the Word of Christ, the gospel, to dwell within us and thus providing the ordering principle for us as God's people. One obvious source to which we turn is Scripture with its manifold witness to Christ, but there are others. We also listen to the historical witness of the church's tradition as it is mediated to us through faithful witnesses. In addition, there is the Word of Christ that comes to us in prayer and service.

2. "Teach each other, and advise each other, in all wisdom" (JB). True community is achieved through mutual

edification (Eph. 4:29). More is implied here than the mere transmission of knowledge, although this is obviously essential. We are told to teach each other "in all wisdom." The teaching called for here should be accompanied with a level of understanding that is truly instructive for ordering our lives.

3. "Sing thankfully in your hearts to the God, with psalms and hymns and spiritual songs" (NEB). Worship is envisioned here not only as adoration to God but also as a way of instructing each other (I Cor. 14:26; cf. Matt. 26:30; Acts 16:25; Eph. 5:19-20; Heb. 2:12; James 5:13).

4. "Giving thanks to God the Father." The text has already urged us to "be thankful" (verse 15), but here our thanksgiving is rendered to God through Christ (cf. 1:12; Eph. 5:20; I Thess. 5:18).

As a final remainder, we are urged to "do everything in the name of the Lord Jesus" (verse 17). This sets the horizon within which the new life is lived and in which the community worships.

Luke 2:41-52

All the lections for today move us beyond Christmas, not only chronologically but practically; it is time now for internalizing the meaning of Christ's coming and for expressing that meaning in personal and social life. This is especially true of Luke 2:41-52 which offers a childhood experience of Jesus as a model of growth toward others and toward God.

Luke's story of Jesus as a twelve-year-old is so normal and natural, so free of miracles, fulfilled prophecies, or special revelations, that some scholars think the narrative may have once circulated independent of the birth stories. Perhaps so, but even if the story were told in circles that did not know the virgin birth stories, Luke certainly knew them but saw no need to bring the language of this event—"his parents," "your father and I"—into harmony with the virgin birth. The fact is, even for Luke and Matthew, the birth stories were not used in the remainder of their Gospels to argue the true identity of Jesus.

What Luke *is* doing with this story is to present both home and temple as formative institutions in the development of Jesus. The family of Jesus is a model of Jewish piety. At every point in Jesus' life, the Law of Moses has been kept: circumcision (2:21), Mary's purification and Jesus' dedication (2:22-40), and now the family's annual pilgrimage to Jerusalem for Passover (2:41). Jesus, being at the age for Bar Mitzvah, accompanies them (2:42). His lingering behind in the temple is not in any way a denial of filial piety but an indirect testimony to the deep faith of the family and the fulfillment of the act of giving the child Jesus to the Lord (2:22-23). Jesus now claims for himself that special relation to God which was symbolized in his dedication as an infant. Up to this point all signs of Jesus' unusual nature or mission have been to or through others: the angel, Mary, Elizabeth, shepherds, Simeon, and Anna, but now he claims it for himself (2:49). To be sure, not too much should be made of the temple scene; Jesus sits among the teachers as a child of unusual understanding (2:47). There is no reason at this point to impute to Jesus full and clear knowledge of his future mission. A sense of Luke's purpose in this story is provided not by reading Jesus' future into this present scene but by reading Luke's model for the story in I Samuel 2. The boy Samuel was given to God by his mother Hannah and in time he was taken to the temple (tabernacle) to live. It was in the temple that he came to an awareness of his special mission. And of the boy Samuel it was said that he "continued to grow both in stature and in favor with the Lord and men" (I Sam. 2:26).

In summary, three statements can be made in reflection on this vignette from Jesus' boyhood, the only record about Jesus between infancy and manhood. First, Luke wants it understood that Jesus was nurtured in a context of obedience and worship. He was from birth to death the true Israelite, unwavering in his observance of the demands of home, synagogue, and temple. Second, at age twelve there were in him the vague stirrings of his own uniqueness. The circle of his awareness and sense of obligation is beginning to widen beyond the home in Nazareth. Third, Jesus' move toward God is not without its tensions in the family. Even though

Jesus returned home with Mary and Joseph and was obedient to them (2:51), three expressions in the story register the tension: "Son, why have you treated us so?" (verse 48); "Behold, your father and I have been looking for you anxiously" (verse 48); "And they did not understand the saying which he spoke to them" (verse 50). Even so, the tension here does not approach that reported by Mark (3:31-35) on the occasion of Jesus' mother and brothers coming for him, having heard that he was beside himself (3:21). The truth that Mark states explicitly and Luke certainly implies in today's lection is clear: family loves and loyalties have their life and place under the higher love and loyalty to God.

January 1 (When Observed as New Year's Eve or Day)

Isaiah 49:1-10; Psalm 90:1-12; Ephesians 3:1-10; Luke 14:16-24

New Year's Eve may be a time for celebration and even revelry, but New Year's Day seems to call for more somber reflection, for taking stock and considering the future. Psalm 90:1-12 puts such reflection into the proper perspective, enabling us to affirm our confidence in the God who is eternal as we recognize our human finitude. The other readings for the day take us beyond ourselves to consider the mission of the people of God to all peoples. In Isaiah 49:1-10 the chosen people are a light to the nations, in Ephesians 3:1-10 Paul speaks about his mission to the Gentiles, and the Lucan account of the banquet has the householder inviting in the ones least expected.

Isaiah 49:1-10

The Old Testament lection includes the second of the Servant Songs in Second Isaiah (49:1-6). The first part of our reading, Isaiah 49:1-7, is assigned for use on Tuesday of Holy Week. In that context the stress might well be on the understanding of the servant as an individual, the one sent to set us free. But in the present setting, and especially with the addition of verses 7-10, the corporate understanding of the servant as Israel is unmistakable. The chosen people are set free in order to be a light to the nations.

The passage includes two distinct parts, the Servant Song in verses 1-6 and the speech in verses 7-10 (which actually continues through at least verse 13). The speaker throughout is a prophetic voice, identified in verses 1-6 as the servant, probably the same one designated by God in the first Servant

Song (Isa. 42:1-4). The passage begins with a summons to hear (1*a*), and presents a message from God. The initial addressees, at least through verse 6, are "the coastlands," the "peoples from afar" (verse 1). In Second Isaiah these expressions refer to the peoples of the world in general and the Gentiles in particular. In verses 7-10 the address seems to have shifted to Israel and concerns their imminent release and then their mission to the world.

Following the call to hear, the servant tells how he was called and equipped for his task (verses 1*b*-3). Like Jeremiah he was designated before birth (Jer. 1:5) and called by name (see also Isa. 43:1). Metaphorical language ("sword," "polished arrow") indicates how God fitted him out for his duty of communicating his message ("mouth"). The servant knows who he is and whose he is because God said, "You are *my* servant" (verse 3).

There are three more elements in the Servant Song: (1) the servant's initial response to his vocation was frustration, but he affirmed his trust in the Lord (verse 4); (2) a messenger formula that introduces the subsequent speech is filled out by subordinate clauses describing the Lord's purposes (verse 5); and (3) God's speech to the servant, to be overheard by the nations, is the crux of the passage: Israel is to be restored and "you" will be a light to the nations, "that my salvation may reach to the end of the earth" (verse 6).

The second part of the reading (verses 7-10) continues the divine address through the prophet—note the messenger formulas in verses 7 and 8. It consists almost entirely of proclamation of salvation to the chosen people. Israel, once "deeply despised, abhorred by the nations" will be vindicated by her faithful Lord (verse 7). Then God turns to speak directly to Israel (verses 8-10). The good news, the "day of salvation" is God's answer to Israel's prayer (verse 8). Proclamations of salvation as release from captivity and return to the promised land are combined with indications of Israel's new destiny. The Lord says to the prisoners, "Come forth"—that is, be free—and to those in darkness, "appear"—that is, be visible (verse 9). He then describes the manner of the return from Babylon—food, pasture, no hunger or thirst, springs of water along the way (verses 9-10).

And with all that, there is the other gift, that they are given "as a covenant to the people" (verse 8).

Israel's destiny, in the vision of Second Isaiah, is clear. Could that vision suggest a New Year's vow for us? Could we, as a people chosen by God, affirm that God's concern to set prisoners free, to bring light into darkness, has no bounds?

Psalm 90:1-12

New Year's Day, like a birthday, is concentrated or distilled time. On these days, we confront the reality that "time like a river bears all its sons and daughters away." Each New Year's Day is a signpost along life's roadway reminding us of the inevitable movement of time and the inevitable mortality of our lives. Psalm 90, a communal lament, gives voice to some of ancient Israel's reflection and anxiety about the shape of the chronological dimensions of human existence.

This section of Psalm 90 opens with a confession (verses 1-2) and concludes with a petition (verses 11-12). In between these two pillars there is talk about God, in hymnic form (verses 3-6), and talk about humanity, in the form of a description of distress (verses 7-10). In speaking of God, however, the discourse turns to humankind and in speaking of humanity's distress, the composer cannot avoid speaking about God. The God-human relationship with its frequently taunting and tearing tensions is nowhere more poignant and overwhelming than in the realization of the death-bound character of human life. When all things are seen as functioning under the supervision of God, as in ancient Israel, life as chronological and debilitating seem too much.

When this psalm sets out to speak of God, in verses 3-6, it presents the Deity as the one who, unhindered and untouched by time, places human life under such strictures of time. God is the one who "uncreates" humans and returns them to the dust from which they came. It is God who sweeps humans away and cuts human life so short. The brevity of people's lives is seen as the work of one for whom there was no beginning and for whom a thousand years of evenings and mornings are no more than a still clearly remembered yesterday or a watch in the night—something that passes while one sleeps without even awareness that it has come and gone. Unlike humans, when time passes, God doesn't. (The minister should be aware of and give expression in preaching to the human feeling of hostility toward God that permeates this psalm.)

Two or perhaps three depictions metaphorically describe the shortness of human life in verses 3-6. Life ends in the dust from which it emerged (verse 3). Its stay and span are like the grass that grows and flourishes only to fade and wither. While it is here, it is somewhat like a dream, insubstantial, experienced, but unabiding, fleeting, raising questions of its reality, not forgotten but soon gone, impermanent, and once gone, irretrievable.

In speaking about human beings, in verses 7-10, the psalm cannot avoid speaking about God. Life, with its short span, is lived under divine scrutiny. This means, according to the psalmist, that people experience God's consuming anger and overwhelming wrath (verse 7). It also means that humans live their lives as sinners—open iniquities and secret sins are known to God who reacts against them in wrath and anger (verse 8). Even if life has the benefit of longevity and one lives out the normal ideal span of seventy years—or beyond the normal eighty years—these will be full of toil and trouble, soon gone, soon forgotten (probably the connotation of "to fly away").

The pessimism (or extreme realism) of verses 3-10 are somewhat muted by the opening confession of the psalm (verses 1-2) as well as the petition in verses 10-12. The opening lines confess and affirm God as dwelling place ("home" or "refuge" are also possible as translations). That is, God is home. The frailty and mortality of dying humans can lose some of their threat in the shadow of the everlasting and undying God. Perhaps all of verses 3-10 should be read in light of the affirmation of verses 1-2. If so, it would mean that the great divisions between God and humans—God as everlasting and undying, humans as created and mortal; God as holy, humans as beset with public and private sins—still remain but confidence in God as home allows the worshipers to live with some security and assurance. (It must be remembered that this psalm was penned before ancient Israelites developed a belief in immortality or resurrection from the dead.)

The petition in verses 11-12 asks for a wise heart, for the ability to live confidently even in light of the realization that all human life is bounded by death and touched by divine wrath. A wise heart is one that knows how to number the days—either to realize how short life is and thus to contemplate its brevity and/or to apportion its life to make the most of what comes its way.

Only this psalm is attributed to Moses (see the psalm's heading). Such attribution probably stems from a period in Jewish exegesis of the psalms when there was an effort to relate at least some of the psalms to individual persons. One can imagine that the heading was added so that interpreters might look at this psalm against the background of the events in Deuteronomy 34. Moses stands on Mount Pisgah, viewing the Promised Land and knowing that he will never enter it. Death awaits him (compare Deut. 34:7 with Ps. 90:10). The pains and disappointments of life torment him. Failures bring life to an end without full fruition. In such conditions, he exemplifies the general thrust of Psalm 90. Such is at least one way of looking at the psalm.

Ephesians 3:1-10

Before we look at some of the themes unfolded in this passage, a few preliminary remarks are in order. We are struck first by the rather abrupt gap in thought between verses 1 and 2. As the passage opens, Paul begins a prayer on behalf of his Gentile readers, but the very mention of Gentiles prompts a rather lengthy interruption that extends from verses 2 through 13. This detour in his train of thought actually constitutes the heart of today's epistolary lection, since the prayer is not resumed until verse 14.

For this reason, the lection could easily be extended to include at least verses 11-12. These verses round out the thought and introduce themes that can profitably be explored in the context of the New Year. For example, at a time when we reflect on the nature of our commitments and how we carry them out, we might choose to explore the way in which God achieved the divine purpose of the universal church in spite of all the contingencies of human history. Verse 12, with its mention of the boldness and confidence we have through our faith in Christ, may easily set the stage for establishing a firm basis for new beginnings made possible through faith.

The central theme of the passage is the divine revelation made to Paul that the Gentiles are included as full-fledged members of the people of God (verse 6). Three times this is referred to as a "mystery" (verses 3, 4, 9). As used here, "mystery" is not a riddle to be solved but refers to that which has been hidden or veiled and is now revealed or unveiled. It presupposes the thought-world of Jewish apocalyptic in which the will of God could be envisioned as "hidden for ages" (verse 9) but unfolded either gradually, in stages, or abruptly in a single, astonishing moment of revelation.

Our text insists that this mystery was hidden for a long time, unknown and unavailable "to the sons of men in other generations" (verse 5). With the dawn of the messianic age and the outpouring of the Spirit that accompanied it (cf. Acts 2), the Spirit of God opened up the will of God and revealed it to the "holy apostles and prophets" (verse 5), and finally to Paul by a special act of grace (verse 7). His special apostolic calling was to "preach to the Gentiles the unsearchable riches of Christ," and to unfold to every one that it was God's original intention for there to be *one* people of God that would include Jews and Gentiles alike on equal footing. Here, our text echoes the overall theme of the Epistle to the Ephesians with its dramatic view of the church universal.

We should note that throughout the epistle, even as here within today's passage, the thought that Gentiles are to be included fully as "fellow heirs, members of the same body, and partakers of the promise in Christ Jesus through the gospel" is a matter of sheer wonderment. By the time this epistle was written, it was an achievement that had already occurred, but even in retrospect it is viewed as a miracle of grand proportions.

As we reflect on this development in early Christian history, we are reminded that the impossible is achievable, even in the face of insurmountable odds. New Year's Day may serve as an occasion for the modern church to reflect on this remarkable achievement in the ancient church, and the Apostle Paul's role in it as the one in whom the vision of the one church as the Body of Christ received its clearest and most forceful articulation.

Equally important is it to remember that all this happened as an expression of the divine will, not simply as the result of strategic planning on the Apostle's part. Today's text speaks clearly of a firm, resolute God who brings about the divine will even though it takes ages and remains invisible to earthly and heavenly spectators. But this God unfolds the content of the mystery in God's own time. The church might well take its cue as it becomes the means through which God's manifold wisdom is now displayed to cosmic spectators.

The Apostle's final request, before he resumes his pastoral prayer, is that we not lose heart (verse 13).

Luke 14:16-24

As Luke reminded us in 2:41-52 that Jesus grew beyond the bounds of home and temple, so in today's reading, he reminds us of the inclusive breadth of the church's love and welcome. In fact, all the lections witness to God's embrace of the nations. If Christmas were kept around hearth and home, it can be *kept* there no longer.

Since Luke 14:16-24 is found in Matthew 22:1-10 in an enlarged, more dramatic, allegorized, and probably more familiar form, the preacher will have to work to prevent the sermon from gravitating in that direction. The listeners may also need some help in this regard. Our text is not the parable of the banquet but the parable of the banquet according to Luke 14:16-24. Unlike Matthew who places the parable within the disputes between Jesus and the religious leaders during the final days in Jerusalem, Luke locates it within the travel narrative (9:51–18:34); that is, on the way to Jerusalem.

According to Luke, Jesus told this parable "at table." It is a portion of a section beginning at 14:1 which contains four units of table talk (verses 2-6, 7-11, 12-14, 16-24), the whole being set in the home of a ruler of the Pharisees (14:1). "Table talk" was in that culture, and remains today, a literary device for gathering materials on a single theme. However, for Luke, meals in the ministry of Jesus and in the life of the church served purposes far more important than literary. Eating together not only bridged the gulf between the haves and have-nots (16:19-31), but also was the sign of the unity of the people of God (Acts 10:1–11:3 is one example). Small wonder that for Luke Christ is known in the breaking of bread (24:35).

The parable is prompted by a pious phrase from someone at the table with Jesus (verse 15), obviously a person feeling quite confident of a reserved seat at the messianic banquet. Again, unlike Matthew, Luke's parable is simple and life-size: a man gives a banquet, invites many, and sends his servant for them at the time of readiness; they excuse themselves for a variety of reasons; the angry host replaces them with street people and transients on public roads. The threefold rejection is common in storytelling, even though in the extracanonical Gospel of Thomas (Logion 64) there is a fourth rejection of the invitation by tradesmen and merchants. The new guests are "the poor and maimed and blind and lame" (verse 21), Luke's phrase for the kingdom people (14:13). Matthew 22:10 has "both bad and good."

The interpretation of the parable depends to some extent on where it ends. If, as some believe, Jesus' story ends at verse 21, then Luke's typical use of the reversal to announce Good News is the format here: the first are last, the last are first, or insiders are out and outsiders are in. This analysis regards the rather awkward verses 22-24 as allegorical elaboration to extend the meaning to say that there is no place for those who reject the offer to come back later and get in. Historically interpreted, this would mean the Jewish people, the original guest list, said no to the invitation, Gentiles were invited, and the opportunity for Israel was no longer there. If this is Luke's meaning in verses 22-24, whether or not these verses were originally in the parable, then it certainly means that in Luke's mind, the mission to Jews was over. Paul certainly did not think so (Rom. 11), and it is difficult to believe that Luke, whose view of the kingdom was so inclusive, could speak a final no to any person or group, and certainly not in the name of Jesus.

It would be a mistake, in any case, to regard the parable solely as a sketch of salvation history: prophets gave the original invitation; Jesus as servant calls those invited; they refuse; Jesus calls the Gentiles. Luke's concern is more than historical. The parable addresses the church wherever it has become "the establishment," and wherever it is content to utter the pious phrases (verse 15) in a false confidence of its own salvation, with no thought of inviting to the table the poor, maimed, blind, and lame. But the zeal of the preacher should not be unleashed against the absentees, as though their excuses for not attending were thin and empty. They were not. The economic pressures expressed by the first two, and the recent wedding of the third are honored in most societies. Such is the nature of the forces against which we contend: they are not petty and silly, but reasonable and well argued. But such also is the nature of God's invitation: it has priority, not simply over our worst but also our best agendas.

Second Sunday After Christmas

Jeremiah 31:7-14 or Ecclesiasticus 24:1-4, 12-16; Psalm 147:12-20;
Ephesians 1:3-6, 15-18; John 1:1-18

Except for Jeremiah 31:7-14, the readings assigned for this day focus on the mystery of the Incarnation, guided mainly by the theme of the Word made flesh from John 1:1-18. The passage from Ecclesiasticus 24 reflects some of the Old Testament thought which stands in the background of the prologue to the Fourth Gospel, personified wisdom as with God from the beginning and active in history. Psalm 147:12-20, a hymn of praise, is a very fitting response to Ecclesiasticus 24 and an anticipation of John 1 in its threefold reference to God's word (verses 15, 18, 19). Similar motifs occur in the epistolary text, with its allusion to divine election before the foundation of the world, and the hope for a spirit of wisdom.

Jeremiah 31:7-14 stands a bit to the side of the other texts, but it carries forward the mood and spirit of the celebration of Christmas. The passage is filled with announcements of salvation, that the Lord has saved, gathered, consoled, and ransomed a people from sorrow to joy.

Jeremiah 31:7-14

There is legitimate disagreement among commentators concerning the historical provenance of Jeremiah 31:7-14. The final form of the so-called Book of Consolation (Jer. 30–31), of which the unit is a part, certainly comes from the era of the Babylonian Exile. In that context our reading corresponds to the message of Deutero-Isaiah: it is an announcement that the captivity is over and the Lord is bringing the exiles home. However, the Book of Consolation was composed of various materials, many of which were earlier than the Exile, and it is most likely that the text before us came from Jeremiah in the seventh century B.C. The good news of these verses then would have originally concerned not the Judeans in Babylon but the Israelite victims of the Assyrian Empire following the fall of Samaria in 722/21 B.C. "Jacob," "Israel," "Ephraim," and the "remnant of Israel" thus applied specifically—in the words of the southern prophet—to the northerners who had been taken away to "the north country" (verse 8), that is, to Assyria.

It is tempting to identify the passage as a hymn of praise, because of its initial calls to "sing aloud with gladness," "proclaim, give thanks" (verse 7). It is, however, prophetic speech from beginning to end, as the messenger formulas ("thus says the Lord") and the oracle formula ("says the Lord") indicate.

The two parts are verses 7-9 and verses 10-14. In the first part the prophet cites the words of God directly, announcing to the scattered ones that they will be returned. Even those least able to travel, the blind, the lame, pregnant women, and women in labor (verse 8) will return. Especially noteworthy is the Lord's affirmation that he is Israel's "father" (verse 9; see also Deut. 32:6 and Hos. 11).

In the second part the prophet calls for the nations to hear that the one who scattered Israel will gather them, and they will come and sing in Zion (verse 12). Mourning will be turned into joy (verse 13), and celebrations will break out. Faces will shine in the presence of the Lord's goodness, and there will be abundant food (verse 12). The prophet's point of view is Jerusalem, and even the temple on Mount Zion. He seems to envision a reunion of the long-divided people in the Holy City.

The reasons for this joyful celebration, the point of these unbridled announcements of salvation, is not some Garden of Eden, some transformation of nature. On the external level it is only the return to earlier conditions, to a time when the people lived as one, and were free from foreign domination. But if we look elsewhere in the Book of

Jeremiah we can recognize that the prophet expects God to effect a deep transformation. The Lord, he promises, will "give them a heart to know that I am the Lord; and they shall be my people and I will be their God" (Jer. 24:7). God will make a new covenant, and "write it upon their hearts" (Jer. 31:31-33). Could there be better reasons for celebration?

Ecclesiasticus 24:1-4, 12-16

For information concerning the authorship, historical circumstances, and the perspective of Ecclesiasticus, and some observations about wisdom literature in general, see the comments on Ecclesiasticus 3:3-7, 14-17 on page 78.

Ecclesiasticus 24 is an extended poetic discourse on wisdom. First, wisdom herself speaks on her relationship to Israel and promises to satisfy all who desire and follow her (verses 1-22). The poem seems to be modeled on the one in Proverbs 8:22–9:12. Second, the teacher, ben Sirach, explains the intimate relationship between the law of Moses and wisdom and then gives his personal testimony concerning his pursuit of wisdom (verses 23-34).

Verses 1-2 introduce wisdom personified as a woman. She will speak with pride and in praise of herself in the "assembly of the Most High . . . in the presence of his host." These expressions allude to the ancient tradition, also well-known in ben Sirach's time, of the heavenly council, with God surrounded by angelic attendants. Among all these wisdom's glory shines.

As the speech opens, wisdom asserts that she originated "from the mouth of the Most High," that is, "I am the word which was spoken by the Most High" (NEB). She then indicates indirectly that, though she was created by God (verse 8), she was present with God at the time of creation; "covered the earth like a mist" (verse 3) is an allusion to the creation accounts in Genesis 1–2. She has dwelt in "high places," that is, in the divine heavenly abode, but has been active in history. The "pillar of cloud" must be a reference to the pillar of cloud and fire that led Israel out of Egypt and through the wilderness (Exod. 13:21-22), and came to the tabernacle when Moses spoke with God (Exod. 33:9-10). It is strongly suggested that wisdom was the means by which God was present in the saving events and the avenue for the revelation of the Law (verse 10).

Wisdom then, in obedience to the divine command (verse 8), "took root in an honored people, in the portion of the Lord" (verse 12). Israel did not seek wisdom, but she came as God's gift. Her speech goes on to compare her growth and development to the flourishing of all sorts of trees in their natural locations (verses 13-16).

It is clear that "wisdom" here means more than practical learning based on experience. She is not the divine attribute we encounter in the book of the Wisdom of Solomon (see especially 7:25-26), but she is viewed almost as God's presence in history and nature. Along with other wisdom teachers, ben Sirach is wrestling with the question of God's distance from and yet presence in the world. His understanding approaches but does not parallel the Logos of the prologue to John.

The central point of the poem comes after our assigned reading, in verse 23: "All this [that is, wisdom] is the book of the covenant of the Most High God, the law which Moses commanded us. . . ." The Torah is wisdom, and wisdom is the Torah. One encounters the wisdom of God by studying and following the law. This point is directly related to the teacher's goal of justifying the ways of Israel to a Hellenistic Jewish audience, most likely those tempted by Greek learning and wisdom. True piety, he argues, leads to genuine wisdom.

Psalm 147:12-20

Psalm 147 gives the impression of being two (verses 1-11 and 12-20) or even three (verses 1-6, 7-11, and 12-20) self-contained units. The ancient Greek translation, the so-called Septuagint, considers the work two separate psalms (verses 1-11 = Ps. 146; verses 12-20 = Ps. 147 in the enumeration of the Greek versions as well as the Catholic Vulgate) and associated both with the postexilic prophets Haggai and Zechariah, whose preaching aided in the reconstructing of the temple.

Two themes dominate the psalm throughout: God's power in the world of nature and his support and care for the chosen people. The pervasiveness of these themes throughout the psalm would suggest that we are dealing with one composition not a combination of more than one psalm.

Verses 12-20 open with a call to praise which is then followed, as in most hymns in the Psalter, with the reasons why God is worthy of praise, in this case, by Jerusalem/Zion. The reasons offered are a complex of matters related both to Jerusalem—the elect, the chosen, the particular—and to the larger world—the earth, the nations, the universe.

First of all, this portion of the psalm celebrates Yahweh's particular care of the Holy City. The city's protection is insured and its population increased (verse 13). Within the region, well-being is to be found and foodstuffs abound (verse 14). All of this is what one would assume to be expected, that is, these reflect what should have been the normal state of existence. Here the normal is thus seen as a blessing. For Jerusalem, the most fought over city in the world, for matters to be ordinary and normal could be seen as extraordinary and abnormal.

Second, the psalm speaks of the created orders, the world of nature, as responsive to and shaped by the word of Yahweh (verses 15-18). The sending of the word is depicted as a command to which the earth responds (verse 15). The snow, ice, and frost of winter, which too are the work of God, melt before the word and spirit (wind) of God and produce water for the earth (verses 16-18).

Finally, the word is made known to the chosen people and becomes embodied in the statutes and ordinances given to Israel (verse 19). That is, the Law or Torah is an incarnation of the special will of God and is given only to Israel. "He has not dealt thus with any other nation; nor made known to them the ordinances" (verse 20).

In Psalm 147, the word comes as a creative command, as a transforming power, as a special incarnation, and as a unique gift to Israel. Christmas and the prologue to the Fourth Gospel also speak of the divine word and supplement the views of this psalm.

Ephesians 1:3-6, 15-18

Today's epistolary lection consists of two selections taken from Paul's opening hymn of blessing (verses 3-14) and prayer of intercession for his readers (verses 15-23). Naturally, they should be read in the overall context of chapter 1, but as they stand, they may be considered as two parts of the prayer, each with a different focus.

1. *The prayer of blessing to God* (verses 3-6). This magnificent eulogy directed to God reminds us of similar prayers of blessing offered to God as they rehearse the works of God done on our behalf (II Cor. 1:3-7; I Pet. 1:3-9). It should be noted that this was a well-established form of Jewish prayer *(Berakah)*, and one that is still in use in various modern Jewish prayer books. In such prayers, God is the object of praise, and the normal pattern is to list the various ways in which God has acted for the benefit of the one offering the eulogy. In this brief section, three such acts of God are mentioned.

First, God has "blessed us in Christ with every spiritual blessing in the heavenly places" (verse 3). For Paul's readers, and for us, God's blessings have been mediated through Christ, the one through whom the promise of Abraham came to fulfillment (Gal. 3:14). But the focus here is "the heavenly places" (cf. 2:6; Phil. 3:20), for the concern in Ephesians is to show that the work of Christ encompasses the entire cosmos. This was an effective way to combat the notion, common in some Christian circles, that Christ was just another of the many angelic beings that inhabited the heavens. Thus, the stress here is that all spiritual blessings are located exclusively in Christ who has been exalted to a position of incomparable preeminence in the heavens (1:20-23).

Second, God "chose us in him before the foundation of the world" (verse 4). Here God is the object of blessing as the One who is responsible for our election (cf. II Thess. 2:13), but there is particular emphasis that God's choice of us was part of the divine will even prior to creation (John 17:24; I Pet. 1:20). The church is thus envisioned as having been part of the original intention of God, not an afterthought. This has the reassuring effect of linking the church with the divine purpose even before the beginning of time. It should be noted that God's call was not simply to designate a people, but to give them a distinctive character: to be "holy and blameless before him" (cf. 5:27; Col. 1:22).

Third, God "destined us in love to be his sons through Jesus Christ" (verse 5; cf. Rom. 8:29; I Pet. 1:2). In a sense, this extends the previous thought of God's election, but with more specific reference to our becoming God's children (cf. John 1:12; Gal. 3:26; I John 3:1). As we all know, the gift of childhood is prompted as an act of love, and the play on words here should be noted: God's love was bestowed on us through the Beloved Son, and this abounds to the praise of God's glorious grace (1:12, 14: Phil. 1:11).

In sum, God is praised for having blessed us, having chosen us to share the divine character of holiness, and having destined us to become the children of God.

2. *The prayer of intercession for the church* (verses 15-18). At the outset we might suggest that this section be extended through verse 19, a more logical ending (cf. JB and NEB).

Before specific prayers are offered on behalf of the church, Paul acknowledges their faith and love (cf. Col. 1:4; also Philem. 5; Rom. 1:8), and the presence of such witness can only be an occasion of unceasing prayer and thanksgiving (cf. Col. 1:9). Accordingly, he prays for three things in their behalf, all of which are to be given by God, the Father of glory (cf. Acts 7:2; Rom. 6:4).

First, "a spirit of wisdom and of revelation in the knowledge of him" (verse 17), or "spiritual powers of wisdom and vision, by which there comes the knowledge of him" (NEB). What is called for here is more than everyday wisdom that comes with experience and age, so-called practical wisdom. Rather Paul calls for a special capacity for spiritual discernment that enables us to see and know the will of God. And this, after all, is a divine gift that comes not from within us but from beyond us.

Second, enlightened hearts by which we can know the hope to which we have been called (verse 18). This too is a matter of spiritual perception. It requires that the "eyes of our hearts" be enlightened (cf. Matt. 6:22 and parallels). With the eyes of our inner selves opened so that our spiritual vision is clear, we are able to gain a better sense of our vocation. In doing so, we discover that the call of God thrusts us into the future, but does so with confident hope (Eph. 4:4; Col. 1:5, 27). As it turns out, our hope is to share in the rich legacy bestowed on us by God through Christ: "the inheritance in the saints" (cf. Rom. 9:23; 10:12; 11:33; Eph. 3:16; Col. 1:27; Phil. 4:19).

Third, the "vast resources of his power open to us who trust in him" (verse 19, NEB). Along with the capacity for spiritual discernment and a vision of our destiny, Paul prays for the church to realize that our faith in Christ introduces us to an unlimited reservoir of strength and power. As the following verses make clear, it is the resurrection faith that is the source of such power.

In summary, Paul's prayer is for the church to acquire the capacity for spiritual discernment and understanding, to develop a clear vision of the hope that lies at the heart of our vocation and directs us toward our inheritance, and to realize the vast resources of power that lie at our disposal as a result of our faith in the risen Lord.

John 1:1-18

The reader is referred to the second additional lesson for Christmas for comments on John 1:1-14. It is not likely that the additional lesson for Christmas and the lesson today would both be used in the same season. The preacher will want to plan whether to use the Prologue to John during Christmas, and if so, when. If the decision is for today, then the fact that the lection continues through verse 18 calls for two statements beyond the comments on John 1:1-14.

First, the mood or tone generated by all the lections for today bear directly on the interpretation of John 1:1-18. The prophet sings the coming of God to Israel to restore and turn mourning into joy. The wisdom writer recites the ways in which the coming of God's wisdom and revelation is pleasant and refreshing. The epistle declares God's eternal purpose now revealed is to bless and to grant us the inheritance of children loved. This joyous and celebrative note is appropriate also for the Good News of John 1:1-18. Too often preachers allow themselves to get buried under the theology of this text and in turn bury rather than buoy the listeners in the sermons based on it.

Second, in the movement of John 1:1-18, verses 14-18 constitute a unit with its own integrity which is worthy of full treatment in the sermon. The opening and closing verses (14 and 18) state the content of the Christian witness. Notice the introduction of "we" and "us" into the text. In other words, this is what we believe: in Jesus of Nazareth we have experienced God. The God concealed in mystery and unseen, is not only known but made available in Jesus Christ. The fundamental human hunger (14:8) is now satisfied (14:9).

However, verses 15-17 remind us that not everyone has experienced God in Jesus of Nazareth. The Christian confession is therefore made with courage, because there are not only detractors but other religious groups who experience God differently. Verse 15 is aware of the presence of the John the Baptist group which followed him rather than Jesus. Verse 17 recognizes the presence of the synagogue and the commitment of many to Moses. That the Christian faith is not unanimous does not call for silence born of intimidation, but courage born of the quiet confidence of one's belief. But courage does not mean prejudice or hostility toward those who do not share in the affirmation, "We have beheld his glory, glory as of the only Son from the Father." After all, verse 16 is also true of the disciples of Jesus: "And from his fulness have we all received, grace upon grace."

Epiphany

Isaiah 60:1-6; Psalm 72:1-14; Ephesians 3:1-12;
Matthew 2:1-12

In the West, as early as the fourth century, Epiphany has been the festival commemorating the visit of the Wise Men to the baby Jesus. The account of that visit in Matthew 2:1-12 is thus the center of attention on this day. Because the visit of the Magi is regarded as the first appearance of Jesus to the Gentiles, Ephesians 3:1-12, which reflects upon the mission to the Gentiles, is a fitting epistolary reading. The responsorial psalm actually anticipates the themes of kingship in Matthew 2:1-12. This ancient Israelite prayer for God's blessings upon the king is now heard over this new "king of the Jews" (Matt. 2:2). Isaiah 60:1-6 doubtless appears here because of its reference to gold and frankincense (verse 6), but it contributes more than that through its mood of celebration and its cry, "Arise, shine; for your light has come," which describes the appearance of the Lord.

Isaiah 60:1-6

Isaiah 60:1-6 begins a distinct section (chapters 60–62) in the literature associated with Third Isaiah (Isa. 56–66). Verses from the concluding unit of the section (Isa. 62:6-7, 10-12) are among the lections for Christmas (Second Proper). The three chapters contain poetic proclamations of salvation that must come from early in the postexilic period, yet some decades later than Second Isaiah (Isa. 40–55). The Exile is over, and perhaps the temple is built (Isa. 60:7), but the people live in relative poverty.

The tone of the passage is set by the imperatives in verses 1 and 4: "Arise, shine," and, "Lift up your eyes and see. . . ."

Who is the speaker, and to whom are the words addressed? In view of the contents, and considering the verses that follow our reading, the speaker is a prophetic voice speaking about God's self-manifestation. In the original historical context, the addressee is probably Jerusalem; the name occurs in verse 1 in the Septuagint (cf. NEB). The city, with its inhabitants, is the location of the divine revelation.

In verses 1-3 the prophet skillfully employs metaphors of light and darkness to proclaim the epiphany of the Lord. The language is powerful and evocative, but restrained. There are limits to what can be said about the appearance of God. Jerusalem is to arise and shine because its "light" has come. In the next poetic line "glory of the Lord" parallels "light." The appearance of the Lord's glory is like that of light in the darkness, like the rising of the sun at dawn. The images of darkness borrow from the language of Isaiah 9:2: "The people who walked in darkness have seen a great light." Here those upon whom the light shines will themselves shine, with reflected light, so that "all nations" will stream to the source of the light.

It is noteworthy that the prophet describes neither a specific event nor a vision of the Lord. Rather, the appearance of God is like the dawn, bringing an overwhelming light. Moreover, the epiphany is of "the glory" of the Lord. This is not unlike Ezekiel's experience of the presence of the Lord. After describing the vision in detail he summarizes: "Such was the appearance of the likeness of the glory of the Lord" (Ezek. 1:28).

In verses 4-6 the prophet calls for the people, presumably of Jerusalem, to look at what is happening, and will happen. Their sons and daughters shall come, along with the wealth of the nations. When they see what is happening they will "be radiant" and rejoice (verse 5). The stream of the exiles and of the tribute from all over the world will testify that the Lord has shined on the people of the Holy City. The wealth from west and east is not for the people of Israel, but is tribute to their God.

To what can one compare the appearance of God, the epiphany of the Lord? The more ancient traditions of the Old Testament spoke more directly, of the awesome theophany accompanied by dramatic upheavals or transformations in nature. In our text it is the glory of the Lord that appears like the sunrise. That appearance corresponds to the appearance of salvation, and is followed by celebration and the procession of all the nations to stand in the light. Finally, we should not miss the point that the ones to whom the light has come, the ones who can see it and celebrate its appearance, are those who are in the darkness.

Psalm 72:1-14

Epiphany celebrates Jesus' manifestation to the world. Psalm 72, a part of the ancient Hebrew enthronement of the Davidic kings, was a communal prayer at the coronation requesting that the Davidic messiah (the newly crowned king) would be the object of universal adoration and praise. Thus, the central motif of Epiphany finds some of its counterparts and foreshadowings in the royal rituals of ancient Judah.

The ideology and expectations that surrounded the Davidic king ruling in Jerusalem are practically all represented in this psalm. They find embodiment in the form of petitions requesting God's blessing upon the ruler. Among these features are the following: (1) the king was considered the representative of God's justice and righteousness; he was the channel through which these flowed to the people (verses 1-2); (2) he was the source of prosperity and blessing for the people (verses 3, 6-7); (3) the king was especially responsible for defending the weak and disenfranchised members of society—the widows, the poor, the oppressed, the fatherless (verses 4, 12-14); (4) he was promised a universal rule extending from one end of the earth to the other, that is, a rule with worldwide dominion (verses 9-11); and (5) although only alluded to in verse 1*b* of this psalm, the king was also the divine son of God, a status to which the king was elevated on the day of his coronation (see Ps. 2:7).

In line with the concerns of Epiphany, we shall note in our discussion of this text only those verses concerned with the king's or the messiah's dominion (remembering that the ruling Judean monarch was the anointed or the messiah).

The claims and requests that were made on behalf of the Judean king are very similar to those known from other major Near Eastern powers. Both the Egyptian pharaohs and the Mesopotamian kings claimed the right to rule over the entire world and saw their positions as god-ordained and divinely upheld. All seem to have drawn on what was a common court style and rhetoric. It is quite clear, however, that the prophets, for example, took such forms of expression seriously and the expectations associated with the earthly Davidic king were projected into the future in the people's depiction of the coming Messiah. What was proclaimed as reality in the royal cult was preached by some prophets as a future vision.

Some means that were used to give expression to the expectations of the king's universal rule were mythologically based; others were anchored in more realistic geography. The expressions "sea to sea" and "from the river to the ends of the earth" could be classified as mythological, being based on a particular view of the world which conceived of the earth as surrounded by seas. The references to Tarshish and the isles and the rulers of Sheba and Seba were ways of talking about western and eastern extremes of the known world at the time. All of these expressions, both the mythological and the more realistic were ways of saying "everywhere." Rulers from throughout the known world were to accept the rule of the Judean king and show such submission by bringing gifts and paying tribute. Actual enemies, it was hoped, would bow down and offer obeisance by licking the dust, that is, by falling on their faces.

The ancient royal theology threw a richly embroidered purple robe over the shoulders of the Judean ruler and in so doing anticipated the expected universal rule of the messiah.

Ephesians 3:1-12

This epistolary lection is traditionally read at the Epiphany because it carries through the theme of the manifestation of Christ to the nations as part of the eternal purpose of God. With its special emphasis on the inclusion of the Gentiles as full-fledged members of the people of God, it echoes the theme of the universality of God's sovereignty found in each of the other readings (Isa. 60:3; Ps. 72:8-11; Matt. 2:1-12).

In form, these verses actually constitute Paul's prayer on behalf of his Gentile readers; or, more accurately, an interruption of Paul's prayer. In verse 1, Paul the prisoner begins a prayer "on behalf of you Gentiles," but the mere mention of the term "Gentiles" leads to a digression. The next twelve verses unfold Paul's apostolic vocation as a mission directed to the Gentiles and one in which he was carrying out the original intention of God. After an elaborate expansion of this theme, the prayer resumes in verse 14.

As is well-known, the Epistle to the Ephesians is widely regarded as pseudo-Pauline, yet there are many genuine Pauline reminiscences in this passage. The setting presupposed is imprisonment, though we do not know where or when (cf. 4:1; Phil. 1:7, 11; Philem. 1, 9-13; Col. 4:18; II Tim. 1:8; 2:9). He is depicted as a steward of God's grace entrusted with divine mysteries that have been revealed to him. It is clear that the historical Paul thought of himself and his apostleship in such terms (I Cor. 4:1; 9:17; cf. Col. 1:25). To view this trust as divinely bestowed by God's grace also reflects Paul's own outlook (Rom. 15:15; I Cor. 3:10; Gal. 2:9; cf. Eph. 3:7-8; Col. 1:25). In addition, to speak of the gospel as "the mystery of God" that was formerly hidden but is now revealed recalls genuine Pauline sentiments (Rom. 16:25; I Cor. 2:1, 6-16). We also hear other Pauline echoes, such as his insistence on being the "least of all the saints" (verse 8; cf. I Cor. 15:9-10; also I Tim. 1:15). Thus, the words and sentiments of our text come from Paul, at least in some sense. We are simply not sure how directly they come to us from him.

But in the liturgical context of the Epiphany, the authorship of this passage is less a concern than how it speaks to us about Christ's manifestation. Several features of the passage are worth noting in this regard.

First, we should note that the gospel of Christ is presented here as a "mystery." Paul speaks here of the "mystery of Christ" (cf. Col. 4:3), noting that he had received it by revelation (verse 3; Gal. 1:12). The specific content of this mystery is given in verse 6: "How the Gentiles are fellow heirs, members of the same body, and partakers of the promise in Christ through the gospel." Thus that which has been "hidden for ages" (verse 9) is God's intention that the "unsearchable riches of Christ" be preached to both Jews and Gentiles. The language of manifestation, or "epiphany," is even more explicit in Colossians 1:26: "the mystery hidden for ages and generations but now made manifest to his saints."

In this respect, we notice a slight shift in the way "mystery" is used, as compared with the genuine Pauline Letters. There it is used in a more general, undefined sense (I Cor. 2:1, 6-16; Rom. 16:25), whereas in Ephesians and Colossians it has specific reference to the inclusion of the Gentiles within the plan of God (Eph. 1:9, 3:9; Col. 1:26-27; 2:2). Thus, by this stage of development of the Pauline tradition, the manifestation of God to the nations is seen as part the "divine economy" (*oikonomia*; cf. 1:10; 3:2, 9).

Second, Christ is to be seen as the turning point in the divine drama, the moment of revelation when God's eternal purpose became fully known. Underlying our passage is a twofold scheme: "once formerly hidden . . . but now fully revealed" (cf. verse 5). There is the recognition that a dramatic shift has occurred in the history of salvation, and that Christ is the hinge on which history has turned. It is in this regard that our text surfaces some of the central themes of Epiphany, for this is the time when we recognize that darkness gives way to light, hiddenness to openness, mystery to revelation, ignorance to knowledge. Our text affirms that the mystery of Christ "was not made known to the sons of men in other generations" (verse 5), and this reminds us that the coming of Christ was a watershed in the divine economy. We stand this side of the apostles and prophets to whom the Spirit revealed this mystery, and now it is possible for everyone to see what was invisible to previous generations (verse 9).

Third, the scope of God's manifestation through Christ as depicted in our passage is cosmic. We have already noted that it is universal, including both Jews and Gentiles. But more than that, today's text affirms that God's mystery has now been unveiled "to the principalities and powers in the heavenly places" (verse 10; cf. 1:21, 2:2; 6:12; also Rom. 8:38; I

Cor. 15:24; Col. 1:13, 16; 2:10, 15; I Pet. 3:22; Heb. 2:5). The light that has shone through Christ has shone not only on earth but has lit up the heavens as well. If the Gospel reading for today focuses on God's manifestation on earth, the epistolary reading extends this revelation into the heavens.

This text already points us in the direction of mission, for the Epiphany often begins a period when the church reflects on its mission, not only in the sense of proclaiming the gospel to the nations but also in the sense of working for peace and justice within the social order. This perspective should provide numerous homiletical possibilities as our text directs us to think about the manifestation of Christ to the nations.

Matthew 2:1-12

Epiphany, the season for celebrating the manifestation of Christ to Israel and to the nations, is always observed with the use of Matthew 2:1-12. The story of the visit to the Magi gathers up and dramatizes the emphases of this period between Christmas and Lent: the revelation of Jesus Christ as king and the coming of the nations to worship him.

The story has its antecedents in both Jewish and Gentile cultures, although it is not easy to know which directly and which indirectly (if at all) influenced Matthew. The idea that the birth of great leaders would be accompanied by celestial signs was fairly widespread in the Mediterranean culture of Matthew's time. A more immediate background is provided by several Old Testament texts: Isaiah 60:1-6 which speaks of kings coming to worship Israel's God, bringing gifts of gold and frankincense; the story of Balaam, the strange seer from the East (Num. 23–24) who saw a star "come forth out of Jacob" (Num. 24:17); and the account of Moses being saved from the wicked pharaoh's slaughter (Exod. 2:1-10). In addition, Josephus reports (*Antiquities* II: 205-6, 215) a legend to the effect that an Egyptian scholar predicted the birth of a savior of Israel, a prediction that upset the pharaoh and caused him to summon the astrologers. However, the preacher will not wish to linger too long in background materials as though Epiphany means "proving" Matthew 2:1-12.

111

In Matthew's hands, the story of the visit of the Magi is related hardly at all to the birth narrative (1:18-25), but rather launches a new cycle of stories. Both 1:18 and 2:1 are introductions to stories rather than 2:1 continuing what was begun in 1:18. In fact, 2:1 introduces "Herod the king" who is the catalyst in a series of five stories. Note:

    2:1-6   —In the days of Herod the king
    2:7-12 —Herod summons the Magi
    2:13-15—Herod threatens the Christ Child
    2:16-18—Herod slaughters the Bethlehem children
    2:19-23—Herod dies

Herod's plotting, jealousy, rage, and death are not only the dark backdrop but also the precipitating forces in all the stories about Jesus as a child.

The preacher who treats this lection, therefore, cannot be unaware of the prominence of Herod, the Idumean half-Jew whose service as an officer in the Roman army was rewarded by the gift of Palestine as his kingdom. Of course, attention will be given to the two concerns of Matthew that are unrelated to Herod. One is the certification that Jesus of Nazareth was indeed born in Bethlehem as the prophet Micah had foretold. Jesus is of Nazareth, not because the family lived there prior to Jesus' birth (as in Luke), but because they moved there later to avoid the threats of Archelaus, Herod's son and successor in Judea where Bethlehem was located (2:19-23). But by reason of birth, says Matthew, Jesus qualifies as the ruler out of Bethlehem who would govern Israel (2:4-6). The second concern unrelated to Herod is the visit of the Wise Men, the Chaldean astrologers. Perhaps deliberately unnamed and unnumbered (later legends), they represent all those from all nations who will come, as Isaiah prophesied (60:1-6), to bow before Christ the King. Matthew is in close touch with his Jewish roots, to be sure, but he is not without his convictions concerning the Gentile mission (4:14-16; 28:18-20).

But having said that, Herod must be dealt with. The story is that of two kings: Herod the king and "he who has been born king of the Jews." Matthew handles Herod in two ways: (1) he sets him and all his displays of power within prophecy and the larger purposes of God and (2) Matthew renders

Herod, for all his destructive power, finally powerless over the true king, Jesus Christ. Herod died, says Matthew, but in a real sense he is still alive, the personification of all the forces arrayed against the way of God's love and grace in the world. The church should be realistic enough to know he is there and he is powerful; the church should be trusting enough to know he is not *finally* powerful.

Baptism of the Lord (First Sunday After Epiphany)

Isaiah 61:1-4; Psalm 29; Acts 8:14-17; Luke 3:15-17, 21-22

The Lucan account of the baptism of Jesus, with the descent of the Holy Spirit and the voice from heaven, is the obvious focus of attention on the day that commemorates the baptism of the Lord, but the other readings have important contributions to make as well. The lection from Isaiah 61:1-4 is highly appropriate in its focus upon the mission of the one anointed and endowed with the Spirit of the Lord. Moreover, this passage anticipates the Gospel reading for the Third Sunday After Epiphany, Year C, in which it is quoted. Psalm 29 is a hymn praising the power of the voice of God, as expressed both in the words of the messenger of Isaiah 61:1-4 and the voice from heaven in Luke 3:22. The passage from Acts echoes the motifs of the Word of God and the Holy Spirit.

Isaiah 61:1-4

Commentators on Isaiah 61:1-4 have long noted the similarity of this poetry from Third Isaiah to some of the Servant Songs of Second Isaiah. God endows the servant with the spirit (Isa. 42:1), calls him to effect restoration and proclaim good news (Isa. 49:1-6), and gives him the words to sustain the weary (Isa. 50:4). Our reading comes from an individual or group that continued the prophetic role into the postexilic period in Jerusalem.

Isaiah 61:1-4 (or 1-3) is the introductory section to a poem which includes the entire chapter. Standing in the center of that poem, which is an announcement of restoration, is the proclamation to the people of Judah that they are "priests of the Lord," "ministers of our God" (verse 6). The speaker in verses 1-4 is not identified, but must be a prophetic figure who alludes to a vocation or designation by God. In verses 5-7 he turns to address the people directly, and in verses 8-9 the Lord speaks. This movement from prophetic or messenger speech to direct address to the quotation of God's words is not unheard of in earlier prophetic literature.

Verses 1-3 contain the self-introduction of the herald or messenger, and in spelling out his mission already begin to proclaim the good news. The language for the designation of the herald is somewhat unusual in a prophetic context. Endowment with the spirit and anointing traditionally were associated with the designation of the king (II Sam. 23:1-7). Spirit and anointing grant divine authority and power to the speaker. For him to proclaim the words is to effect the events.

The mission is spelled out with a series of infinitive clauses dependent upon "anointed me," broken only by the parallel "he has sent me" (verse 1). Almost every infinitive is followed by an indirect object. Thus the anointed one is to give an effective word of good news to someone (individual or group) in trouble or distress: good news to the poor (RSV fn), binding up the brokenhearted, liberty to the captives, release of those in prison.

Especially remarkable is the proclamation of "the year of the Lord's favor" (verse 2). This is almost certainly an allusion to the Year of Jubilee. While there must be some ancient practice behind the legislation, it seems unlikely that the Jubilee as described in Leviticus 25:8-55 was ever a social reality. Here it provides some of the important images for the age of the reign of God. In that time all who are poor will hear good news, those who are bound—including slaves and debtors in prison—will be set free, and mourning clothes will be replaced by garments fit for celebration. The "day of vengeance of our God" here stresses not revenge—though that emphasis certainly can be found elsewhere—but the restoration of balance, the establishment of justice.

The vision of the future becomes concrete in verse 4. "They" are the people of Judah who have returned from the

Exile and are facing the task of rebuilding not only the fallen structures of Jerusalem and the other towns of the territory, but their lives and institutions as well.

What is the aim, the goal, of this transformation? Why is good news proclaimed to the poor, the brokenhearted, the captives, and hope to the people huddled in the ruins? The series of infinitives characterizing the herald's mission had concluded in verse 3b with a purpose clause that provides the answer. First, all this happens so that the people may be given a new name, signifying a new reality: "Oaks of righteousness, the planting of the Lord." Second, the good news is proclaimed that the Lord "may be glorified." This God is the one who is glorified when mourners are comforted, captives are set free, the poor hear good news, and even when ruins become habitable.

Psalm 29

The accounts of Jesus' baptism in the waters of the Jordan report that a heavenly voice spoke on the occasion. Psalm 29 has been selected for reading on the celebration of Jesus' baptism because it too speaks of waters and of a heavenly voice.

This hymn celebrates the manifestation of divine authority and power as these are revealed in the lightning and thunder of a storm that sweeps into Palestine from the Mediterranean Sea (verse 3), passes through Lebanon (verses 5-6), and moves into the desert of the south (verses 7-8).

A number of surface features about this psalm are noteworthy. First, the sevenfold repetition of the term "voice" gives the psalm a staccato quality (see Rev. 10:3). Second, the voice of God creates disturbances and manifests its power over the waters (verse 3), trees (verse 5), mountains (verse 6), the desert (verse 8), and animals (verse 9 which can be translated "makes the hinds to calf and brings ewes to early birth"). Practically the whole of the natural order becomes involved. Third, neither humans nor the chosen community of Israel play any real role in the psalm and are mentioned only at the end of the psalm. Fourth, the psalm moves from the heavenly world of the sons of gods to the world of humanity via the imagery of the storm. One might say the psalm moves from *Gloria in Excelsis* to *Pax in Terris,* from "Glory to God in the Highest" to "Peace on Earth" (see Luke 2:14). Fifth, a polytheistic, mythological worldview is assumed throughout the text. The "sons of gods" ("heavenly beings" in the RSV) are called upon to praise God (Yahweh) in the heavenly realm. Yahweh sits enthroned upon the waters, the turbulent powers of chaos that threaten world order.

The whole of the psalm supports the assertion that God is in charge. The thunder, lightning, and storm are manifestations of God's voice speaking from the cosmic abode of the Divine. In spite of the turbulence in the world of nature, God is enthroned as king (verse 10); in fact, the rainstorm only demonstrates the fact, it does not challenge it.

Acts 8:14-17

In this tiny vignette we are told how the Samaritans received the gift of the Holy Spirit at the hands of the apostles Peter and John. It is set within chapter 8 of Acts which records the spread of the gospel into the regions of Samaria, just as the risen Lord had predicted (Acts 1:8). We are told that the death of Stephen had precipitated an intensive wave of persecution against the church in Jerusalem (8:1). As a result, its members fled for safety to the surrounding regions of Judea and Samaria, while the apostles remained in Jerusalem.

The leading role in evangelizing Samaria was played by Philip the evangelist, one of the seven men chosen by the apostles to assist them in caring for the needy (6:1-6). Like the others, he was commended because of his good reputation, along with his possession of a full measure of the Spirit and wisdom (6:3). His preaching in the regions of Samaria met with great response, as "multitudes gave heed to what was said by Philip" (8:6). Along with his preaching, he performed signs and wonders, which included acts of exorcism and healing the paralyzed and lame (8:7). So impressive were the signs he performed that even Simon Magus, the Jewish magician who had won a considerable hearing among the

Samaritans, believed and was baptized. Even though later in the narrative Simon's faith proves to be fraudulent, at this point in the narrative he serves as living proof of the effectiveness of Philip's preaching.

What puzzles us about today's lection is that Philip's preaching, for all its power and effect, was deficient in one crucial respect: it did not bestow the gift of the Holy Spirit. Elsewhere in Acts, when converts are baptized they ordinarily receive the Holy Spirit at the same time, or shortly thereafter (Acts 2:38; 10:47; 11:15). Here, however, we are told that the Samaritans "had only been baptized in the name of the Lord Jesus" (verse 16). This reminds us of twelve disciples later described in the narrative as having heard only of the baptism of John (19:1-7). However, as soon as they were baptized "in the name of the Lord Jesus" (19:5), they received the Holy Spirit through the laying on of hands by Paul (19:6).

The Acts narrative makes clear that "baptism in the name of the Lord Jesus" and the reception of the Holy Spirit through the laying on of hands are two distinct acts, and they may be separated by a considerable space of time. In today's text, the Spirit is bestowed by Peter and John, the two apostles who have played the leading role up to this point in the story (Acts 3:1, 11; 4:13, 19). In one sense, their action here diminishes the role of Philip in the narrative, for it makes clear that bestowing the Spirit in this manner did not lie within his power. But the other side is that their action legitimates the preaching among the Samaritans by linking it with the apostolic circle who had been with the risen Lord. In this way, the spread of the gospel beyond Jerusalem receives the apostolic imprint even though it is being carried out by lesser figures such as Philip.

In spite of these wrinkles in the text, some important points emerge.

First, here as elsewhere in Acts baptism and the laying on of hands are closely associated. As was the case in the baptism of Jesus, it was the bestowal and reception of the Spirit that was crucial, for this signified that the presence of God had been conferred in the one case on Jesus, in the other cases on those who believed in Christ as the Son of God. It is this, after all, that gives baptism its true significance, for in becoming children of God, even as Jesus was acknowledged as the Son of God, we come into possession of God's very own Spirit.

Second, the conferral of the Spirit occurs in response to prayer (verse 15). Among other things, this suggests that God does not bestow the Holy Spirit as if it were an automatic response that occurs without reference to the earnest pleading of the individual. At this point, today's epistolary lection is tied closely with the Lukan version of the baptism of Jesus, which is distinctive in its own right for the way in which it depicts the descent of the Spirit as occurring while Jesus was in the midst of prayer (Luke 3:21-22). To be sure, in Acts this is not a consistent pattern, for at other times the Holy Spirit descends in the act of preaching (10:44; 11:15; cf. 19:6).

Celebrating the baptism of Jesus enables us to see more clearly the meaning of becoming God's child, since among other things, it provides a special occasion for us to ponder the significance of the prophetic proclamation, "The Spirit of the Lord is upon me" (Isa. 61:1).

Luke 3:15-17, 21-22

A traditional subject for Epiphany is the baptism of Jesus as presented by one of the Gospels. However, when Luke is the Gospel, the subject is more correctly "What happened at Jesus' baptism," for, as we shall see, the baptism itself is noticeably subordinated to the heavenly attestation to Jesus as God's Son, the opening of the heavens, and the descent of the Holy Spirit, to which both Isaiah 61 and Acts 8 testify. In fact, the psalm for today (29) praises God's glory through flood, wind, and fire, elements which serve in biblical language as symbols for the Holy Spirit.

The Gospel lection is in two parts: Luke 3:15-17 and 21-22. Verses 15-17 deal with John the Baptist, but it is not his person that is central here. Even though verse 15 expresses the general public interest in John, Luke actually removes John from the scene prior to the account of Jesus' baptism (verses 18-20). Neither John nor the Jordan River appear in

Luke's story of the baptism. Luke's interest in John at this point is in his witness to the larger and vastly different ministry of the One coming after him. Even though John does not identify that greater one as Jesus—that identification is in the Fourth Gospel—the reader makes that association naturally enough. The greatness of the One to come is pointed out in the contrast between water baptism and baptism with the Holy Spirit and fire. Because of the overlay of Christian interpretation, both by the writer and the reader, it is difficult to know what John understood by "Holy Spirit and fire." Since "spirit" can also be translated "wind," and since the elaboration in verse 17 is about the wind separating wheat and chaff, perhaps the central thrust of John's message concerns the coming judgment; that is, while John's ministry involved a purging by water, the One to come will purge with wind and fire. But even if that is John's understanding, wind and fire are for Luke symbols of the Holy Spirit (Acts 2:2-3), and the Holy Spirit is for Luke and other early Christians the promised gift of Christ to the believers (Acts 1:5, 8; 2:38).

Verses 21-22 focus not upon Jesus giving the Holy Spirit to others but upon his receiving it at baptism. As mentioned earlier, Luke subordinates the baptism itself to other concerns. John is already in prison (verses 18-20), Jesus comes among all the people (verse 21), and the baptism is set in a subordinate clause, along with prayer (verse 21). This minimal attention to Jesus' baptism may be due in part to some early Christian difficulty with, if not embarrassment over, the fact that Jesus was baptized. Matthew 3:13-15 addresses that problem, as did later Christian writings which turned the baptismal scene into a spectacle with bright lights, fire on the surface of the water, and a heavenly voice explaining the divinity of Christ. But Luke's scant attention to the baptism itself is also motivated by a desire to give major attention to the Epiphany qualities of the occasion. The opened heavens signaled the launching of a new age. The heavenly voice addresses Jesus, as in Mark 1:9-11, not the people, as in Matthew 3:13-17. However, the descent of the Holy Spirit has a public dimension in that it comes "in bodily form" as a dove.

The voice from heaven, in identifying Jesus, combines Psalm 2:7, used at the coronation of Israel's king as God's son, and Isaiah 42:1, a description of the servant of God. Jesus is the Servant King or the Sovereign Servant. The use of Isaiah 42:1 indicates that the coming of the Holy Spirit is not to make Jesus the Son of God—Luke affirmed that in the birth story—but to empower the Servant for his task. This view is confirmed in 4:16-30 where Luke clearly states that the Holy Spirit was an anointing for public ministry. Some manuscripts of Luke 3:22 use the remainder of Psalm 2:7, "today I have begotten you," opening the door to an adoptionist view of Christ as Son of God.

The preacher will want to notice the reference to prayer in verse 21. The prayer life of Jesus is a matter of real importance for Luke (5:11; 6:12; 9:18; 9:28-29; 11:1; 22:32, 39, 46; 23:34, 46). But not the prayer life of Jesus alone. Just as Jesus was in prayer when the Holy Spirit descended, so the church, awaiting the promised power of the Spirit, was (Acts 1:8, 14) and should continue to be constant in prayer.

Second Sunday After Epiphany

Isaiah 62:1-5; Psalm 36:5-10; I Corinthians 12:1-11; John 2:1-11

The dramatic manifestation of the power of God is the dominant theme in the readings for this day. The Gospel lections for the season call attention to the beginning of the ministry of Jesus. The account of the miracle at the wedding in Cana in John 2:1-11 is, according to the Fourth Gospel, the first of Jesus' signs, when he "manifested his glory" (verse 11). In this context the lection from I Corinthians 12:1-11 calls attention to the manifestation of God through the gifts of the Spirit. In Isaiah 62:1-5 the brightness of a vindicated Jerusalem reveals God's grace. Psalm 36:5-10 is a hymn of praise for God's steadfast love, faithfulness, righteousness, and judgment, the one in whose light "we see light" (verse 9).

Isaiah 62:1-5

A striking number of the Old Testament readings for this season are taken from the coherent section of proclamations in Isaiah 60–62. (For discussion of the unit as a whole see the commentaries for Epiphany and Christmas, Second Proper.) Unlike Second Isaiah, who announces the release of the Babylonian exiles and their return to Judah, Third Isaiah in these chapters proclaims the restoration of the people in general and the city of Jerusalem in particular. He sees no single dramatic political event on the horizon, but an inner transformation of the people.

The passage is a prophetic speech, basically a proclamation of salvation to Zion and, by implication, Zion's people. But it begins with what almost amounts to a vow by the prophet himself: he will not keep silent, will not rest until Zion is vindicated. These lines, which parallel verses 6-7, suggest a note of lament and petition to God. The prophet, like many before him, has assumed an intercessory role on behalf of the people.

The imagery for Zion's vindication and salvation has been encountered frequently in Third Isaiah. It is the image of light, as in Isaiah 6:1-3 (see the commentary on the texts for Epiphany). The brightness of this vindication will be seen by "the nations," by "all the kings" (verse 2). Royal metaphors continue with the picture of Zion held like a "crown," a "royal diadem" in the hand of God.

All of that concerns the revelation of the transformation that God has effected. The transformation itself is the subject of the remainder of the passage; it is characterized as God's gift of a new name (verses 2*b*, 4-5). Though developed poetically, the proclamation concerning a new name is similar to the earlier prophetic reports of symbolic actions. There is the account of an action or the divine instructions to perform one followed by the interpretation of its meaning. There are numerous such accounts, and it is striking how many of them concern names (Isa. 7-8; Hos. 1:2-9). The prophet promises a new name from the mouth of God (verse 2*b*), gives new names as reversals of past conditions (verse 4), and gives a metaphorical explanation of the meaning of the names (verse 5).

The names, old and new, symbolize the nature and reality of Yahweh's relationship, past and future, to Zion and Zion's children. Formerly they were Forsaken, their land Desolate. Could there be a more powerful statement of the absence of God? For the prophet and his original hearers, the Exile was accepted as divine judgment, the time when Yahweh turned aside from them. But now they will be called, "My delight is in her" (in Hebrew *Hephzibah*) and the land "Married" (in Hebrew *Beulah*). This symbolic naming to indicate new realities of relationship is seen also in Hosea 1-3, especially 1:6-9 and 2:16-17. The Book of Ezekiel concludes with a new name for Zion, "The Lord is there" (48:35; see also Jer. 33:16).

The renaming of Zion and the land means that Jerusalem's children will return and claim her, like a young husband takes a wife. Moreover, it signifies that God will rejoice over his people as a bridegroom over a bride (verse 5). Such intimate metaphors were possible within the framework of a covenantal relationship between God and people in which the initiative was God's. The new names thus announce and confirm a new election of the people. It makes a difference what one is called, especially if the name is given by God.

Psalm 36:5-10

These hymnic verses of Psalm 36 are sandwiched between a description (addressed to a human audience) of the wicked person (verses 1-4) and a plea for protection against evildoers (verses 11-12, actually begun already in verse 10). Thus we have a psalm with most of the features of an individual lament.

Before examining verses 5-10, which celebrate the epiphanies of God and their accompanying blessing, a side glance should be given to the opening and closing sections. The description of the evildoer in verses 1-4 may be seen as a negative contrast to the description of divine benevolence in verses 5-10 and as a counterpart to how the worshiper would like to be viewed. In most cultures, portraits of the villainous character serve an educational and moral function just as much as the descriptions of the hero type. Such typologies allow a person to engage in self-assessment and character imitation. (Note that in Western movies, one of America's basic forms of morality plays, the villian as well as the hero is a character figure.) According to the psalm description, the evildoer is one who has no fear of God, believes that his iniquity will not be found out, speaks deceitfully and without normal restraints, and even while awaiting slumber upon the bed plots schemes. In other words, the evil person is one who fundamentally considers him/herself to be an exception to the rule. What applies to others are irrelevant in his/her case and anything can thus be excused. Arrogance, the self-assurance of one's existence as an exception to the rule and evil frequently go hand in hand (see verse 10).

The closing petition (verses 10-12) has the worshiper requesting divine protection so as not to become the object of abuse or the casualty of someone else's arrogance and wickedness. To fall prey to such a state is to be at the mercy of another, to lose one's freedom and dignity (verse 12).

The hymn-like section at the heart of this psalm testifies, in direct address to God, to the benevolence and protection of the Divine. In expressing this sentiment, the psalm writer compares God's qualities to features of the natural world—the heavens, the clouds, a mountain, the great deep (the cavernous, watery deeps beneath the earth). Yet, the one who receives such benefactions is placed in the same category as an undomesticated animal—"man and beast thou savest" (verse 6c). What may initially strike us as odd in such a comparison or classification might not appear so if we give it some thought. The beast receives its blessings, its food, its livelihood without setting out to please God or anybody; it makes no effort to measure up to any standard; it simply drinks in the benefits that come its way from the created order controlled by God. The writer is suggesting something similar in the case with humans.

Verses 7-8 extol the extravagance of God's benefits bestowed in the temple, the place of worship. Not only is God like a protective bird under whose wings one can find shelter but also his house is a place of abundance. What is said in verse 8 should be seen against the background of temple services and sacrifices. Many of the sacrifices were consumed by the worshiper who offered them. After the priest had received his share of the sacrifice (his salary!) and the fat and other portions were burned on the altar, the remainder went to the worshiper who cooked and consumed it in the company of family, friends, and others. The sacrifice or the animal's meat had to be eaten on the day of or the day following the sacrifice (see Lev. 7:11-18). Sacrificial worship was thus very much like a family or communal barbecue. It was a period of gluttony when the normal drive to consume food was countermanded. Thus the psalmist can praise the pleasure, the hedonism of those times in the house of God when food abounded and drink flowed in abundance (see I Sam. 1:1-18).

I Corinthians 12:1-11

With today's epistolary lection, we begin the semicontinuous reading of I Corinthians 12–15 that takes us through the Eighth Sunday After Epiphany. It should be remembered that the Epistle lessons for the Sundays after Epiphany in all three years are taken from First and Second Corinthians. Thus at this time of the liturgical year we are allowed to look at the way one early Christian community appropriated the Christian gospel in a very concrete setting.

Today's lection introduces a three-chapter unit in the epistle (chapters 12–14) that deals with the question of "spiritual gifts" (verse 1), or perhaps "spiritual persons." The openings words, "Now concerning . . . ," suggest that the Corinthian church had inquired of Paul about this topic, and in what follows we have his instructions in which he responds to their question. It is well-known that the question of "spiritual gifts" was of special concern to this church. At least, the topic is addressed more fully in the Corinthian Letters than in any other New Testament writing.

Early on in the letter, Paul wrote to reassure the church that they were not deficient in this regard (1:7). From what we can gather, some members of the church were experiencing the Spirit in highly visible ways, with the result that other members who were not similarly endowed with the Spirit felt that their faith was severely lacking. Paul's concern is pastoral: he seeks to reassure the whole church in its faith, and to relate each of the members, regardless of his or her particular form of spiritual endowment, to the rest of the members in ways that edify the whole church.

In the opening section of today's lection (verses 1-3), Paul reminds his readers of their former pagan status, when they worshiped "dumb idols" (cf. Hab. 2:18-19; Ps. 115:4-5; III Macc. 4:16; Acts 17:29). Regardless of their previous motivations, they were "led astray" by these false gods. In their new life in Christ, they are now reminded that there are proper bounds within which the Holy Spirit works. It is simply not enough to claim that one is speaking "in the Spirit." Rather, we must ask what the Spirit prompts us to say. If it is "Jesus be cursed," we can be assured that God's

Spirit is not responsible for such an imprecation. But if it is "Jesus is Lord," we can be just as assured that God's Spirit is the ultimate motivation.

We are not sure what actual situation, if any, is reflected in this passage. One possibility is that some Christians, in moments of ecstasy, were actually calling down curses on Jesus. Such a scenario is conceivable if we allow that certain Corinthian Gnostics disparaged the human figure Jesus and devoted themselves instead to the "spiritual Christ" (cf. I John 4:2–3). Their curse would then mean: "The historical, or the fleshly, Jesus be cursed." Another possibility is that behind these words we hear the accusations of the Jewish synagogue charging that a crucified Jesus is accursed under the law (Deut. 21:22-23). Or, it may be that Paul is stating a theoretical possibility, and not reflecting an actual situation at all.

The important point to note is that it is not enough simply to claim to be speaking "in the Spirit." We must ask *what is* said "in the Spirit." In this case, Paul insists that the Christian confession, "Jesus is Lord," serve as the fundamental criterion by which we weigh spiritual utterances (cf. Matt. 7:21; Luke 6:46; John 13:13; Rom. 10:9; II Cor. 4:5; Phil. 2:11; Col. 2:6).

In the second section of today's lection, Paul turns to a discussion of spiritual gifts. It should be noted that he prefers to use the term *charismata*, since it conveys the idea that they are bestowed as a gift of grace (*charis;* cf. Rom. 12:6; also Heb. 2:4). The fundamental point he makes in this section is that there is a diversity of gifts. They are referred to in different ways: "varieties of gifts . . . varieties of service . . . varieties of working" (verses 4-6). Yet, for all their variety, in every case they have a single source: the same Spirit, the same Lord, the same God. His conviction is summarized in verse 11: "All these are inspired by one and the same Spirit, who apportions to each one individually as he wills."

These words are well worth hearing, for Paul insists here that diversity of gifts, functions, and service is part and parcel of Christian community. As will become clear later in these chapters as he discusses the gift of tongues, some in the church were elevating one gift to a position of supreme importance above all the rest. According to them, there was one supreme gift to which every one had to aspire. Not many, but one. For them, all should seek the same gift. For Paul, each should recognize his or her individual gift and use it for the good of all. The Pauline word for us is that diversity is a given. What's more, it is God-given. We should not think of diversity as an obstacle to be overcome but as a resource to be used.

Besides affirming the value of diversity, Paul instructs us about the proper use of these gifts: they are "for the common good" (verse 7; cf. I Cor. 6:12; 10:23; 14:26). Here he attacks the robust individualism within the church. The Spirit gives us gifts not for the sole benefit of personal enrichment, but so we can enrich the faith of others. As we will see later, this becomes an important criterion for judging the worth of particular gifts. Do they contribute to community, or do they destroy community by establishing tiny cells of spirituality wholly unrelated to one another, and in the end, insensitive to one another?

The various gifts are mentioned in verses 8-10. To determine precisely what each gift entailed, and how they differed from one another, the preacher will need to consult concordances and commentaries. It is worth noting, however, that tongues are mentioned last, no doubt intentionally by Paul to place it at the bottom of the list. For this situation, it least commended itself because it contributed least to corporate solidarity.

John 2:1-11

The lections for this second Sunday after Epiphany join not only in announcing the manifestations of God among us but do so with festive spirit and with gifts in abundance. This is especially true of the story of the wedding in Cana, recorded only in the Gospel of John.

That John 2:1-11 is an Epiphany text is evident both by direct statement and by symbolic clue. The direct statement occurs in verse 11, "manifested his glory," and the symbolic clue is the opening phrase in verse 1, "On the third day." If one tries to understand the third day as a chronological reference, the calculation is confused by the use of "the next day" to mark each of the three preceding events (1:29, 35, 43). However, as a resurrection symbol, the third day is appropriate to signal a revelation event. In fact, the next account in John, the cleansing of the temple (2:13-22), is also a "third day" story (verses 20-21) in that the temple cleansing is, in this Gospel, a death-resurrection sign. Given the favorable reception accorded Jesus in Galilee and the rejection in Jerusalem, it is not coincidental that the wedding is set in Galilee and the "funeral" (2:13-22) in Jerusalem.

Approaches to the Cana story in terms of its sources are not very fruitful. The Dionysius cult in Syria had stories of gods turning water into wine, and Philo of Alexandria characterized the Logos as giving the people wine instead of water. However, whether the Evangelist was aware of such background stories is unclear, and even if he were, interpreting a text on the basis of sources is of limited value. More pertinent is the question, What is John saying about Jesus in the Cana wedding story?

It seems clear that John is not attempting to *prove* a miracle was performed, as, for example, Matthew attempts to prove the resurrection (28:1-15). Were that John's purpose, surely more details would be provided. Who issued invitations to the wedding? Why was the family of Jesus there? What gave Jesus' mother (never called by her name in this Gospel) reason to believe Jesus could relieve the wine shortage? Did she expect a miracle or a purchase? Or did she expect him and his friends to leave and thereby relieve the short supply? From where did the servants get approximately one hundred fifty gallons (six jars holding eighteen to twenty-seven gallons each) of water, a major task in itself? If proving a miracle were John's purpose, surely more witnesses to the miracle would have testified to its having occurred. But neither the servants nor the wine steward knew what happened. Who, then, believed the sign? Jesus' disciples (verse 11).

Let us, then, allow the Evangelist to make his point. First of all, the writer wants it understood that Jesus performed his signs according to God's will (5:19, 30; 7:6; 8:25) and not in response to any person's wish or need. While his mother is an unwitting helper in this first sign, Jesus does not act at her bidding. He distanced himself from her (verse 4), indicating that his ministry would be according to "his hour" (verse 4), a recurring theme in this Gospel. When his brothers urged him to go up to Jerusalem, he said it was not his hour, and then he went (7:1-9). When Martha and Mary sent word to Jesus about their brother's illness, he tarried two days before going (11:1-7). In John's Gospel, Jesus speaks and acts not in response to any claims of kinship, friendship, or even need, but at his own initiative as God's will is revealed to him. This pattern may seem to be without compassion, but something more than compassion is involved. In the Cana story as well as in those involving his brothers and his friends, Jesus meets the need but he does more. Compassion alone might provide wine, but sovereign grace does more: it reveals God in what is done and confirms the disciples' faith in Jesus.

Second, the Evangelist is saying that a sign is not a miracle to amaze or an offer of proof for his teaching. The sign was a window through which God was revealed. To attend to the miraculous and to miss the revelation would be no more than curiosity wallowing in the unusual.

And, finally, a sign is not evident to all, and bears an uncertain relation to faith. At Cana, Jesus manifested his glory and those who believed were already his disciples (verse 11). On other occasions it is said, "Many believed in his name when they saw his signs" (2:23), but obviously being present was not sufficient to generate faith. In fact, Jesus said to Thomas, "Have you believed because you have seen me? Blessed are those who have not seen and yet believe" (20:29).

Third Sunday After Epiphany

Nehemiah 8:1-4a, 5-6, 8-10; Psalm 19:7-14; I Corinthians 12:12-30; Luke 4:14-21

Thematic connections among the lections for this day are not easy to discern, and it is not necessary to impose them upon the readings. Each passage has enough to say in itself, and any one offers rich possibilities for the preacher. The Old Testament text and the responsorial psalm concentrate upon the Law, the book of the law read by Ezra to the people, the Law of Moses, the divine instructions for life. The Lucan account of Jesus in the synagogue in Nazareth—including the citation of Isaiah 61:1-2, the Old Testament lesson for the First Sunday After Epiphany—continues this season's interest in the youth and early ministry of Jesus. The epistolary text from I Corinthians 12:12-30 is Paul's classical statement of the church as many members but one body in Christ.

Nehemiah 8:1-4*a*, 5-6, 8-10

Our Old Testament reading contains the essential elements of the report (Neh. 7:73*b*–8:18) of Ezra's reading of the book of the law to the people assembled in Jerusalem after the return from the Exile. Important as the report is in itself, it is only part of a larger account of ceremonies in Jerusalem. After the law was read the people engaged in prayers of confession and fasting, and then renewed the ancient covenant with their Lord (Neh. 9–10).

The account is filled with ritual and ceremonial allusions. The people are assembled in the square before the Water Gate, part of the newly rebuilt walls of Jerusalem. Ezra is identified as a priest (verse 2). The date ("the first day of the seventh month") probably refers to the calendar of religious events. The position and posture of Ezra and the people indicate a solemn occasion: he stood on or at a wooden pulpit or platform, surrounded by others (verse 4), opened the book where all could see him do it (verse 5), pronounced a blessing or invocation, and all responded by saying, "amen, amen," lifting up their hands in prayer and prostrating themselves (verse 6). Then he read clearly and the Levites "gave the sense" (verse 8). Finally, Ezra declared the day to be one of sacred celebration (verses 9-10).

The ceremony must be distinguished from the rituals of the temple. It included all the people who could understand—men, women, and young people—and it did not take place in the sacred precincts. The patterns of speech and action suggest that while we may have the report of an event that took place once, the ceremonies were not invented for the occasion but depended upon more ancient tradition. Compare this reading with the one reported in II Kings 22. Certainly this activity of reading, teaching, and responding to the law is like that in the later synagogue, and some of the practices are doubtless older. When one considers the broader framework which leads to the renewal of the covenant one can compare the events with accounts such as that in Joshua 24, in which Joshua led the people in the renewal of the Sinai covenant. In any case, religious services that concentrated upon the reading and interpretation of the scriptures came to be central in the synagogue, and from there formed the basis for the Christian service of the word.

The most important theme here concerns the reading and interpretation of the book of the law. It is not possible to know what book or books Ezra actually read. The author of the Books of Chronicles/Ezra/Nehemiah uses the expression to refer to the Torah, or the Pentateuch. There is no suggestion that all these books were read: Ezra read "from it" (verse 3), and the time given would limit how much could be read. Clearly, in the time of the author—if not already in the time of Ezra—it was widely held that the Torah was sacred scripture, soon to be fully recognized as canon.

Given the degree of reverence for the book of the law, it is all the more remarkable how the book is treated. Notice that it was "read clearly," and then the Levites "gave the sense" and "gave instruction in what was read" (verse 8, with NEB). It is not enough to hold it in reverence, or just to read it publicly. It also must be explained and taught. The role of the Levites here is not unlike that reflected in the Book of Deuteronomy, in which ancient laws are presented, explained and reinterpreted, and then laid upon the hearts of the people. The meaning of the ancient scripture must be made plain in a new time.

Psalm 19:7-14

Psalm 19 is concerned with two major topics: the world of creation, the heavens and the sun especially (verses 1-6), and the way of the law or Torah (verses 7-10). The present lection focuses on the latter part, the hymn in praise of Torah, but it also includes the prayer portion of the psalm, addressed directly to God (verses 11-14).

Verses 7-9 contain a series of six affirmations in praise of the law that follow a common pattern. The first line of each of the affirmations begins with a different synonym for the law, is followed by a declaration, and a participial construction defining a function of the law. The following are the synonyms: law, testimony, precepts, commandment, fear, and ordinances. The clauses or adjectival declarations are: perfect, sure, right, pure, clean, and true. The functions of the law are given as: reviving the soul (or renewing life), making wise the simple (educating the unlearned or simpleton), rejoicing the heart, enlightening the eyes (we would say "restoring strength"; see I Sam. 14:24-30), enduring forever, and righteous altogether.

Verse 10 is an adulation of the law stated in the form of a "more . . . than" saying. Here the law is compared to two items and their distinctive qualities: more desired than gold (in ancient as in modern times, the most coveted of metals) and sweeter than honey or the honeycomb (the ancients' primary source of sweetening).

A twofold function of the law is affirmed in verse 11. Negatively, the law functions to warn and thus to aid one in right living (11*a*). Laws such as the Ten Commandments functioned not to tell one what to do but as signposts at the periphery of experience warning that one should not go beyond a certain point. The law thus served to define the boundaries within which one could operate and live safely. It served as a canopy under which one could live. It functioned to provide a reading on one's location in the larger world of experience. Positively, the keeping of the laws is related to rewards (11*b*). Rewards should be seen here not as something presented by God like trophies for winning a race but as the results or consequences inherent in obedience to Torah itself. Law's shaping of life and the shape of the life produced are its rewards. Obedience to Torah means that one has experienced what is promised in the declarations of verses 7-9.

Verses 12-14 constituted the petition proper embodying the requests of the worshiper. Since it is difficult for one to be certain when errors occur and hard to avoid the pitfalls of self-delusion, the worshiper asks to be kept from certain fallacies. Two types of conditions or sins are singled out: (1) hidden faults that are not obvious to the undiscerning eye; those personality factors and unseen attitudes that can corrode character or shape the personality in distorted ways; and (2) presumptuous sins, acts that one may commit as if they were some bold adventure in courage, some venting of a true, primeval drive, or some daring experiment in being one's own person. Hidden faults and presumptuous sins are the two extremes by which one may step beyond the law and the goals of Torah.

The final request (verse 14) likewise employs extremes: doing (words) and thinking (meditation of the heart) are ways of speaking about a totality.

In preaching from the Old Testament, and from such psalms as 19, the Christian preacher should be attuned to the values inherent in the law and expound the qualities of life lived according to Torah.

I Corinthians 12:12-30

In the previous section, Paul has stressed the common source of the various manifestations of the Spirit in the church. He now turns to discuss the paradox of the one and the many as it is experienced in Christ.

First, the one (verses 12-14). For Paul, it was axiomatic that there was one body, the church (Rom. 12:5; I Cor. 10:17; Eph. 1:23; 4:4; Col. 3:15). But besides being one in number, the church also exhibits another level of oneness. The one Spirit, viewed here both as the agent of baptism and the source of spiritual sustenance, brings about a kind of unity that eliminates ethnic and social differences. Thus, Jews and Greeks, slaves and free, share a common initiation by the Spirit through which they achieve a level of oneness: they become one body (Gal. 3:28; Rom. 10:12; Col. 3:11). In this respect, the church is like a human body. It has many parts, but they function as part of a single entity (cf. verse 27; Rom. 12:4).

Second, the many (verses 15-30). In this section, the other side of the paradox is discussed: "the body does not consist of one member but of many" (verse 14). Unity does not exclude diversity. The two may exist together, but they must be properly understood. To help explain the nature of the "many," Paul cites the well-known example of the human body, an analogy used by Greco-Roman authors to illustrate the nature of the state.

As used here, this example enables Paul to make two points. (1) The human body has many parts with many different functions. It is absurd to think that there could be only one part with a single function. Thus, "there are many parts, yet one body" (verse 20). (2) The parts are interdependent. They are many, but not in the sense that there are many pebbles in a box. Rather, they are organically related. The pain one part experiences is experienced by the other parts. They form an ecology of suffering and rejoicing (verse 26).

By this point, Paul has established, largely through the use of the analogy of the human body, that the one can encompass the many; in fact, that it is impossible to speak of *one body* in any meaningful sense unless we grant the existence of its many parts. Oneness does not mean sameness. Unity does not mean uniformity.

Having elaborated on the one and the many, Paul now applies his remarks to the church: "Now you are the body of

135

Christ and individually members of it" (verse 27). He does not say: "You are a body of Christians," as if we are a group with a common identity. Rather, his claim here appears to be metaphysical not metaphorical, even though this point is hotly disputed among commentators. If Paul here is making a fundamental claim about the nature of corporate Christian existence, he is asserting that the risen Lord finds concrete manifestation among us, the church. Whether the best way to conceive of this is to think of the church as the extension of the exalted body of Christ is debated. Even this may not be emphatic enough to account for Paul's bold claim here. But however we conceive of this claim, we should see the church as the Body of Christ in some *real* rather than metaphorical sense.

Accordingly, God has constituted the church with a variety of gifts, services, ministries, offices, and functions. These are elaborated in verses 28-30. As applied to the church, Paul's earlier point now receives concrete application. There is one church, but it cannot exist if there is only one part with a single function. Then it becomes grotesque. We can only speak of oneness if we recognize diversity.

The overall direction of Paul's remarks in this chapter is clear. There is not one spiritual gift to be sought as the summum bonum of Christian existence. There are many gifts, each with its own form and function, uniquely able to contribute to the whole.

These words of Paul, when taken seriously, keep the church from developing a cookie-cutter mentality. The missionary thinks everyone in the church should become a missionary. Likewise, the teacher, church musician, and so forth. We all live with the tyranny of the specialties, each of us looking at the whole through the lens of our particular gift, wondering why everyone does not aspire to it as we do. But should every person in the church be a teacher? Paul thinks not. His is not a monochrome vision of the church.

Luke 4:14-21

Luke 4:14-21 joins Nehemiah 8 and Psalm 19 in affirming the revelation of God in the Word which is read in the assembly of believers. The act of reading and hearing the Word of revelation provides a theme most appropriate for Epiphany.

Our Gospel lection consists of two parts: verses 14-15 and 16-21. Verses 14-15 function in three ways: (1) they provide a transition both in terms of location and of activity from Jesus' wilderness temptation to the launching of the Galilean ministry; (2) they continue the attention on the power of the Spirit in Jesus' ministry in Galilean synagogues before focusing upon one of the synagogues in particular, the one in Nazareth; and (3) they set the general context of Jesus' ministry in Galilean synagogues. It is important also to receive the report of Jesus' rejection in Nazareth and the attempt on his life (verses 28-29) against the backdrop of wide reputation (verse 14) and most favorable reception (verse 15).

The second part of our Gospel, verses 16-21, poses for the preacher a small problem. These verses are in fact a portion of a unit extending through verse 30. However, verses 21-30 (verse 21 is an overlap) constitute next Sunday's reading. The preacher is thus faced with the task of treating a single narrative on two separate occasions. Is this problem insurmountable or is a violation of the text inevitable? No. There are two characteristics in the text which offer some justification for the division: first, verses 16-21 record the first movement of the synagogue service, Jesus reading the Scripture, while verses 22-30 provide Jesus' sermon on the text and the congregation's response. The division is somewhat natural. Second, verses 16-21 tell of a positive response to Jesus while verses 22-30 report a very negative response. The contrast is so sharp that some scholars have suggested that Luke is here conflating two stories from the tradition. We can, therefore, confine ourselves to verses 16-21, and it will be important not to steal from verses 22-30, thereby robbing next Sunday's message of its punch.

Clearly the event Luke here describes is the same as the one recorded in Mark 6:1-6 and Matthew 13:54-58, although the accounts differ so much that one must conclude Luke is following a different source. More importantly, however, is the different purpose to which Luke puts the story. Both Mark and Matthew place the rejection in Nazareth (actually only Luke names the town) well into Jesus' ministry, while

Luke locates it at the beginning, prefaced with only a general comment about Jesus coming into Galilee, teaching in the synagogues (verses 14-15). In fact, Luke sacrifices chronology in the service of another purpose, for even though Jesus goes to Capernaum later (4:31-37), our story assumes he has been there and his ministry is widely known (verse 23). Although admittedly awkward, this placing of the Nazareth event first is Luke's way of making it programmatic, a preview of all Jesus' ministry which will now unfold. Perhaps it will sharpen our focus if we press the impact of verses 16-21 into a series of brief summary statements.

1. Jesus' ministry is in the power of God's Spirit, both in his movement and his activity (3:22; 4:1-2; 4:14; 4:18). Luke's model here is probably Elijah whose itinerary as well as power came from the Spirit (I Kings 18:7-16).

2. All Jesus' ministry was inside, not outside the bosom of Judaism and the traditions of his people. Here Jesus affirms by his faithfulness the Sabbath, the Scriptures, and the synagogue. He is, according to Luke, a reformer and not an opponent of his heritage.

3. By reading Isaiah 61:1-2, Jesus has not only announced fulfillment of prophecy (verse 21) but has defined what "messiah" means. Isaiah 61 is a servant song, and if "anointed me" is taken literally ("christened," "made me the Christ or Messiah") then the Christ is God's servant to turn the hopes of the poor, imprisoned, and oppressed into reality. The Messiah will bring the amnesty, the liberation, and the restoration of the year of jubilee (Lev. 25:8-12).

4. The "someday" of hope is now the "today" of fulfillment (verse 21). For Luke's church and for us it is still "today" and preaching which turns "today" into another vague and distant "someday" has not listened carefully to the text.

Fourth Sunday After Epiphany

Jeremiah 1:4-10; Psalm 71:1-6; I Corinthians 13:1-13;
Luke 4:21-30

The Gospel reading continues the account of the first events in the ministry of Jesus with the semicontinuous readings from Luke. Jeremiah's report of his vocation is good preparation for the Lucan emphasis upon the parallels between the role of Jesus and that of the Old Testament prophets: gracious words came out of his mouth, and no prophet is honored in his own country. Psalm 71:1-6, an individual's prayer for deliverance, responds in particular to the election of the prophet "from his mother's womb" (verse 6 and Jer. 1:5), but it supports the theme of conflict with opponents in the Gospel lection. First Corinthians 13 reminds us that the gift of love is even greater than that of prophecy or tongues.

Jeremiah 1:4-10

It is appropriate that we consider the vocation reports of the prophets—Jeremiah today and Isaiah next Sunday—in the context of the beginning of the ministry of Jesus. We are encouraged to reflect not only on the prophetic aspects of that ministry but, like the first disciples, also upon our own response to God's vocation.

The calls of prophets and other servants of God are very private matters. That is especially true of Jeremiah, who reveals throughout his work so much of his personal turmoil. It is all the more remarkable, therefore, to learn that Jeremiah's report of his call has a great many features in common with other Old Testament vocation reports. These include the reports of the calls of Moses (Exod. 3:1–4:17), Gideon (Judg. 6:11-24), Isaiah (6:1-13), and Ezekiel (Ezek. 1–3). All these report an encounter with God, a commission to do the Lord's will or speak the Lord's word, and a ritual act or sign symbolizing the designated role. In all cases except Ezekiel the one who is called objects to the vocation, and then is reassured. We may conclude from the persistence of this feature in vocation reports that resistance is not linked so much to individual personalities as it is to the experience of standing in the presence of the Holy One, and being called God's servant. It goes with the office, even verifying that one is called by God, to feel unworthy or inadequate.

Some of the vocation reports (Isa. 6; Ezek. 1–3; cf. I Kings 22:19-22) give accounts of the Lord's heavenly throne. Jeremiah's report, like that of Gideon and Moses, focuses rather upon the encounter with the word of God, as verse 4 explicitly states. The pattern of the report is that of a dialogue between Yahweh and the prophet. The initial divine speech (verse 5), remarkably, announces past events. Even before Jeremiah was formed in the womb he was known by Yahweh, consecrated and appointed "a prophet to the nations." Jeremiah's response (verse 6) is an objection that he does not know how to speak, that he is too young. Yahweh then reacts (verse 7) to both of the objections, but more to one than to the other. He simply tells the prophet not to say that he is only a youth; and to the question of Jeremiah's speaking ability, God announces that he will command him to speak, and will tell him what to say. Then Yahweh responds with the promise of deliverance to an objection that had not been voiced, fear of opposition: "Be not afraid of them." This allusion indicates that the purpose of the account was to respond to opposition from the people. Prophets reported their vocations in order to establish their authority to speak.

At this point the dialogue is over and the ritual of ordination begins. As befits designation for the prophetic role (see Isa. 6:5-7; Ezek. 2:8–3:3), Yahweh touches Jeremiah's mouth and gives him the message he is to deliver (verses 9-10). It is a message of both judgment and salvation.

One of the most important aspects of this report concerns the meaning and authority of the prophetic word. In the first place, it is clearly indicated from beginning to end that the words of the prophet are to be those the Lord gives him. That self-understanding persists not only in Jeremiah but in all other Old Testament prophets as well: they are messengers bearing revelations from their God. Second, it is equally clear that the prophetic words are not idle talk but powerful. To have the words of God in one's mouth is to be "set over nations . . . to pluck up and to break down" (verse 10). As in Genesis 1, when God speaks, it is so. No wonder that one called by God to speak such a word would be reluctant to take on the task. Have the church and our culture completely lost the sense of such words as powerful? Which words, if any and by whom, do we consider to be effective?

Psalm 71:1-6

Psalm 71 is a complex lament in which a description of trouble (verses 7-11) occurs along with various appeals for help (verses 2-4, 12-13, 17-18), statements of trust and confidence (verses 1, 16, 19-21), and vows to perform certain actions in the future (verses 14-15, 22-24).

The first six verses have been selected to accompany the other readings for the day because of the parallels between these verses and statements in the call of Jeremiah. Psalm 71 seems to be a prayer of an aged man, perhaps a king, at a time of sickness or approaching death. The person's youth is reflected upon as a time that inaugurated a lifelong devotion and fidelity to Yahweh.

The psalm opens with a statement of confidence and trust (verse 1a) but quickly shifts to a request (verse 1b). Throughout verses 1-6, this same interweaving of trust and appeal for cure occurs. The enemies of the person are the wicked, the unjust, and the cruel. As bargaining power to secure help in old age (verse 9), appeal is made to the fidelity that has characterized life since birth. Like Jeremiah and Paul, the psalmist is willing to affirm a special status or at least a special relationship with God from birth.

I Corinthians 13:1-13

Ordinarily, this chapter is read as a poetic hymn to love, and as such is all too easily removed from its immediate context. Some scholars argue that it breaks the train of thought introduced in chapter 12, and consequently should be treated as an excursus with no thematic relation to what precedes or what follows. But a strong case can be made for seeing it as intrinsic to the discussion of spiritual gifts introduced in chapter 12 and continued in chapter 14.

How then does it function? A clue is provided by the earlier discussion of eating sacrificial meats in chapters 8–10. There Paul introduces the topic about which the church had inquired (chapter 8), but midway in the discussion he presents two examples for the church, one positive (his own apostolic behavior, chapter 9), the other negative (Israel, 10:1-22), and finally resumes the discussion (10:23–11:1).

The discussion in chapters 12–14 unfolds in similar fashion. The topic about which the church inquired is introduced (chapter 12). Then he provides his own apostolic behavior as an example for the church (chapter 13), after which he returns to the discussion of spiritual gifts, contrasting the gift of tongues and the gift of prophecy (chapter 14). Read this way, chapter 13 is to be seen primarily as a discussion of Paul's own apostolic behavior.

Accordingly, it divides into three parts. In part one (verses 1-3), he characterizes various aspects of his own apostolic behavior. Note that he consistently uses the first person singular, and that each of the items relates directly to his own apostolic behavior: speaking in tongues (14:6, 18); prophecy (14:6; mysteries (2:1, 7; 4:1; 14:2; 15:51; Rom. 11:25; 16:25); knowledge (8:1-2); faith to remove mountains, that is, power to work miracles (Matt. 17:20; II Cor. 12:11-13); giving up his possessions (I Cor 4:11; II Cor. 6:10); handing over his body for the glory of his ministry (reading the textual variant; II Cor. 4:7-12; Gal. 6:14). Each of these is best understood in direct reference to Paul's own behavior. If any of these apostolic acts is not motivated by *agape,* it is of no value, least of all to Paul himself. *Agape* serves as the fundamental mainspring of his apostolic work.

In part two (verses 4-7), Paul characterizes *agape*. The contrast between *agape* and *eros* is well-known, and there is an abundant literature on the significance of *agape* in antiquity. What each of these characteristics stresses is the self-giving, sacrificial dimension of *agape*, and this fits well with Paul's earlier insistence that *agape* builds up, while *gnosis* puffs up. Love, as Paul understands it, eventuates into a form of life that does not insist on its own way, is not egocentric, but is self-giving. This was the way of Christ (Phil. 2:4), the expected norm of Christian behavior (I Cor. 10:24), and the earmark of Paul's apostleship (I Cor. 10:33).

In part three (verses 8-13), Paul presents *agape* as the supreme eschatological reality, that which "never ends" (verse 8). By contrast, the other gifts of the Spirit, such as tongues, knowledge, and prophesying, are partial and temporary. But what which transcends time is *agape*. "It is the future eternal light shining in the present. It therefore needs no change of form. It is that which continues" (Barth). When set against "that which is perfect" (verse 10), the end time, love endures, since it represents most vividly that part of God that has reached from the future into the present through the Christ-event (cf. Rom. 8:39).

But how does this relate to the Corinthians' situation. Paul urges, "Make love your aim" (I Cor. 14:1). Their task is to translate the eschatological reality of love into a congregational life-style that fosters corporate edification instead of individual self-interest (I Cor. 14:5, 26).

One of the chief tasks faced by the preacher in dealing with this all too familiar text is to make it concrete. Preaching on I Corinthians 13 can all too easily become an exercise for poetic soaring rather than an occasion for addressing the pressing problems of the church. The homiletical move here should not be into the clouds but onto the earth, for here, after all, was where God's love finally became manifest.

Luke 4:21-30

All the readings for today declare that we are fully known of God, even from the womb. In that understanding is great comfort, for being known of God does not mean that one is known or accepted by one's contemporaries. In fact, being known of God in the sense of being chosen for special service sometimes stirs hostility in others, even in those whom one may seek to serve. While this is the testimony of Jeremiah, the psalmist, and Paul, it is especially true of Jesus in Luke's record of his visit to Nazareth. Epiphany, the celebration of the manifestation of Christ to the world, has its darker side.

The reader is urged to review the comments on verses 14-21, last Sunday's Gospel lection. There is nothing in those verses to justify the opinion of some that verse 22 should be taken as a negative response to Jesus. Those who chart the congregation's reaction to Jesus as moving from favor (22*a*), to disfavor (22*b*), to violence (28) are presuming to read a mood of doubt in the words, "Is not this Joseph's son?" A better case can be made that there was a radical shift from favor to violence. But whether there is doubt or injured pride in the congregation, Jesus understands them as expecting a demonstration for the hometown folk of the extraordinary work being reported from Capernaum. Jesus also understands that proximity and familiarity tend to be blinding privileges. Luke reports as much on other occasions. The people of Nineveh and the queen of the South will judge the generation which did not heed one greater than Jonah and Solomon (11:29-32), and those who appeal to enter the kingdom on the grounds that Jesus taught in their streets and ate in their homes will be turned away (13:26-27). In fact, the woman in a crowd who declared a blessing on Jesus' mother was corrected: "Blessed rather are those who hear the word of God and keep it!" (11:27-28). The warning to the church in these statements is quite clear.

Jesus' response to the congregation's expectation makes it evident that the problem is far deeper than simply blind familiarity. If the citizens of Nazareth assume certain privileges for themselves, that error is joined to a more serious one: a possessiveness that resents Jesus taking God's favor to others beyond Nazareth, especially to Capernaum, a town very likely having a heavy non-Jewish population. Such is the clear implication of the two stories Jesus told. Many widows in Israel were suffering under the prolonged drought. Elijah brought relief to one, a foreigner in

144

Sidon (I Kings 17:1–18:1). With many lepers suffering in Israel, Elisha healed but one, a Syrian (II Kings 5:1-14). These two stories were, of course, in their own Scriptures and quite familiar. Perhaps this accounts in part for the intensity of their hostility; anger and violence are the last defense of those who are made to face the truth imbedded in their own tradition. Such truths will not go away even after the one who pointed to them has been removed. Those at war with themselves and what they know to be true often make casualties even of those who seek their good. It is a common theme in Luke that the quarrel is not really between Jesus and Judaism or between the church and the synagogue. The tension lies between the synagogue and its own Scriptures.

The synagogue, now a mob, attempted to stone Jesus. The law permitted that stoning could be either by throwing stones at a person or throwing a person against the stones (verse 29). Jesus' escape, not described in detail (verse 30), is reminiscent of the elusive Elijah and anticipates the escapes of Peter (Acts 12:6-11) and Paul (Acts 16:25-28).

The event in Nazareth foreshadows Israel's rejection of Jesus and the taking of the message to Gentiles. However, it is important to notice that here Jesus does not go elsewhere because he is rejected; he is rejected because he goes elsewhere. Luke's point is that Israel should have understood. Readers of Luke's Gospel expect Christ to go to the nations, having a certain word in the matter as early as Simeon's prayer over the infant (2:29-32). But Israel, says Luke, knew of God's grace toward the nations as early as the covenant with Abraham (Gen. 22:18; Acts 3:25). The tragic difference between knowing and really knowing has not departed from God's people, even to this day.

Fifth Sunday After Epiphany

Isaiah 6:1-8 (9-13); Psalm 138; I Corinthians 15:1-11;
Luke 5:1-11

As the semicontinuous readings from the Gospel of Luke and from First Corinthians continue in this season, the lections do not always present a single or even dominant theme for the preacher. However, a motif present in one way or another in most of these readings is a concern with the power and authority of the word. In Isaiah 6 the prophet reports his call, and the harsh words he is to proclaim. The responsorial psalm is a song of thanksgiving from the temple, the location of Isaiah's vision. First Corinthians 15:1-11 is Paul's summary of the gospel that he had preached, and through which God works. In Luke 5:1-11 the people crowded to hear from Jesus "the word of God," (verse 1), he taught them from the boat, and at the "word" of Jesus, Simon let down the nets again. Moreover, the Gospel account of the call and response of the apostles parallels in significant ways the vocation of Isaiah and his response.

Isaiah 6:1-8 (9-13)

Like the Old Testament lesson for the previous Sunday (Jer. 1:4-10), Isaiah 6 is the report of a prophet's vocation. While Jeremiah's account concentrates upon the encounter with the word of Yahweh, Isaiah 6 closely parallels Ezekiel 1–3. Both are reports of visions of the Lord's heavenly throne. Similar also is the scene described by Micaiah ben Imlah in I Kings 22:19-22: "I saw the Lord sitting on his throne, and all the host of heaven beside him. . . ." Neither Isaiah nor Ezekiel sees God directly, but both have the sense of being on the outskirts of the heavenly throne room and hearing the

146

deliberations going on there. Such Old Testament imagery is indebted to ancient Near Eastern traditions concerning the heavenly court. In those polytheistic traditions the court includes the chief god and the other deities; in the Old Testament God holds court with his messengers (see also Job 1:6-12).

The date formula that begins Isaiah's report also sets the mood. "The year that King Uzziah died" would have been 742 B.C., but that king's death signaled the end of an era of relative independence for Judah. During most of Isaiah's lifetime his nation lived under the threat of Assyrian domination. The prophet was active for some forty years, from the date given here until at least 701 B.C.

The date formula, however, is mainly a preface to the description of the vision of Yahweh as king on a throne (verses 1-4). That his "train" filled the temple suggests that the prophet stands at the entrance to the sacred precincts, and probably that the ark of the covenant was understood as the symbolic throne of Yahweh. Other aspects of temple worship are the antiphonal hymn of praise sung by the seraphim, and the fact that the "house"—that is, the temple—was filled with smoke, probably from offerings. The seraphim who attend the Lord must cover both their "feet" (a euphemism for their nakedness) and their faces because no one can see God directly and live.

Isaiah responds to the scene with a cry of woe (verse 5), similar to a confession of sin and an expression of mourning for both himself and his people. Confronted with the presence of the Lord he knows that he is unclean, although by the priestly criteria he would have been judged ritually clean before he approached the temple. In reaction to his confession one of the seraphim performs a ritual of purification combining word and deed. He touches Isaiah's mouth with a coal from the altar and pronounces that his guilt is removed and his sin forgiven. This ritual parallels those in the vocation reports of both Jeremiah and Ezekiel in that all of them concern the mouth of the ones called to speak for God.

The vision report reaches a climax when the prophet overhears Yahweh asking the heavenly court whom he shall send, and the prophet steps forward (verse 8). The remainder of the chapter consists of the Lord's terrible commission to the prophet to bring a word of total judgment, interrupted only by the prophet's unsuccessful prayer of intercession.

Viewed in the context of other vocation reports, the purpose of this account becomes clear. The authority of the prophets to speak frequently was challenged (see Amos 7:10-17), especially if their message was one of judgment. Since prophets had no "official" standing comparable to that of, for example, priests, their right to speak in the name of the Lord was open to question. The vocation reports were their responses. Because of a call from God, the prophet was not only entitled to speak but compelled to do so. In the case of Isaiah 6, the prophet specifically justifies his harsh message by reporting his vocation.

A great many features of this passage cry out for proclamation. There is first of all the emphasis upon the sacred, including its cultic dimensions. One should therefore not drive a wedge between the prophetic and the priestly. It is in the temple that Isaiah experiences the awe-inspiring presence of the Lord, is aware of his uncleanness, and is purified. The holiness of God—the radical difference between the divine and the human—is a persistent theme in the words of Isaiah. Second, there is the call itself and the prophet's response. God does not address Isaiah directly, but the one purified by the divine messenger is able to hear the call and accept the commission. Note the sequence: encounter with the presence of God, confession, purification, and overhearing, and then acceptance of the commission. Third, there is the theme of the effectiveness of the word of God, and of the word of God through human expression. As with Jeremiah, the prophet is empowered with words that will prevent repentance and will bring judgment. Are there any modern words that have—or are believed to have—such power?

Psalm 138

This psalm may be subdivided into three parts. Verses 1-3 thank and praise God; verses 4-6 extol the grace and glory of

God and their impact on the rulers of the world; and verses 7-8 express trust in God.

The general tone of the psalm clearly identifies it as a thanksgiving. It differs, however, from most thanksgiving psalms in two ways: (1) there is no description of the trouble or the distress from which the person was rescued (see verse 3 which refers to an appeal to God at an earlier time of distress), and (2) the psalm is addressed directly to the Deity throughout (verse 8*a* is possibly an exception) whereas most thanksgivings are addressed to a human audience.

The person offering thanks in the original usage of this psalm was probably the king. This is suggested by the references to the kings of the earth in verse 4 who hear the words of Yahweh's mouth, perhaps words spoken by the Judean king. Also, the king was especially the man of God's right hand (verse 7; see Ps. 110:1).

Several elements in the psalm call for elucidation:

1. The reference to "before the gods" (verse 1) could mean one of several things. Ancient translations read "before the angels," "before kings," or "before judges." If the reference is to pagan gods, then the worshiper could be saying no more than, "I sing your praise in an alien culture." If the reference is to heavenly beings (see Pss. 29:1; 82:1), then the phrase could denote worship before the heavenly council of God.

2. To bow down toward the temple does not imply that the worshiper is in some foreign land or away from Jerusalem. This could be a reference to worship or activity at the temple gate, near the main altar, or in the temple courtyard.

3. The lowly may not refer to a class—the poor, the downtrodden, or others in similar conditions—but could be a self-designation, even of a king—the lowly over against the divine.

4. The verb translated "to know" in verse 6*b* may mean, on the basis of an Arabic parallel, "to humble." Thus "the haughty he humbles from afar."

The statement of trust in verses 7-8 gives expression to a serene confidence—almost. Verse 8*c* still resorts to petition even after the statement of assurance. Note that the psalm does not assume that life will be free of distress and problems but only that God will preserve one through them all.

Trouble and enemies are the givens in life; grace and preservation to endure and overcome them are the sustaining gifts.

I Corinthians 15:1-11

Since this passage served as the epistolary reading for Easter, Year B, we provided there some basic observations about its overall structure and certain of its prominent motifs. We will not repeat those observations here.

One of the chief difficulties we face in preaching on this text during the season after Epiphany is that we tend to think of it almost exclusively as an Easter text, suitable for proclamation only in that liturgical context. But even if the words we hear above all the rest are "he was raised on the third day" (verse 4), we do well to remember that every Sunday is in one sense a celebration of the Easter faith.

There is, however, another approach to preaching this text in a post-Epiphany setting. In some traditions, the period after Epiphany has become an occasion for the church to think about mission in ways that are all too humanistic in their orientation. Today's text seriously challenges this stress on human agency in several important respects.

First, the gospel is presented as that which the church has received (verses 1 and 3). Paul readily acknowledges that the gospel he preached had preceded him in time. He inherited it from his predecessors in faith. He had not created it, but had received it as a gift of grace (verses 10-11). Standing within the succession of faithful witnesses beginning with Cephas and the Twelve (verses 5-8), he places himself within the tradition as a faithful tradent, or one who transmits the sacred message. Elsewhere in his writings, he reflects the same distance between himself and the sacred tradition he had received, and consistently respects this distance (I Cor. 7:10, 12, 25, 40; 9:14; 11:23; 14:37; I Thess. 2:13).

By recognizing this, we are instructed by this passage, for it reminds us that the gospel is not something we create. It is before us, prior to us, and possesses an absolute existence all its own apart from us. At this point, we do well to listen to the dialectical theologians who stress the priority of the Word of

God that comes to us from outside us and beyond us. For all its immediacy, the gospel is not our own. We can receive it, and in turn give it, but only as God sees fit to give it.

This same emphasis is seen in verses 5-8, where Paul rehearses the "appearances" of the risen Lord to the succession of witnesses. Quite often, the questions we bring to this part of the text arise from our concern with historicity. We thus find ourselves asking about the nature of the risen Lord's body, the form in which the disciples saw him or experienced him. From there, the discussion becomes one of modes of validation and verification.

While these questions are legitimate in their own right, they do not deserve to set the agenda entirely. Equally important is it to recognize the fundamental truth-claim being made here: that the Easter faith was not a matter of the disciples' own discovery but a divine revelation. It was that which came to them from without, not from within. That this is the case is seen by the fact that it continued to be revealed beyond Easter morning. That it extended through time into Paul's own time suggests that it cannot be measured or contained by time and history in any ordinary sense. Put simply, this text proclaims a basic Christian truth: the Easter faith created disciples; the disciples did not create the Easter faith.

Second, the gospel is that "in which we stand and through which we are being saved" (verses 1-2). When we acknowledge that the gospel is that in which our own existential identity is anchored, we are again acknowledging its prior claim on us. The faith of the gospel provides the fundamental reference point for Christian existence, so much so that we are continually encouraged to establish our stance in and toward life by faith (Rom. 11:20; I Cor. 10:12; 16:13; II Cor. 1:24; I Thess. 3:8). By finding our center of gravity within the gospel, we experience there the saving power of God that both gives us salvation and leads us to salvation (Rom. 1:16; 10:9; I Cor. 1:18, 24). Or, in Paul's own words, "By the grace of God I am what I am" (verse 10).

Approached this way, today's epistolary text can enable us to bear witness to the gospel as the gift God bestows, the revelation God unfolds, and the work God does.

Luke 5:1-11

Today is one of those extraordinary Sundays on which all the readings speak with a single voice. Isaiah has the vision of God, is struck by his own unworthiness, but nevertheless is sent to preach. Paul sees the risen Lord, realizes he is unfit to be called an apostle because he persecuted the church, but by God's grace he works harder than any of the others. And in Luke 5:1-11, Simon Peter gets a glimpse of the power and knowledge of Christ, falls before him in the profound grip of his own sinfulness, but even so, is called by Christ to become a fisher of men.

Our text, Luke's version of the call of the first disciples, is clearly an Epiphany story. Both Matthew and Mark tell of Jesus preaching from a boat in order to get away from a pressing crowd (Matt. 13:1-2; Mark 4:1), and they both record the call of the first disciples from the life of fishing on the sea of Galilee (Gennesaret in Luke). However, Mark (1:16-20) and Matthew after him (4:18-22) place the event early, making it all the more remarkable since the backdrop for their call consists only of a general statement about Jesus coming into Galilee preaching. In Luke, however, the call comes after Jesus' ministry in Nazareth (4:16-30), an exorcism in a synagogue in Capernaum (4:31-37), healing Simon's mother-in-law (4:38-39), many healings and exorcisms in that city (4:40-41), preaching tours (4:42-44), and such a growing popularity (4:37) that the crowds were pressing against him (5:1). This location of the story allows Luke to say two things about Jesus calling disciples.

1. His own success made helpers necessary, a fact that became even more evident later in the sending out of the seventy (10:1-2). The work of Jesus is thus prophetic of the church's successful spread of the gospel as Luke reports in Acts, a fact which also required the enlisting of more workers (Acts 11:19-26).

2. The disciples Jesus calls are responding to a Jesus who has demonstrated power to which they are witnesses. They follow a transcendent and compelling Christ in Luke, not a new preacher of an approaching kingdom as in Mark and Matthew.

In this sense, then, Luke's account is closer to that of John (21:1-23) which is a resurrection appearance narrative, and therefore, not surprisingly, an Epiphany narrative. In John also the story focuses on Simon Peter even though other disciples are present. In Luke 5:1-11, Simon Peter appears for the first time in this Gospel, even though he is mentioned by name in the earlier account of Jesus healing his mother-in-law (4:38-39). The story so thoroughly centers on Simon that his partners are unnamed and unnumbered until the end of the story. James and John are then named (verse 10), but not Andrew, Peter's brother. The remarkable catch of fish recalls the stories of miraculous provisions in the Elijah-Elisha stories (I Kings 17; II Kings 4:1-7, 38-41, 42-44), the prophets who have already proven to be a favorite resource for Luke (4:22-30). Luke's comfort with miracle stories—quite unlike Paul—is well known. However, even he is aware of the ambiguous role of miracles in the generation of faith and in their power to prompt discipleship (11:14-19). He also knows that non-Christians can work wonders (11:19; Acts 8:9-11). However, for Luke, the power of God not only characterized the ministry of Jesus but also was essential in the mission and witness of the church (Acts 1:8; 4:33).

Before the demonstrated power and knowledge of Jesus, however, the response of Peter is not one of powerlessness or ignorance. (Why could we not do it? Why did we not know where the fish were?) Simon's skill as a fisherman is not the issue; rather it is Simon's sin as a human being unworthy to be in the presence of the Lord. His sin does not disqualify him, however, for the same power that caused him to fall on his knees, now lifts Simon into Jesus' service. But not as a better fisherman; rather as one who will be "catching men" (verse 10). The word translated "catch" meant "to take alive in the sense of rescuing from death." The prominence to which Simon Peter later rose surely never erased from his memory the day he knelt in a smelly fishing boat at the feet of Jesus.

Sixth Sunday After Epiphany (Proper 1)

Jeremiah 17:5-10; Psalm 1; I Corinthians 15:12-20;
Luke 6:17-26

The readings from Luke and I Corinthians continue, each raising different issues. Luke 6:17-26 begins the "Sermon on the Plain" with a series of blessings and woes, in part parallel to the Beatitudes (Matt. 5:3 ff). Both the Old Testament lection and the responsorial psalm use the same kind of expressions as in Luke to stress the contrast between the righteous and the unrighteous, between weal and woe. First Corinthians 15:12-20 turns our attention to Paul's argument concerning belief in the resurrection. It does to some extent suggest some of the eschatological tone of the Gospel reading.

Jeremiah 17:5-10

The authorship and historical circumstances of Jeremiah 17:5-10 are uncertain. The chapter as a whole does not develop a consistent theme but includes a variety of materials, some of which (verses 14-18 in particular) correspond to Jeremiah's thought and language. The concern with the heart in verses 9-10 is consistent with Jeremiah's perspective. The wisdom sayings of verses 5-8 are unusual in Jeremiah, but there is nothing in them that is explicitly contrary to the prophet's views.

Our reading contains two major parts, verses 5-8 and 9-10. The first part begins with an introductory messenger formula, "Thus says the Lord," but what follows is neither prophetic nor divine speech; the Lord is spoken of in the third person. What follows the introduction is a neatly balanced and concise wisdom speech, extended sayings giving the two sides of a coin. The first (verses 5-6) points out that the one "who trusts in man," who turns away from the Lord, is cursed, and then it compares that one to a shrub in the desert. The second (verses 7-8) gives the antithesis. The one who trusts in the Lord is blessed, like a tree planted by the water. The parallels of this section to Psalm 1, both in form and contents, are strong and obvious. The view of most scholars that Psalm 1 is later than and dependent upon this passage is probably correct.

The second section (verses 9-10) also contains two parts, the first a proverbial-like saying on the human heart as "deceitful" and incomprehensible, and the second a divine speech in which Yahweh affirms that he knows the heart of everyone and gives according to their ways.

A number of themes or issues present themselves for homiletical reflection:

1. As in other Old Testament prophetic and wisdom literature from the time of Jeremiah onward, the focus is upon the inner life of the individual. God is concerned with the heart, the thoughts and beliefs of the person. Note, however, that the passage concludes by pointing out that the Lord looks also "to the fruit of his doings," to what emerges from that inner life.

2. Perhaps the key word in this text is "trust" (verses 5, 7). This trust does not mean belief in propositions, but commitment, devotion. The verb must have an object, and that is the decisive point: to trust in what is human or to trust in God, that is the question.

3. The passage raises the question of divine retribution, as does the reading from Luke. *Does* God give to everyone according to what they have done? One who preaches on such texts is obligated in the first instance to let the text have its say. Here that would include reflection in the context of verses 5-8 as well, which suggest that those who trust in what is human and those who trust in God have their reward. To do the one is to live an arid life; to do the other is to live the abundant life. Having examined the perspective of the text, then one might reflect on the extent to which the viewpoint corresponds to experience and to the rest of the biblical canon.

Psalm 1

Psalm 1 which opens the Psalter might just as well be an introduction to the Pentateuch for it focuses on legal piety and Torah observance. The psalm opens in beatitude form although the actual content of the psalm expands such a form beyond its bounds and becomes a poem of admonition.

The psalm profiles two types of persons, the righteous and the wicked and thus reflects a pattern frequently found in the Old Testament. Obviously, the intention of the text was to encourage emulation of the righteous and to discourage imitation of the wicked. As such, the psalm is a sharp call for commitment to a certain pattern of life, a pattern based on study and meditation on the Torah and observance of its commandments.

In such depictions of opposite attitudes to life, there is no neutral ground, no neutral corners. The two ways lead in two different directions and one cannot walk in both paths. The decision for Torah is the decision to take upon oneself the shield and protection, the ordering and regulation of the Torah. To refuse Torah is to choose chaos, impermanence, the lack of a mooring for life.

In depicting the righteous person, the psalm does so in a series of negative characteristics (verse 1). The righteous does not follow the counsel of the wicked, does not take the path of sinners or join the company of the insolent. The positive description (verse 2) describes the righteous as making the law a fundamental concern of life, an object of meditation day and night.

Verse 3 may be read as the promise conditional upon the Torah piety described in verse 2. The righteous becomes like a tree, fruitful, productive, predictable.

The description of the wicked on the other hand presents them as unstable, insecure, open to the whims and winds of the moment, carrying in themselves no weight of character (verse 4). Thus sinners or the wicked will be unable to stand in judgment, that is, they will be either unable to serve as judges and participants in legal suits or else cannot survive the judgment of their (righteous) peers.

Finally, the two ways are summarized. The way of the righteous God knows (cherishes, upholds, aids) but the way of the wicked is on its own, doomed, perishing, headed for chaos.

I Corinthians 15:12-20

There can be no doubt that in rehearsing the outlines of the early Christian kerygma in the previous section Paul is operating at the most elementary level. But he does so purposely. He begins at ground level: the Easter faith is the fundamental axiom of Christian preaching. The story begins there, and from there moves both backward and forward. Thus, he can begin his argument, "Now if Christ is preached as raised from the dead. . ." (verse 12). True, this axiom is stated as an "if clause," but its content is stated in such a way that it is assumed to be real. With this claim, we are at the fulcrum of the Christian faith. On this, everything turns.

Clearly, there were some members in the church at Corinth saying that "there is no resurrection of the dead" (verse 12). Even if Paul observes this with a note of incredulity, he does not for a moment take the claim lightly. If we ask what precisely they were claiming, there are several possibilities.

First, that there is no life after death. This position was advocated in both Jewish and non-Jewish traditions. The Sadducees were the most notable example of the former (cf. Matt. 22:23-33 and parallels), the Epicureans of the latter.

Second, that there is no resurrection of the body. One well-established tradition of Greco-Roman thought regarded the body as a tomb in which the soul was incarcerated. Accordingly, the notion that the body would be raised or revivified was regarded as offensive and unattractive. To believe that the soul housed in the body was immortal was a most attractive option and was widely held. It is conceivable that some people in the Corinthian church held this philosophically acceptable position, and thus found it impossible to believe in a resurrection of the physical body (cf. verse 35).

Third, that there is no future resurrection. While some believed in resurrection, they conceived of it not so much as a

157

future event but as a form of existence that could already be experienced in the present. This was apparently the position taken by those Christians who believed "that the resurrection is already past" (II Tim. 2:18). This view is known to have existed in certain Gnostic circles in the second century, and it may have occurred in certain forms in the New Testament period (cf. I Cor. 4:8-9). Those who would adhere to this third position would gladly affirm belief in the resurrection, but would be unwilling to conceive of it as something to be realized at a future time, after death.

We cannot be sure which of these positions, if any, is being taken by the Corinthian Christians. In any case, we should notice Paul's response. In essence, he argues *reductio ad absurdum*, insisting that if this position is correct, it has implications that even the adherents would be unwilling to admit. Thus, Paul insists, if there is no resurrection, three things follow:

1. Christ has not been raised (verses 13, 16). It is impossible to deny resurrection in principle, while at the same time affirming the resurrection of Christ in particular. We cannot have it both ways. We cannot affirm in one breath that Christ has been raised and deny in a second breath that resurrection is by definition impossible. Both stand or fall together. From the form of Paul's argument, it appears that those against whom he is arguing have expressed no doubts about Christ's own resurrection, only about their own. Perhaps Christ was for them a special case. But, Paul insists that Christ's resurrection and that of all humanity are on a continuum.

2. Paul's preaching is vain (verse 14-15). Since the Easter faith constituted the central feature of his preaching, Paul's own gospel would be vitiated and he would turn out to be a false witness "misrepresenting God." His own integrity is at stake.

3. The church's faith is in vain (verse 14). Here Paul argues from their own experience of the Easter faith. He presupposes that their existence in Christ is a given from which he can argue and which they cannot gainsay. The logic of his argument is this: You are a community of the Easter faith, having been brought into existence by believing in the resurrection of Christ. This you cannot deny. Yet, if resurrection in principle is disallowed, you are calling into

question your own existence. Hence, "your faith is futile and you are still in your sins" (verse 17). Moreover, you must despair over those of your fellow Christians who have died, for their fate is hopeless.

This line of reasoning may appear odd, even unconvincing to us, because it seems to beg the question. Yet for Paul Christian existence had such palpable, undeniable concreteness that it could function as the given in the argument. Consequently, our text concludes with a strong reaffirmation of faith: "But in fact Christ has been raised from the dead, the first fruits of those who have fallen asleep" (verse 20). Here we are near the heart of the gospel he preaches (Rom. 8:11; I Cor. 6:14; II Cor. 4:4; Gal. 1:1). By identifying Christ as the "first fruits" (15:23; Col. 1:18; Acts 3:15; 26:23; I Thess. 4:13), he asserts the continuity between Christ's own resurrection and our own. Our destiny is indissolubly linked with his.

Luke 6:17-26

The texts for today join in describing the conditions of those living under God's favor (blessing) and those under God's disfavor (curse or woe). On the lips of members of the faith community addressing one another, a blessing is a celebration of someone's pleasant and happy circumstance, and a curse or woe is a lament over someone's plight. However, when spoken by God or by one who speaks for God, blessings and woes are more than descriptive; they are pronouncements which declare in effect that those conditions will prevail. On the lips of Jesus Christ, therefore, the blessings and the woes of our Gospel lection can be taken as the "official" proclamation of the way life will be among the people of God. In other words, as an Epiphany text, Luke 6:17-26 does more than suggest how to be happy, not sad. In fact, the passage does not contain exhortations, as though these are conditions that are the result of effort, and the preacher will want to guard against slipping into phrases such as, "We ought to be hungry now," or, "Let us not laugh now lest we later weep and mourn." Blessings and woes are to be heard with the assurance that they are God's word to us, and God will implement them.

It is a bit difficult to follow the sequence of events in Luke here, given the changes from Mark's order and from Matthew's location of the sermon which we know in that Gospel as the Sermon on the Mount. Luke's order of calling the Twelve (6:12-16) and healing the crowds (6:17-19) is a reversal of Mark (3:7-19). Luke also shifts the scene from the sea (Mark 3:7) to a level place (6:17). Although the sermon beginning at verse 20 is later in Luke than in Matthew, there are similarities in location. Matthew places his version of the sermon after the call of four disciples and a general statement about Jesus' ministry (4:18-25) while Luke sets his version after the call of twelve disciples and a general statement about Jesus' ministry (6:12-19). Luke's sermon is but one-fourth the length of Matthew's, but it is clear that, given the differences appropriate to their own views and reader needs, both writers are working with much the same material.

What accents in this text, far more familiar to the church in its Matthean parallel, impress themselves upon the reader? First, there seems to be a theological use of geography. The mountain is the place for prayer to God and choosing those "whom he named apostles" (verse 13), a designation for the Twelve that is very important to Luke. Being selected on the mountain and in prayer, they are a special group, as Acts 1 bears out. Having chosen the twelve leaders (a new Israel?), Jesus now moves to the plain below with all the people. With them he identifies, as he did at his baptism (3:21). Only after coming off the mountain to the people and having healed them all (verse 19) does Jesus preach this "inaugural" sermon on life in the kingdom.

The sermon opens with four beatitudes and four woes, reminiscent of the blessings and curses set before Israel (Deut. 11:26, 28). Luke's beatitudes are not only briefer than Matthew's (5:3-11), they also pronounce favor upon persons who are entirely different. All four beatitudes bless the deprived: the poor, the hungry, those who weep, and those despised and rejected. This is not surprising, given Luke's special attention to the poor, the captive, the oppressed, the wounded, the lame, the halt, and the blind (4:18-19; 14:12-14). The four woes are pronounced on those whose lives are the very opposite of the blessed: the rich, the full, the laughing, and the socially accepted. This contrast, combined with that of setting *now* over against the future, puts the entire passage in an eschatological frame of reference. As Luke stated as early as the "Magnificat" (1:46-55), the arrival of the kingdom in its fullness will be marked by a complete reversal in the fortunes of the rich and poor, the powerful and the powerless, the full and the empty.

To say that Luke here contrasts present and future is not to say that he is urging disciples to sit and wait for that blessed future. Christ's presence has already launched the reign of God's love and care. As Jesus said in the synagogue at Nazareth, "*Today* this scripture has been fulfilled" (4:21). The Messiah who will come *has come*, and it continues to be "today" among the followers of Jesus.

Seventh Sunday After Epiphany (Proper 2)

Genesis 45:3-11, 15; Psalm 37:1-11; I Corinthians 15:35-38, 42-50;
Luke 6:27-38

The Old Testament text doubtless was selected because it reinforces the main concerns of the Gospel lection from Luke 6:27-38, in which Jesus teaches that one should love one's enemies. Joseph, in his forgiveness of his brothers, becomes an example of such love, of lending without thought of return. Psalm 37:1-11 responds to a major theme of Genesis 45:3-11, 15, God's providential care. The confident tone in the psalm may be heard to support Paul's faith in the resurrection expressed in I Corinthians 15:35-38, 42-50.

Genesis 45:3-11, 15

Genesis 45:1-15, from which our reading is taken, is a key episode in the Joseph story (Gen. 37, 39–50). In fact, it contains the account of Joseph's revelation of his identity to his brothers and is the climax of the narrative, the point at which the main tensions of the plot are resolved and the purpose of the events disclosed. That purpose is not easy to understand without considering this episode in its larger context.

The Joseph story, although similar in some respects to the other narratives in Genesis, is quite distinctive. The fact that it is a long, highly developed story, with a coherent plot from beginning to end, has led many scholars to compare it to the short story or novella. There is serious interest in human personalities and emotions, such subtle points as the awareness that foreigners may need to communicate through translators, carefully constructed sub-plots, and literary techniques such as foreshadowing. Moreover, unlike most of the other narratives in Genesis, this account shows the differences between the characters in their youth and their maturity. One needs only to compare the Joseph of our passage with the one in Genesis 37. A spoiled brat has become generous and compassionate. The reader can also sense that the brothers are bent with age and the effects of their struggles.

While the story as a whole is a unity, it bears the marks of the combination of the older sources, J and E. Careful reading of our passage will reveal evidence of such a combination. It is not clear, for example, whether Joseph's display of emotion was private or heard by the Egyptians. He twice tells the brothers who he is, and—perhaps indicating that something has dropped out—he asks if his father is still alive (verse 3) but proceeds to give instructions to bring him to Egypt without hearing the answer.

The brothers, jealous of Joseph, had sold him into slavery, where he had not only survived but prospered. His special talents and skills had taken him, as he says, to the second highest office in Egypt. (The language of verse 8 and elsewhere indicates that the narrator sees him as the Grand Vizier.) Egypt, and the entire region, is suffering the period of famine foreseen by Joseph, so the brothers come looking for food. The tension had been allowed to grow: How will the conflict be resolved? Our text shows the answer, and also makes it clear that the plot—the development of the story—had actually been taking place on a different level.

The passage before us, except for verses 3*b* and 14-15, is a speech by Joseph. It is filled with the emotion of the reunion. When Joseph says who he is, the brothers are "dumbfounded" (NEB) by fear and unbelief. Will Joseph, who now is so powerful, repay them with what they did to him? The brothers quickly learn what we, the readers, know already, that he will forgive them. But, significantly, Joseph gives what amounts to a theological explanation for his attitude and his actions: "God sent me before you to preserve life. . . . God sent me before you to preserve for you a remnant on earth . . ." (verses 5, 7). That is the point of the

narrative as a whole, expressed somewhat more compre-
hensively in Genesis 50:20: "As for you, you meant evil
against me; but God meant it for good, to bring it about that
many people should be kept alive, as they are today."

Thus the movement of events, so transparent on the
human level, is the expression of a gracious divine purpose,
which in the end becomes plain. The two main themes of the
passage then come together. Those who understand and
have confidence in God's providential care are able to love
even their enemies. Who knows, God may be in the process
of using the wrath of human beings to praise him.

Psalm 37:1-11

Psalm 37, which reads in many ways like a miniature
version of the book of Proverbs, contains numerous parallels
to the Gospel lesson from Luke. Both are collections of
sayings that admonish and invite one to try to follow a certain
life-style.

Several assumptions may be ssen as foundational pillars
undergirding the teachings of the psalm.

1. The world and life are assumed to be reasonably
well-ordered and to make sense if understood in proper
perspective. This seems reflected in the well-ordered form of
the poem itself—an alphabetic composition.

2. A strong and necessary interrelationship is presumed to
exist between actions and results, between deeds and
consequences. That is, a particular type of pattern of action is
assumed to lead to predictable results.

3. What appears to contradict this view of the world and
behavior, such as the success of the wicked or the triumph of
the unrighteous, is only a temporary state, an illusory
condition which will soon pass.

4. When the world and human society do not seem to
conform to the pattern, in that temporary disruption of the
normal state of affairs, one should remain faithful and
endure the momentary absence of proper conditions.

5. Ultimately, the good, the right, the proper will be
rewarded—"the meek will possess the land" (verse 11*a*)—
and prosperity will be the reward of the diligent.

Various ways of speaking of the human situation and of the proper conduct of life are found in these opening verses of the psalm. Verses 1-2 contain two prohibitions followed by the motivation or reason why, in this case why one should not act a certain way. Verses 8-9 contain two imperatives followed by the reason why one should act a particular way. Verses 10-11 contrasts two consequences of behavior patterns.

Let us look at some of the practical advice offered in this psalm. First, throughout the psalm, one is warned against jealousy and the agitation of life that comes from being obsessed with the success of others. "Fret not yourself" occurs several times (verses 1, 7, 8). The resentment of others which underlies jealousy and anger is seen as self-defeating and as ultimately a denial of faith in God's justice. Freting tends only to produce evil (verse 8*b*). Second, being jealous, especially of the wicked and wrongdoers, is bad because their success is doomed and their fate foretold. Third, the best attitude in life is one that trusts in God, does good, and waits patiently. Fourth, those who are not given to anger, not overcome by wrath, and not "torn-up" over others' status—that is, the meek—will possess the land and enjoy its fruits.

This psalm must have offered encouragement and provided sound advice to those in ancient Judah who may have doubted the value of their commitments in light of the success of the wrongdoers. At the same time, it held out hope for a change for the better and affirmed the age-old conviction that sowing and harvesting are intimately related in spite of all evidence to the contrary.

I Corinthians 15:35-38, 42-50

In what form will we experience resurrection life? It is a question Christians have asked in every age, and continue to ask. It addresses one of the central mysteries of the faith. The question could hardly be ignored in chapter 15, Paul's most extensive and systematic treatment of the question of the resurrection of the dead.

The question is posed here on the lips of an imaginary interlocutor. The style of Paul's treatment is diatribal, and this suggests that it is an objection or question with which Paul wishes to deal rather than an actual question being raised in the Corinthian church. It is not for this reason merely a hypothetical question. As phrased in our text, the question runs, "How are the dead raised? With what kind of body do they come?"

The background which gives rise to this set of questions is probably one that drew a sharp distinction between the body and the soul. In Greek thought, it was common to believe in the immortality of the soul. The soul could easily be conceived as having an eternal existence, without beginning or end in time. As such, it could come to inhabit the body, and in some instances it was felt that this cycle could occur several times, or become reincarnated in different bodily forms. The physical body was thus viewed as a temporal dwelling with little significance in comparison with the eternal soul. Because the body consisted of physical matter, like the rest of earthly existence, it was difficult for most Greeks, and some Jews, to conceive of its resurrection. Once the living body becomes a corpse, how can we speak of its being raised? Should we envision life being breathed back into the corpse so that the person is revivified and literally lifted up into the heavens? These are the natural questions Greeks would put to the Christian teaching of resurrection.

In the first part of today's epistolary lection, Paul addresses these questions by citing an example from nature, a common form of illustration in diatribal teaching. For him, the process through which a grain of wheat was sown into the ground and eventually shot up through the ground as a stalk of wheat perfectly illustrated the Christian understanding of resurrection. This metaphor may have even originated with Jesus himself (John 12:24). The grain of wheat provided a helpful image in at least three respects.

First, it illustrated that in nature we see one form of existence (seed) transformed into another form of existence (plant). In appearance, form, and substance, each form differs radically from the other; and yet, there is continuity between them. Even in its transformed state, the stalk of wheat is still the same entity as the grain of wheat. In spite of their different form, they are a single organism.

Second, the change between the forms is brought about by a "death." Before the transformation can occur, the seed must be buried in the ground. As it is placed in the ground, it has the germ of life within it, but this life is only potential. It does not, and cannot, blossom forth into full life until it "dies." The grain of wheat thus shows how a single living being, by dying, can be transformed from one mode of existence into another mode of existence. So understood, death is not the end of life, but a point of transition from one form of life into another.

Third, it is a process under the control of God (verse 38). It was a common assumption in antiquity that the cycles of nature occurred under divine auspices, however differently God may have been viewed. In our text, of course, it is the Genesis creation story that informs Paul's own view (Gen. 1:11-12). The important point is this: in nature life forms do not undergo change willy-nilly, but occur according to a divinely ordered pattern.

In the second part of today's lection (verses 42-50), Paul uses the metaphor of the grain of wheat to illustrate how our form of existence is transformed in the resurrection. It may help to summarize his remarks by noting the ways in which he envisions the two different modes of existence:

it is sown:	it is raised:
perishable	imperishable
in dishonor	in glory
in weakness	in power
a physical body	a spiritual body
a man of dust	a man of heaven

As with the grain of wheat, so with our existence. It can be conceived as having two different forms, the one we experience this side of death, the other we experience the other side of death. They are radically different because they are of a different order. Yet there is continuity as we move from one form of existence to the other.

But how can we be assured that this is the case? Because Christ himself has already experienced this change. Here, Paul draws on the creation story again as he contrasts "the first man Adam" with Christ, "the last Adam" (verse 45). They differ in one crucial respect: the first Adam "became a living being" while Christ became a "life-giving spirit" (verse 45). The man Adam experienced life at one level, primarily as a recipient of biological life. Christ, the second Adam, through the resurrection came to experience life at a completely different level. As a recipient of resurrection life, or life with a capital "L," he became Life-giver. His existence as exalted Lord is already imperishable, in glory, in power, fully spiritual, and heavenly. As full possessor of resurrection life, this transformed mode of existence, it is fully his to give and ours to receive.

Our text makes clear, then, resurrection is not at all "unnatural," for it involves a process we witness in nature's own cycle of life. Just as the grain of wheat is a parable of our own life and destiny, so Christ is the first to illustrate its full truth.

Luke 6:27-38

The Gospel lesson continues the teaching of Jesus in the sermon on a level place (6:17), Luke's parallel to Matthew's sermon on the mount (chapters 5-7). Verses 27-38 follow immediately the blessings and the woes with which the sermon begins (verses 20-26). Matthew's version of verses 27-38 present the content in a different order (5:39-42; 44-48; 7:12; 7:1-2). This difference in order, the shifts from plural *you*, to singular, to plural again (verses 27-28, 29-30, 32-36), and the packing of many instructions on diverse and very weighty matters into a very brief span persuade the reader that Luke (and Matthew) draw upon a compilation of teachings rather than a single sermon delivered on a single occasion.

The most noticeable differences between Luke 6:27-38 and the Matthean parallels are two: First, Luke's "he [God] is kind to the ungrateful and the selfish" (verse 35) expresses Matthew's "he [God] makes his sun rise on the evil and on the good, and sends rain on the just and on the unjust" (5:45). Although in different images, both affirms the radical nature of grace which finds its reason in God and not in the merits of its recipients. Both Matthew and Luke elaborate this theme in parables which portray not only God's graciousness but the offense that is felt by those who regard impartiality as unjust. To the offended in Matthew's parable of vineyard workers, grace says, "Do you begrudge my generosity?" (20:15), and to the offended in Luke's parable of the prodigal, grace says, "It was fitting to make merry and be glad, for this your brother was dead and is alive; he was lost, and is found" (15:32). The second noticeable difference between Luke and Matthew is that Luke's, "Be merciful, even as your Father is merciful" (verse 36) is in Matthew, "You, therefore, must be perfect, as your heavenly Father is perfect" (5:48). But again, the difference is more apparent than real. If one is not misled into thinking of Matthew's "perfect" as moral flawlessness but rather lets the context provide understanding, then the two statements make the same affirmation about God and offer the same admonition. Of course, lesser differences occur, such as Luke's preference for the term "sinners" (verse 32-34) while Matthew speaks of tax collectors and Gentiles (5:46-47).

Luke 6:27-38 consists of three units, as the paragraphing in major English translations reflects: 27-31, 32-36, 37-38. The first unit lays down the general principle that kingdom people do not reciprocate, do not draw their behavior from that of those who would victimize them. Following the statement of principle are numerous examples of forms of mistreatment: hating, cursing, abusing, striking, stealing, begging. The important point to notice here is that these teachings assume the readers/listeners are victims not victimizers. Jesus offered no instruction to followers who would strike, steal, hate, curse, and abuse others because such is not kingdom behavior. But to those who are vulnerable and likely recipients of the world's abuse, Jesus gave teachings on how not to be a victim: take charge of your life and the situation by taking the initiative in loving, caring, giving. This unit concludes with Luke's version of the Golden Rule (verse 31), found not only here and in Matthew (7:12) but also in Homer, Seneca, Tobit, II Enoch, Philo, and elsewhere. For a principle to be widely embraced and widely stated does not make it any less valid or binding.

The second unit (verses 32-36) repeats the principle of the first unit; that is, one is not to reciprocate in responding to others. However, the principle was first applied in relation to those who violate us and here it is applied in relation to those who treat us favorably. In other words, just as one's behavior is not determined by the enemy, neither is it determined by the friend. Christian behavior and attitude are prompted by the God we worship who does not hate in response to hatred or love in response to love. God does not react; God acts in love and grace toward all, and such is the way of those who are children of the Most High (verse 35).

It follows, then, in the third unit (verses 37-38) that the children of God do not judge or condemn, but rather give and forgive. One will notice, however, a bit more justice, a bit more reward and punishment, in this unit than in the first two. But even the balanced fairness of "the measure you give will be the measure you get back" (verse 38) is broken by the image of abundant generosity poured out upon those who give. The phrase "into your lap" (verse 38) refers to the large pocket formed by the fold in a robe above the belt. Even this huge pocket will not contain the pressed down, shaken together, running over blessings that come to those who give generously to others.

God is full of grace, and the final work of grace is to make us gracious, too.

Eighth Sunday After Epiphany (Proper 3)

Ecclesiasticus 27:4-7 or Isaiah 55:10-13; Psalm 92:1-4, 12-15; I Corinthians 15:51-58; Luke 6:39-49

Both Old Testament readings have links with the psalm and with the Gospel lection, but at different points. Both Ecclesiasticus 27:4-7 and Luke 6:43-45 consider the relationship between a tree and its fruit, although the point of the metaphor is different in each case. The proclamation in Isaiah 55:10-13 that God's word will be effective relates to Luke 6:46-49: those who hear and do the words of Jesus will be like a house with a sound foundation. The imagery of trees and fruitfulness appears in Psalm 92. The continuation of the readings from First Corinthians concludes with Paul's thankful affirmations concerning resurrection.

Ecclesiasticus 27:4-7

For information concerning the authorship, historical circumstances, and the perspective of the book of Ecclesiasticus, and some observations about wisdom literature in general, see the comments on Ecclesiasticus 3:3-7, 14-17 under the readings for the First Sunday After Christmas in this volume.

It is always wise for the preacher to consult more than one modern translation of the assigned or chosen texts. That is especially important when preaching or even reading in worship proverbial literature such as Ecclesiasticus 27:4-7. The original sense of sayings often is particularly difficult to capture in another language because they are so pithy or even enigmatic that the meaning sometimes seems to lie between the lines. Moreover, they make extensive use of images, similes, and metaphors from the original culture, and the translators will have to decide whether to translate the words or to find equivalent images or ideas. The New English Bible and the Jerusalem Bible are both clearer and more accurate translations of today's text than is the RSV.

The broader context of Ecclesiasticus 27:4-7 contains teachings and advice about behavior in society. The passage is surrounded more immediately (26:28–27:29) by teachings about good and bad character, how it is tested by circumstances and how one may recognize it in oneself and others. The poetic instruction immediately before our reading (26:9–27:3) meditates on the temptations that business presents for a person, and urges steadfast and zealous piety as the way to avoid dishonesty and its effects.

Ecclesiasticus 27:4-7 itself is an artistically composed wisdom speech that employs three comparative sayings (verses 4-6) to support the concluding instruction (verse 7). Each of the sayings states a conclusion about something that can be observed: the shaken sieve, the potter's kiln, the fruit of a tree. Each then applies its general conclusion to an aspect of human thought or discourse. The first (verse 4) concerns "thoughts" (RSV) or "talk" (JB), the second (verse 5) deals with "reasoning" (RSV), "debate" (NEB), or "conversation" (JB), and the third (verse 6) relates the "expression of a thought" to the "cultivation of a man's mind" (RSV) or to one's "character" (NEB).

The concluding instruction (verse 7) gives direct advice and draws a general conclusion. Ben Sirah advises against praising a man until you have heard him "reason" (RSV), or "in discussion" (NEB). The general conclusion provides the reason for the advice, "for this [reason, discussion] is the test of men." On the surface the instruction is advice for evaluating one's associates, but it also means to encourage a certain behavior. One should work on the ability to reason, to carry on thoughtful discussion, for that is a test of character.

In preaching on this text one may wish to stress the importance of the mind, human reasoning, and rational communication. There may be a tendency to treat such considerations as strictly individualistic. However, not only civilization but any humane society is founded on the use of reason, careful communication, and even lively debate. It is through the use of such capacities that prejudices and preconceptions are challenged. By thoughtful conversation persons know and appreciate one another.

Isaiah 55:10-13

This text concludes the section of the Book of Isaiah (40–55) attributed to Second Isaiah, the prophet of the end of the Exile. In some respects the passage parallels the beginning of the work (40:1-11). Both stress the power of the word of God, and both proclaim the good news that God will bring the people out of Exile and return them to their land. The words would have been spoken originally in 539 B.C., the year before the end of the Babylonian Empire. The first audience was the community in exile.

Our assigned reading is part of the longer discourse that includes all of chapter 55. (Isaiah 55:1-11 is one of the texts assigned for reading during the Easter Vigil.) In language resembling that of a hymn, the chapter consists of admonitions to listen to and believe in the word of God and celebrations of the Lord's word and works. God's grace to the exiles includes food that will satisfy both physical and spiritual needs. The one who seeks the Lord finds life.

Isaiah 55:10-13 consists of two parts, closely related but distinct in both form and contents. In the first part (verses 10-11) Yahweh is the speaker, continuing the previous discourse. In the second part (verses 12-13) the prophet is the speaker.

Verses 10-11 give reasons for following the exhortations of verses 6-7: "Seek the Lord. . . . " The "for" of verse 10 parallels those of verses 8 and 9. This third reason is in the form of an extended comparison between water from heaven—rain and snow—with its effects (verse 10) and the word of the Lord (verse 11). Just as the rain and snow bring about growth, seeds, and bread, so the word of the Lord is effective, accomplishing what the Lord intends. God accomplishes his will through the word, as in Genesis 1 and as in the prophetic announcements.

Verses 12-13 begin with another "for" which may give yet another set of reasons for seeking the Lord. The verses contain proclamations of salvation concerning the exiles and their future. When they go out—from Babylon—in joy and are led in peace, nature itself will join in the celebration. Second Isaiah's poetry is rich in the imagery of creation because of his sense of the cosmic scope of God's work. The thornbush and the brier will be replaced by the cypress and the myrtle. The only point not clear in the concluding verse is the antecedent of the "it" that will be the memorial and sign. It could refer to the people or to the saving event itself, the going out in joy and peace. Salvation, or those saved, will be a perpetual sign, calling to mind the Lord of Israel.

The purpose of this passage is the proclamation of good news. It means to evoke in the hearers and readers confidence in God's word and the joyful celebration of hope.

Psalm 92:1-4, 12-15

This psalm, as the superscription suggests, was used in early Jewish worship services as the Sabbath psalm. Seven psalms, which actually offer a summary of the basic tenets of Judaism, were sung by the Levites at the main temple services during the week: Psalm 24 (Sunday), 48 (Monday), 82 (Tuesday), 94 (Wednesday), 81 (Thursday), 93 (Friday), and 92 (Saturday). In Psalm 92, the Israelite name for God, Yahweh, occurs seven times (given as the LORD in the RSV; verses 1, 4, 5, 8, 9, 13, and 15). This can hardly be coincidental in a psalm intended for use on the seventh day of the week! The ancient rabbis even suggested that Adam was the author of this psalm and that he sang it on the first sabbath in the Garden of Eden.

This psalm is a thanksgiving offering thanks for redemption from enemies (verses 10-11). The first eleven verses are addressed directly to the Deity while verses 12-15, proclamation or preaching, are addressed by the worshiper to a human audience.

Verses 1-4 declare that it is good to offer praise to God, morning and evening. This may be a way of saying that it is good to offer praise "all the time." Or it may reflect the fact that daily sacrifices were offered in the temple in the morning and evening—when music would have accompanied the ritual (verse 3).

Verses 12-15 declare that the righteous, the faithful are securely planted, firmly anchored and will flourish and bear fruit even into old age. God is a rock upon whom life's house may be built with secure confidence, and the passing of time does not diminish the care and the products of life. Note the verbs that describe the faithful in verses 12-15: flourish, grow, bring forth, are ever full. In the imagery of the psalm, the faithful do not plant their house, they are planted in God's house, that is, they are a constant feature in temple worship.

Like the reading from Luke, Psalm 92 stresses the reliability, the trustworthiness of God. "The Lord is upright; . . . and there is no unrighteousness in him."

I Corinthians 15:51-58

This final section of Paul's exposition on the resurrection, or what might be called the Pauline apocalypse, is introduced with the solemn declaration, "Lo! I tell you a mystery" (verse 51). Against the background of Jewish apocalyptic, this would mean that Paul, one of the "stewards of the mysteries of God" (I Cor. 4:1), is now unveiling the secret of the end-time. With an eye to the future, Paul now adopts the stance of the apocalyptic Seer (cf. Rev. 1:1-3).

The essence of the Pauline apocalypse is this: "We shall not all sleep, but we shall all be changed" (verse 51). At the end-time, both the dead and the living will undergo transformation (I Thess. 4:15-17). Throughout this section both groups are in view, and it is possible to interpret his remarks accordingly.

For example, verse 53 may be describing the way in which each group experiences the final transformation. Thus, "this perishable nature must put on the imperishable" means that those who have already died and whose bodies have experienced corruption will be clothed with a transformed, incorruptible nature suitable for resurrected existence. And, "this mortal nature must put on immortality" means that those who are still alive yet destined eventually to die because of their mortal nature will be clothed with an immortal nature suitable for eternal life with God.

In similar fashion, the biblical quotation in verse 55, "O death, where is thy victory? O death, where is thy sting?" would appear to state the victory cry of both groups, the dead and the living. To be sure, it is a rough paraphrase and reinterpretation of Hosea 13:14, which reads in Hebrew, "O Death, where are your plagues? O Sheol, where is your destruction?" and in the Septuagint, "Death, where is your judgment? Hades, where is your sting?" In the prophetic context, Hosea's words are words of judgment, warning Israel of impending punishment.

These prophetic words are appropriated by Paul as words of reassurance to both the dead and the living. As in the Old Testament quotation, the questions are addressed to Death personified. Those who have died in Christ, assured that even in death their corruptible nature will be clothed with a new, incorruptible existence, can finally hurl these words at Death, "Where is your victory?" It looked as if Death had won, but in the end-time Death has no hold on the dead in Christ. In similar fashion, those who are still alive, who have not yet experienced the sting of death, can also claim victory over Death. Through the resurrection, they are able to bypass death and twit Death, asking, "Where is your sting?" So, it is the dead in Christ who finally shout, "O death, where is thy victory?" and those who are alive in Christ who shout, "O death, where is thy sting?" The paraphrase of Isaiah 25:8, "Death is swallowed up in victory" (verse 54), becomes the ultimate cry of vindication of Christians both dead and alive.

We should note that in this Pauline apocalypse, the transformation to resurrected life is instantaneous: It occurs "in a moment, in the twinkling of an eye, at the last trumpet" (verse 52). Part of this vivid imagery is supplied by the Old Testament, where trumpets were used to summon Israel to worship (Num. 10:1-10; Lev. 23:24; II Chron. 7:6; Sirach 50:16), but also to put them on military alert (Num. 10:9; Amos 3:6). Israel was also accustomed to reminders that trumpets would herald the impending punishment to come upon them (Isa. 18:3; Hos. 8:1; Jer. 4:5; 6:1), or that the Day of

Yahweh would be ushered in with the sound of trumpets (Joel 2:1; Zeph. 1:16).

The Christian parousia is envisioned here as the gathering of the elect of God for the Day of Yahweh, but the crucial difference is that God "gives us the victory through our Lord Jesus Christ" (verse 57; I John 5:14). What has been accomplished in the work of Christ is that the three mortal enemies—death, sin, and the law—have finally been vanquished (Rom. 7:13, 25).

It is significant that the Pauline apocalypse concludes with a call to steadfast diligence (verse 58). Thinking about the resurrection can all too easily turn into ill-focused musing about the eschaton. The temptation is to disengage from life and its demands, to lay down our tools, and sit with folded arms, gazing expectantly into the heavens. For Paul, this is not an option. The proper way to prepare for the end is to be engaged in productive work for the Lord (cf. Col. 1:23).

Luke 6:39-49

With this lesson we conclude Luke's "sermon on a level place" (6:17). Upon a first reading of verses 39-49, three statements can be made. First, we apparently are dealing with isolated sayings of Jesus which Luke has chosen to put together in this place. That they are isolated is supported by a lack of internal unity in the subject matter and by the fact that Matthew has this material located in a number of settings. Verse 39 is in Matthew 15:14, verse 40 in Matthew 10:24-25, verses 41-42 in Matthew 7:3-5, verses 43-45 in Matthew 7:16-20 and 12:33-35, verse 46 in Matthew 7:21, and verses 47-49 in Matthew 7:24-27. Second, this difference in the location of a saying of Jesus alters the meaning of the saying. For example, the statement that a disciple is not above but rather is like the teacher (verse 40) is in Matthew a warning to the disciples that they can expect the same mistreatment and persecution Jesus received (10:24-25), whereas in Luke's setting, the statement refers to the fact that disciples become like their teachers. If one learns from blind, hypocritical, and judgmental teachers, then one becomes such a person. In other words, choose carefully your teachers. And third, Luke's reason for joining these isolated sayings to form the sermon's conclusion is not evident to the reader. Perhaps some clarity will come from further investigation.

It is helpful in such passages as verses 39-49 to discern lines of thought within the material which will permit division into sub-units. Here the yield of four segments seems natural and fruitful: 39-40, 41-42, 43-45, 46-49. Verses 39-40 warn of that kind of leadership which presumes to instruct and guide others in matters which the leader has not personally understood, believed, or embraced, and disciples of such leaders cannot expect to be any different or any better. Like teacher, like pupil. Verses 41-42 use the tragicomical scene of a person with a log in the eye attempting to improve the condition of another whose eye has a speck in it in order to address the problem of moral superiority found in those without the faculty of self-criticism. It is not an uncommon trait in helpers of all kinds to be deceived by the altruism of their efforts to attend to the needs of others ("Brother, let me take out the speck that is in your eye"). Looking always to others, not self, can be a beautiful veil protecting one from honest soul-searching. Verses 43-45 underscore the inseparable union of what one is and what one does. More specifically, the union is between what one is and what one says: "For out of the abundance of the heart his mouth speaks" (verse 45). One's words, sooner or later, will reveal character just as surely and naturally as the appearance of fruit announces the kind of tree bearing it. And verses 46-49 concludes the entire sermon by joining confession and obedience. The confession of Jesus as Lord (verse 46) was and is, of course, appropriate. Paul's writings show this to have been one of the earliest forms of the Christian confession of faith (Rom. 10:9; Phil. 2:9-11). However, this confession unaccompanied by the obedience implied in such a confession is shallow emotional exuberance which will not hold firm against the inevitable storms that assail the faithful. Luke's storm is the rising of a stream, quite different from Matthew's wind, rain, and flood (7:24-27). Commentators suggest the differences may reflect the differences in climate and weather in the locales of the two writers.

Do these verses reveal an organizing theme, a theme not imposed upon the material but one prompted by the content? Preachers need to be alert to the integrity of a passage, not only to understand it better but also in order to present it to the listeners with clarity. One would not be far afield to identify as an organizing theme Luke's joining of character and influence. The culture in which the New Testament was written looked favorably upon imitation of one's teacher as a primary mode of learning, and modeling behavior by the teacher as a primary responsibility of the vocation. Many Christian texts support Luke here (Acts 20:17-35; I Cor. 4:15-17; 11:1; Phil. 3:17; Tit. 2:7) as do most congregations. This is not to say imperfections in leaders disqualify them. On the contrary, Luke's point is that blindness to one's own imperfections is the disqualifying factor. The demand is neither for laxity nor rigidity but for honesty in the effort to be obedient to Jesus as Lord.

Last Sunday After Epiphany (Transfiguration)

Exodus 34:29-35; Psalm 99; II Corinthians 3:12–4:2;
Luke 9:28-36

On the day that commemorates the Transfiguration of the physical appearance of Jesus, the Gospel lection that reports the event is the center of attention, but all the assigned readings contribute directly to the same theme. Exodus 34:29-35 is the account of the change in the appearance of Moses' face after he had been on Mount Sinai in the presence of God. The responsorial psalm, a hymn to the kingship of Yahweh, in celebrating the holiness of God alludes to Moses, Aaron, the pillar of cloud, and the holy mountain. Second Corinthians 3:12–4:2 includes Paul's interpretation of the report of Moses' shining face and the veil.

Exodus 34:29-35

Our Old Testament reading is part of a section of the book of Exodus (chapters 32–34) concerning the renewal of the covenant following the rebellion of the people of Israel and the breaking of the original tablets. In many respects the report is parallel to Exodus 19–24, the account of the initial covenant. Consequently, some commentators have seen duplicate traditions or sources concerning the same event, but the matter is disputed. The immediate context of Exodus 34:29-35 is the return of Moses from Mount Sinai with the words of the covenant written upon new tables (34:28).

However one resolves the question of the relationship of Exodus 32–34 to Exodus 19–24, the passage before us contains a distinct and special tradition primarily concerned with Moses. On the surface it appears to be a relatively simple and direct account of the awesome shining face, its effect upon the people, and the solution of the problem with Moses' veil. Upon closer examination, however, the complexities of the story began to appear. When and why did Moses wear the veil? He put it on because the people were afraid to come near him, but he put it on only after he had finished talking with them (verse 33). Does the text mean to describe an event that happened once or a continuing activity? Verses 29-33 are correctly translated in the past tense, for they recount what happened once, following Moses' forty days and forty nights on Mount Sinai with God. Verses 34-35, on the other hand, are properly translated in the present tense, indicating that Moses would take off the veil when he would go in to speak with God, and put it on when he came out to speak to the people. These last verses suggest the tradition not of the revelation on Sinai but of the tabernacle. Thus it appears that the passage is the combination of at least two traditions.

One of the more interesting interpretations of this account is found in the Vulgate, in which the Hebrew verb meaning "to shine" was incorrectly taken to mean "had horns." That is the source of many representations, including Michelangelo's, of Moses with horns.

At one level a major concern of the account is the figure of Moses, and Moses contrasted with the people of Israel, including Aaron. Moses is the only one who can approach God. He is the one who acts as intermediary between God and people. Having interceded on their behalf, he now receives the law and communicates it to the people. Their fear of his changed countenance contrasts with his freedom to talk directly with God. However, even traditions such as this that glorify Moses know their limits. He remained a fully human mediator, not even aware that his appearance had been changed (verse 29).

At another and deeper level the concern of this text is the holiness of God and its effects, a point not even rejected in Paul's treatment of this passage in II Corinthians 3. Moses' face shone "because he had been talking with God" (verse 29). The rays of light are reflections of the glory of God. In the Old Testament view, it is terrifying and dangerous to be in the presence of God. Is it still possible that one who approaches God, who encounters the Holy One, will be transformed so that others can see the effects of that encounter?

Psalm 99

Psalm 99, like Psalms 96–98 which were readings for Christmas Day, is an enthronement psalm. These psalms were probably used in ancient times as part of the celebration of Yahweh's annual reenthronement in the Jerusalem temple at the fall festival (the Feast of Booths or Tabernacles). This particular psalm stresses factors or figures drawn from Israelite history more than do the other enthronement psalms. As a rule the enthronement psalms stressed creation rather than history.

The liturgical character and its employment in worship are evident in the complexity of the psalm. The speaker and addressee change rather frequently. Hymnic speech about God occurs in verses 1-2 and 6-7. Liturgical directions or admonitions are found in verses 5*a* and 9. A cultic shout—"Holy is he"—appears in verses 3*b* and 5*b*. (Verse 9*b* may have once also had this form.) Direct address to God appears in verses 3*a*, 4, and 8. One perhaps should envision the component parts of this psalm as having been spoken by different participants in a dramatic ritual in the temple. The entire congregation or certain Levitical choirs sang the hymnic parts (verses 1-2 and 6-7), another group or choir addressed the Deity directly (verses 3*a*, 4, and 8), priestly participants or Levites encouraged the congregation (verses 5*a* and 9), and the congregation probably joined in the worship with a responsive "Holy is he" (verses 3*b*, 5*b*, and 9*b*; see Isa. 6:3 for the threefold acclamation "holy, holy, holy").

Some expressions in this psalm would need explanation when preaching on it.

1. "Enthroned upon the cherubim" (verse 1*b*) is a description of God dependent on old mythological concepts as well as early Israelite iconography. The cherubim were composite guardian beings associated apparently with the winds or storm clouds and were associated with the ark (see I

Sam. 4:4). They seemed to have initially been conceived as part of the heavenly "transportation" for the Deity. Cherubim were found in the Holy of Holies in the Jerusalem temple as well as engraved on the temple walls (see I Kings 6:23-29; 8:6-7), and God could be understood as enthroned on these figures.

2. The "footstool" of God (in verse 5a) is probably synonymous with the "holy mountain" of verse 9a. The "footstool," however, may also have been identified with the ark (see Ps. 132:6-7). If God sat enthroned on or over the cherubim then the ark that rested between the cherubim may have been considered his footstool.

Two emphases dominate the affirmations and celebrations of this psalm. First, Yahweh reigns as king over the created order and the peoples of the earth (verses 1-4). As king, Yahweh is the embodiment and defender of justice and right order in the world. His rulership is exercised in Zion and it is from here that he rules over the world. Second, God is one who responds to intercession, forgiving Israel's sins and avenging their wrongs (verses 6-8). Moses, Aaron, and Samuel are seen as intercessors (see Num. 14:13; 16:46; I Sam. 12:16-25; Jer. 15:1) whose intercession in the past was successful. God did respond to them and forgive. Verse 8c, which the RSV translates as "but an avenger of their wrongdoings," seems to suggest that God punished the people before forgiving them. The phrase may be understood and translated differently as in the NEB "forgave all their misdeeds and held them innocent") or the JPSV ("exacted retribution for their misdeeds").

The surface parallels between Psalm 99 and the transfiguration story are the mountain imagery, the historical figures from the past, and the awesome holiness that pervades the materials.

II Corinthians 3:12–4:2

Today's epistolary lection is the latter part of Paul's midrashic exposition of the giving of the Law to Moses at Sinai (cf. II Cor. 3:3-11). With its focus on Moses as the one through whom God's revelatory light shone, and its contrast between the fading splendor of the Mosaic revelation and the permanent splendor of the new covenant of Christ, it is an excellent text for the Last Sunday After Epiphany when we celebrate the Transfiguration of the Lord. Although Paul makes no direct reference to the Gospel account of Christ's Transfiguration, which is rehearsed in today's Gospel reading (Luke 9:28-36; cf. Mark 9:2-8; Matt. 17:1-8), his exposition may be said to reflect the faith expressed in the divine voice, "This is my Son, my Chosen; listen to him!" (Luke 9:35).

It is also fitting that today's Old Testament reading is Exodus 34:29-35, since this is the biblical text that informs Paul's midrashic exposition. To make any sense of Paul's remarks, it will be necessary for the preacher to have this text from Exodus firmly in mind.

The central image from the Exodus text that informs Paul's exposition is that of the veil. Moses' encounter with God in receiving the Law on Sinai was such a numinous experience that his face glistened (Exod. 34:29). So blinding was his appearance that he was required to wear a veil when he appeared before the people. But when he returned to God's presence, he removed the veil from his face, thus enabling him to encounter God "face to face."

For Paul, the image of the veil illustrates something else, and more far-reaching. Just as Moses' face was veiled so that Israel would not be blinded by the dazzling light that shone through his face, so had Moses' message become similarly veiled to Israel. Israel had *seen* Moses through a veil, but so had they *read* Moses through a veil. The true form of his face had escaped their view, but so had the true meaning of the words he had received from Yahweh.

It is important to notice that in Paul's exposition in II Corinthians 3, he shifts his use of the image of the veil. He first speaks of the veil that hides the message of Moses, but then speaks of the veil that covers Israel's mind (verse 15). He appears to be saying that God's message given in the Law through Moses was not in itself inscrutable or incomprehensible. Rather, the minds and hearts of the Israelites had become hardened (verse 14; John 12:40; Rom. 11:25; also Mark 3:5; 6:52; 8:17; Eph. 4:18). The real fault lay not with the

Law but with the Israelites' inner faculties of perception, for there is where the light of God's revelation had been shut off.

Paul insists that things had reached an impasse: the Word of God as revealed through Moses to the people of Israel had become short-circuited. What had been intended to give life had only produced death (verse 6). What had begun as a relationship of splendor had dimmed to a flickering light (verse 10). What had been meant to speak to the needs of living, human hearts had been reduced to lifeless letters coldly inscribed on stone (verses 3-6).

This impasse was broken with and through Christ, whose appearance on earth effectively removed the veil (verse 14). Here, the Synoptic account of the Transfiguration symbolizes this dramatic shift, for in the Gospel narratives we see the old way of knowing God through the Law (Moses) and the prophets (Elijah) give way to the dazzling brightness of the transfigured Son of God, upon whom the divine voice bestows its blessing. Once Moses' face glistened before God on Sinai, but on this Christian mountain of revelation, the glistening face of Christ now becomes the focus of attention. The transfigured face of Moses pales beside the transfigured Christ.

For Paul, Moses' reentry to God, where the veil is removed (Exod. 34:29, 35) becomes the prototype for our "turning to the Lord" (verse 16). The image behind verse 16 of our text is Moses reentering the sacred place where he encounters God directly, but in its indefinite form it now encompasses our own encounter with God. What is different in the Christian experience, however, is that we confront the "Lord [who] is the Spirit" (verse 17), and in this encounter we find freedom (verse 17; cf. John 8:36; Rom. 6:18, 22; 8:2; I Cor. 7:23; Gal. 5:1). So, our view of God now takes place "with unveiled face" (verse 18), and through the transfigured face of Christ we gaze at the "glory of the Lord" (verse 18). So dazzling is this experience of God that it has a transforming effect on us, for we find ourselves "being changed into his likeness from one degree of glory to another" (cf. Phil. 3:21; also I Cor. 15:43, 49, 53; Rom. 8:29; 12:2; I John 3:2). Our experience of knowing God, which Christ has made possible, quite literally becomes a spiritual metamorphosis, because it "comes from the Lord, who is the Spirit" (verse 18).

The impact of this new way of knowing and seeing God was empowering: "We do not lose heart" (4:1; cf. Gal. 6:9). As he says in verse 12, "we are very bold." Because of the directness of his encounter with God, his position before God is one of genuine confidence. But there was another effect: it was also sobering. Such an unmediated, pristine encounter with God prevented him from playing fast and loose with God's word (II Cor. 2:17; I Thess. 2:3). All underhanded dealings are excluded when one confronts the living God this directly. No behind-the-scenes negotiating are permitted, for now the proclamation is public and out in the open. These last words are doubtless directed against Paul's opponents in the Corinthian church who had accused him of double-dealing in his apostolic work. But for Paul, the manifestation of God through Christ meant that his own behavior became open to public scrutiny.

For Paul, the light that had shone through Christ did not cease to shine in the earthly ministry of Jesus. It continued to reveal the nature of Christ to the world, and in so doing, exposed the true nature of Christian ministry (II Cor. 5:12; also I Cor. 4:5).

Luke 9:28-36

The Season of Epiphany, which began with the visit of the Wise Men, concludes with the Transfiguration of Jesus. The Transfiguration and its companion story, the baptism of Jesus (Luke 3:21-22), are the foundation for the Christian celebration of the revelation of the Son of God to the world.

Quite clearly Luke follows Mark (9:2-8) in this account, as does Matthew (17:1-8). Like Mark also, both Luke and Matthew locate the Transfiguration story immediately after the confession of Simon Peter and the introduction of the passion into the teaching of Jesus (Luke 9:18-27; Mark 8:27–9:1; Matt. 16:13-28). As we shall notice shortly, this location of the account is significant, as are also the points at which Luke modifies the story as received from Mark.

Hardly any passage in the Gospels has prompted interpretations as widely divergent as has this one. Some scholars confine themselves to questions of historicity and debate whether it occurred on Mt. Tabor or Mt. Hermon. Others understand the experience as a mystical vision that Jesus had, one in which three of his friends were involved. From time to time the theory that the Transfiguration is a displaced resurrection story is seriously entertained, as is the view that this is an artistic expression of the Christian confession that Jesus is Lord and Son of God. Whatever may be the historical event or circumstance prompting the Gospel accounts, two observations can be made with certainty. First, the story as it comes to us has been told after the manner of the theophany recorded in Exodus 24:12-18. The two events share many details: the mountain, the cloud, six days (Luke has eight), Moses, the voice, the glory. In addition, Matthew and Luke describe the face of Jesus as shining like the face of Moses after being in the presence of God (Exod. 34:29-35). Second, the location of the Transfiguration immediately after the first prediction of the passion of Jesus is significant for its interpretation. Just as Jesus, after submitting to the baptism of preparation, received heaven's confirmation as the Son of God, so here, he, after stating his commitment which would lead to Golgotha, is again confirmed as Son of God. The one who will be crucified is not just another martyr in a lost cause; for a moment he is seen by three of his disciples and the reader as the church saw him after the resurrection.

However, our Gospel lection for today is not simply the Transfiguration but the Transfiguration according to Luke. The Lukan accents are important. Instead of "after six days" (Mark 9:2), Luke says "about eight days" (9:28). Possibly Luke is tying the story to the resurrection which occurred on the eighth day, the day after the Sabbath, or he may be reflecting the use of this account in Christian worship which was held on the eighth day. In verse 29 Luke says that the experience occurred while Jesus was praying. Luke had said earlier (verse 18) that Jesus was praying when he asked the questions that led to Peter's confession and the first teaching about his coming death. And even earlier, after Jesus' baptism, Luke says that it was while Jesus was in prayer that he received the Holy Spirit and the voice of divine approval (3:21-22). The major events and critical moments in the life of Jesus were, according to Luke, marked by prayer.

Luke's only extended addition to Mark's account occurs in verses 31-33. Luke alone reports the content of the conversation among Jesus, Moses, and Elijah: they "spoke of his departure [exodus], which he was to accomplish at Jerusalem" (verse 31). That the Law and the Prophets testify to Jesus' suffering, death, and resurrection is an important theme in Luke (24:25-27, 44-46). The three disciples were not privy to this conversation because they were heavy with sleep (verse 32), but they awoke to see the two with Jesus and to see Jesus' glory. They also experienced the overshadowing cloud and heard the voice say, "This is my Son, my Chosen; listen to him!" (verses 34-35). In other words, for Jesus, the experience not only gave heaven's confirmation of who he was but also confirmed that his passion was according to God's purpose revealed in the Law and the Prophets. The "exodus" of Jesus would launch a new exodus for the people of God. For the disciples, the experience permitted them to see who the Jesus on the way to death really was, and to know that he, regardless of what suffering, denial, and humiliation was to come, was Lord, taking precedence over the Law and the Prophets.

The disciples were silent about these things "in those days" (verse 36), not needing Mark's command that they tell no one (Mark 9:9). And that is understandable; the silence following extraordinary experiences makes more powerful the words which eventually break that silence.

Holy Name of Jesus; Solemnity of Mary, Mother of God, January 1

Numbers 6:22-27; Psalm 67; Galatians 4:4-7 or *Philippians 2:9-13; Luke 2:15-21*

Celebrating the beginning of the new year on January 1 goes back to the mid-first century B.C., when Julius Caesar restructured the civil calendar. Prior to that time, March 1 marked the beginning of the new year. From the outset, it was a festive celebration that easily gave way to excesses of various kinds. In response, the Roman church called on Christians to open the new year with prayer, fasting, and penitential devotions. Another way to provide an alternative to raucous festivals was to designate January 1 as a time for honoring Mary the Mother of God. In the Roman calendar the day was designated *Natale Sanctae Mariae*, the Feast of Saint Mary.

Even though the particular emphasis given to January 1 has shifted through the centuries, in modern times, and especially in the Roman church, this day has received a dual emphasis. First, it is a time to recall the naming of Jesus, hence the designation the "Holy Name of Jesus." This aspect of its celebration is closely related to the custom, going back at least to the sixth century, of celebrating the Feast of the Circumcision of the Lord on this day. Second, it is an occasion for commemorating Mary, hence the designation the "Solemnity of Mary, Mother of God."

The selection of readings for this day echoes these themes. The Old Testament reading is chosen because of its emphasis on the bestowal of the Divine Name on the people Israel. Psalm 67 closely parallels Numbers 6:22-27 in the form of the blessing it contains. The epistolary readings in different ways pick up on both themes: the Galatians passage embodies a pre-Pauline tradition in which Christ is confessed as one "born of woman, born under the law," while the Philippians reading lays stress on the exalted name that God bestowed on the risen Lord. The Gospel text, of course, combines both themes: the central role of Mary as the one who pondered the divine mystery in her heart and the circumcision of Jesus as the occasion when he received the holy name.

Numbers 6:22-27

Within the Pentateuch as a whole, Numbers 6:22-27 is part of the laws given through Moses at Mount Sinai. The section of which it is a part began with Exodus 19 and will end in Numbers 10. In terms of literary source, this unit like most of the laws from Sinai from Exodus 25 to Numbers 10, comes from the Priestly Writer (sixth century B.C.). Specifically, the stress on the priesthood of the sons of Aaron (6:23) reveals that writer's point of view. However, in the great body of legislation this passage stands out for its poetic style, suggesting that the blessing itself is much older than the source in which it is found. Its style and content clearly reflect its repeated cultic use.

The unit consists of the Aaronic blessing surrounded by a brief narrative framework. The narrative (6:22) simply but significantly indicates that what follows is a divine speech to Moses. The benediction as a prayer for God's blessing was itself a gift from God. The speech instructs Moses to tell Aaron and his sons—that is, all future priests in the line, down to the writer's day—to bless the people of Israel, it gives them the words of the blessing, and then (6:27) it states the meaning of the act of blessing.

The blessing contains three sentences, each with two parts and each one longer than the one before. Every sentence begins with the divine name, Yahweh, followed by verbal forms that indicate wish or hope, e.g., "*May* the Lord bless you. . ." (TEV). They are then prayers for the well-being of those addressed. Since the form of address is second person singular, the blessing may apply equally to individuals or to a group. The contents concern God's protection (verse 24), gracious care (verse 25), and gift of peace. "Peace" is a comprehensive term, a fitting greeting, that includes wholeness. Priests are to pronounce the blessing but, as verse 27 expressly states, the Lord is the one who blesses.

What does it mean that by pronouncing the blessing the sons of Aaron thus put the divine name upon Israel? One hardly needs to stress the importance of names in the Old Testament. Abram and Sarai were given with the covenant new names (Gen. 17). After struggling through the night, Jacob was given the new name Israel, but the one with whom he struggled would not reveal his name, for in the name is power (Gen. 32:27-29). Yahweh was to be worshiped at the place which he would choose "to put his name" (Deut. 12:5). To put the name of the Lord over the people of Israel is to indicate that others know them, and they know themselves by that name. They are thereby identified with this God, and this God is identified with them.

Psalm 67

This psalm presents the reader or interpreter with what appears to be a twofold dialectic. On the one hand, the psalm is a prayer or speech to the Deity (verses 2-5) and yet it contains speech about God (verses 1, 6-7). In addition, the psalm apparently offers thanks for blessings already received (verses 6-7) and yet requests blessing from God (verses 1-5). The psalm thus has some of the characteristics of a lament (petitions for blessing) and of a thanksgiving.

The tension in the psalm can also be seen in its stress on both the particular (the people of Israel; the "us" of the psalm) and the universal (the nations; the peoples of the world). The request for blessing upon the more restricted community, that is, the "us" of verses 1, 6, and 7, has as its ultimate goal, the recognition of God by foreigners and the praise of the nations.

The analogies between this psalm and Christmas, holy family, and Mary the mother of Jesus might be seen as the following. The birth of a child has very specific, very limited connotations. The child is very particular: the particular offspring of a particular locale. The birth is always to a particular "us." Yet the birth of Jesus is proclaimed as possessing universal ramifications that reach out to the nations and the peoples of the world. The Incarnation is at once a most particular and universal event. At the same time, a birth is a blessing and an occasion for thanks (verses 6-7) and yet it looks forward to the future, to the expectation and intercession of blessings to come.

Galatians 4:4-7

"Born of woman, born under the law." These few words are as close as Paul comes to providing a birth and infancy narrative of Jesus. Yet, for all their remarkable compactness, they capture the essence of Luke's birth narrative. "Born of woman" naturally applies to Mary's giving birth to the Son of God, and it is this phrase that especially commends this epistolary lection for the celebration of New Year's Day as the "Solemnity of Mary, Mother of God." Some scholars believe that the phrase is pre-Pauline, and thus stems from the very earliest stages of primitive Christianity. If it is part of a creedal statement, we can see that quite early on Mary was the object of early Christian confession.

If "born of woman" underscores the humanity of Jesus, "born under the law" underscores his Jewishness. For Paul, this had special significance, since he is concerned to show that precisely because Jesus lived under the Mosaic law he was able to redeem us from the bondage of the law. What Paul says here in shorthand, Luke portrays in narrative form: Jesus circumcised according to the prescription of the Law (Luke 2:21) and brought to the temple for the rite of consecration (Luke 2:22-38). He is the son of parents loyally devoted to life according to the Law of Moses (Luke 2:39-51). Just as the first phrase links the epistolary text with the celebration of Mary as the Mother of God, so does this second phrase link directly with the circumcision and naming of Jesus (Luke 2:21).

Homiletically, these two motifs might be explored by showing how the devotion of Mary, as depicted in the Gospel reading, related to the devotion of Jesus. Both have in common their loyalty to the law of God. We are told that she and Joseph were scrupulously loyal, performing "everything according to the law of the Lord" (Luke 2:39). In the same breath, Jesus is portrayed in terms reminiscent of Samuel, the faithful servant of God (I Sam. 3:19). It would be possible to trace the Lukan portrait of Mary, especially noting her favorable status (in contrast to the Markan portrait) as among those "who hear the word of God and do it" (Luke 8:19-21).

Like mother, like son.

Philippians 2:9-13

If one chooses the Holy Name of Jesus as the focus of attention on New Year's Day, this will be the more appropriate epistolary text. For those who know that verses 9-11 comprise the second stanza of the Christ-hymn that Paul quotes here, it may appear odd to begin the reading at verse 9. But certainly that part of the hymn draws our attention to God's bestowal of the divine name on Jesus.

If this epistolary text is chosen, it provides a strong counterpart to the Gospel reading (Luke 2:15-21), where the name given to the Son of God, according to the angel's prescription, is "Jesus" (Luke 1:31). By contrast, in the epistolary reading the "name which is above every name" (verse 9) is "Lord" (cf. I Thess. 1:1). This is the name bestowed on Jesus because of his resurrection (Rom. 1:4); or, in the words of our passage, because "God has highly exalted him" (verse 9). To be sure, it is the "name of Jesus" before which the universe bows in submission, but the heart of the confession is that "Jesus Christ is Lord." We can begin to see the true significance of this ascription if we remember that in the Greek Old Testament Yahweh was commonly designated as Lord. Thus, for Christians to give Jesus this title was to ascribe him a status normally reserved for Israel's God, Yahweh.

The sequel to this part of the Christ-hymn is well worth exploring in a New Year's Day setting, because it spells out the implications of confessing and submitting to the divine name of Jesus Christ the Lord. Submission to the name implies submissive obedience which is worked out in salvation. It is not, however, the work that we do but the work that God does within us that brings about such obedience. We are reminded that "fear and trembling" accompany God's saving work within us. Not that we become feckless and craven before a vindictive, bloodthirsty God, but that we respect the exalted status and universal dominion of the One we confess as Lord. Such a perspective creates within us a healthy respect for the numinous and holy that prevents us from confessing the name of Jesus blithely and unthinkingly. This day is, after all, a celebration of the *Holy* Name of Jesus. It may be well to call the church to recover this sacred dimension as it launches into a new year.

Luke 2:15-21

Today we return to a portion of the Christmas story, but since the special nature of this service provides the reason for this return, it is appropriate that the nature and purpose of the service guide the approach to the text. Because attention may be focused on Mary's response to the events which surround her child or on the service of naming the child, these two approaches to the text offer themselves, plus a third which will be suggested at the close of these comments.

To give special attention to Mary would be to do no more than Luke himself has done. If Protestants think the Roman Catholic tradition has made too much of her, they could reasonably be charged with a neglect of her. While Luke is more attentive to women in general than are the other Evangelists (note, for example, 8:1-3; 23:27-31; 23:55; 24:10; Acts 1:14), his portrayal of Mary is noticeably distinct. There is in Luke, we remind ourselves, the episode of a woman in a crowd shouting to Jesus, "Blessed is the womb that bore you, and the breasts that you sucked!" to whom Jesus responded, "Blessed rather are those who hear the word of God and keep it!" (11:27-28). But upon reflection, Jesus' response is not a distancing from Mary but an embrace of her on the very grounds on which Luke consistently presents her as blessed: she received and obeyed the word of God. From the beginning, in response to the annunciation by the messenger Gabriel, Mary's relation to all that followed was clear:

194

"Behold, I am the handmaid of the Lord; let it be to me according to your word" (1:38). Elizabeth eulogized Mary as one who believed in God's faithfulness in fulfilling promises (1:45). Mary's own song reflects strong confidence and hope in God (1:46-55). She did not always understand what was said about her child, whether by shepherds (2:19) or by old Simeon at the temple (2:33). Neither did she understand the words and behavior of her son at age twelve (2:48-51). Even so, she kept all these things in her heart (2:19, 51), and she was found among those in Jerusalem waiting in prayer for the Holy Spirit promised by her risen son (Acts 1:5, 14).

If today's service attends primarily to the naming of Jesus, only verse 21 pertains to it. However, the brevity of the text should not be taken as brevity of meaning. First of all, the circumcision and naming of Jesus was according to the law (Lev. 12:3). Luke is careful to point out that the entire life of Jesus from birth, circumcision, dedication, Passover observance at age twelve, regular synagogue attendance, and even through his death and resurrection, was according to the Law of Moses as well as a fulfillment of the Prophets and the Psalms. Jesus is the true Israelite. Second, the naming confirmed the promise of the messenger from God and demonstrated the faith of Mary and Joseph in that promise (1:31; 2:21). And finally, the name itself was significant. Jesus, or Joshua, meant "one who saves." Such was his description to the shepherds in the field (2:11), and so he was and is, as Matthew also testifies (1:21).

However, the preacher may prefer to return to the text as a story and enjoy again its beauty and insight. The story line is simple: the shepherds come to Bethlehem, find Mary, Joseph, and the baby, relate their extraordinary experience, causing all who heard to wonder, and then return to their flocks, glorifying and praising God. They alone experienced both the shining glory and the mangered baby, the angel's revelation and the mother's whispers, the heavenly choir and the stabled animals. Those present at the manger had only the baby; Mary and Joseph had only the baby. But now they had the witness of the shepherds about the baby, and it is that witness which generates wondering, pondering, believing, and praising God.

Presentation, February 2

Malachi 3:1-4; Psalm 84 or 24:7-10; Hebrews 2:14-18;
Luke 2:22-40

This day is the celebration of the event reported in the Gospel reading, the presentation of Jesus in the temple in Jerusalem in accordance with Jewish law. Either of the psalms is highly appropriate, for both enable the church at worship to recreate the scene at the temple. Psalm 84 is a pilgrim hymn in praise of Zion and Psalm 24:7-10 is an entrance liturgy that praises the king of glory. The christological reflections in Hebrews 2:14-18 show a fully human Lord as high priest in service of God. Malachi 3:1-4 is the promise of a messenger of the covenant who will come like a "refiner's fire," after which the offerings—such as those mentioned in the Gospel—will be acceptable to God.

Malachi 3:1-4

For comments on the Old Testament lesson see the discussion of the readings for the Second Sunday of Advent, Year C, in this volume.

Psalm 84

The two psalms selected for reading in celebration of Jesus' presentation at the temple are both concerned with devotion to the temple. Psalm 84 may have been once used in conjunction with making a pilgrimage to Jerusalem at festival time, although verse 9 seems to suggest it was used by the king. Psalm 24 contains words spoken at the time when pilgrims entered the sanctuary precincts.

Psalm 84:5-7 probably talks about the route to Zion taken by pilgrims as they made their way along the roads to the city. At the time of fall festival, some of the early autumn rains may already have fallen reviving the parched land. "Strength to strength" could be translated "stronghold to stronghold," that is, the people move from one village outpost to another.

The piety of the worshiper and the psalm composer can be seen in various ways in the text. One way of analyzing the materials is to note the three groups whom the writer declares "blessed" (or "happy" which is a better translation of the Hebrew word used in all three cases).

1. First, a happy company is the birds that dwell continuously in the temple (verses 3-4). The sparrows and swallows that nest in the sacred precincts have the advantage of constantly dwelling in the house of God where they can ever sing God's praise.

2. Happy are those who go on pilgrim to Jerusalem (verses 5-7). To visit the temple and Zion is to experience happiness and to see "the God of gods."

3. Happy are those who trust in God (verse 12) who find their confidence in him. Here we have a sort of generalizing pronouncement that moves beyond the specificity of temple piety.

Verse 10 may be taken as embodying the overall sentiment of the psalm: to visit the temple and worship in its courts were some of the supreme experiences for the ancient Hebrews.

Psalm 24:7-10

A litany of questions and responses make up the heart of Psalm 24. Originally written for use in temple worship, the following is an outline of the text: (1) hymn in praise of God (verses 1-2) probably sung by the whole congregation; (2) pilgrims' question about entering the sacred precincts of the temple mount (verse 3); (3) priestly response (verses 4-5); (4) pilgrims' reply to the priests (verse 6); and (5) a choral dialogue at the time the gates were opened allowing the people and God, represented by the ark, to enter (verses 7-10).

The reading of this psalm on Presentation Day results from the early church's identity of Jesus with the king of glory who enters the sanctuary.

Hebrews 2:14-18

At one time, especially in the Western church, this feast day was oriented toward Mary, and this was reflected in its name "Purification of the Blessed Virgin Mary." But because this appeared to threaten the doctrine of the sinlessness of Mary, in modern times the Roman church reverted to the more ancient understanding of the Eastern church which celebrated this day as the "Presentation of the Lord." This more nearly conformed to its various designations in the East: "Coming of the Son of God into the Temple" (Armenian); "Presentation of the Lord in the Temple" (Egyptian); "The Meeting of the Lord" (Byzantine). The shift in title reflects a shift in emphasis: it is intended to be a feast of the Lord and not a feast honoring Mary.

With this focus on the presentation of the Lord, which, according to scriptural prescription, took place forty days after his birth (Lev. 12:2-8), this feast day has an incarnational cast. Celebrated on February 2, the fortieth day after Christmas, it serves to mark the end of the Christmas season. While the Gospel reading provides an account of the Lukan story of the presentation of Jesus in the temple (Luke 2:22-40), the epistolary reading serves to anchor the redemptive work of Christ in his Incarnation. This text should not be forced in a false harmony with the Gospel reading, since each reflects a different theological interest. Nevertheless, there is a certain irony in the fact that the child who is presented in the temple "according to the law of Moses" finally becomes the merciful and faithful high priest officiating in the heavenly temple, making expiation for the sins of the people.

Several features of today's epistolary lection are worth noting.

First, the solidarity between Christ, "the one who sanctifies" and all humanity, "those who are sanctified" (verse 11). In the previous verses, several Old Testament texts are placed on the lips of Christ to show that he identifies completely with all of God's children (Ps. 22:22; Isa. 8:17-18). As such, he was born a member of the human family, sharing completely in our nature as "flesh and blood" (verse 14; Rom. 8:3, 29; Phil. 2:7). Just as it is the lot of every member of the human family to die, so did he experience death.

The effects of his death, however, were far from ordinary. For one thing, it was God "for whom and by whom all things exist" who made Jesus the "pioneer . . . perfect through suffering" (verse 10). In addition, through death he passed through the heavens and became the exalted Son of God (Heb. 4:14). Because his death was both uniquely exemplary and triumphant, he destroyed death as the stronghold of Satan (verse 14; John 12:31; Rom. 6:9; I Cor. 15:55; II Tim. 1:10; Rev. 12:10). In his death, he delivered "all those who through fear of death were subject to lifelong bondage" (verse 15). The incarnation of Christ eventually meant the freedom of all humanity from the fear of death.

Second, Christ as the merciful and faithful high priest (3:1; 4:14; 5:5, 10; 6:20; 7:26; 8:1; 9:11; 10:21). Because of his complete obedience, he demonstrated his true fidelity as the Son of God (5:8-9; cf. I Sam. 2:35). Because of his complete identification with the entire human family through his becoming "flesh and blood," he can be thoroughly sympathetic with the human condition. His own suffering and testing qualifies him to assist us in our sufferings and testing (verse 18; 5:2; cf. Matt. 4:1-11 and parallels; 26:36-46 and parallels).

In his role as high priest, Christ makes expiation for our sins (verse 17). His unique experience as one of God's earthly children makes it possible for him to plead in our behalf (5:1; Rom. 3:25; I John 2:2; 4:10; cf. Exod. 4:16).

Christ as a heavenly high priest, officiating in the heavenly temple and pleading in our behalf, can easily become a lofty image, far removed from the world we know and live in. Oddly enough, Christians have always found it easier to worship such an elevated Christ, enthroned high above the heavens. It is far more difficult for us to envision a Christ who became like us *in every respect* (verse 17). Yet today's epistolary text makes this unqualified claim about Christ who was concerned not with angels but with the descendants of Abraham (verse 16). Given a choice between the company of angels and the company of humans, Christ plumps for flesh and blood. Why shouldn't we?

Luke 2:22-40

The service of the Presentation of Jesus had its Gospel basis in Luke 2:22-40. This story and the one which follows (2:41-52) are found only in Luke.

Between the accounts of Jesus' birth and the beginning of his public life as an adult, Luke places three stories: the naming of Jesus at his circumcision (2:21), the presentation of Jesus in the temple (2:22-40), and the visit of Jesus to the temple at age twelve (2:41-52). All of them have as one clear purpose the demonstration that Jesus' family was careful to keep the Law of Moses and to observe all the practices appropriate to a pious, God-fearing Israelite family. Mary and Joseph were especially concerned to see that all the rites of passage for a firstborn male child were meticulously observed. If as an adult, as a teacher, preacher, and prophet Jesus was in tension with his tradition, it was not, says Luke, because the observance of that tradition was lacking in his life. On the contrary, Luke repeatedly points out that it was his religious tradition which nurtured in him the insights that brought him into conflict with flawed and hollow practices of that tradition.

The presentation story itself (2:22-40) consists of three parts: the framing story (verses 22-24, 39-40) into which are inserted the responses of Simeon (verses 25-35) and Anna (verses 36-38). The framing story itself makes three points vital for Luke's theology. First, the temple and Jerusalem are of central importance for Jesus and the early church (24:47-52; Acts 1:4; 2:46, and others). Second, the law of the Lord is observed (mentioned no less than five times in our text, verses 22, 23, 24, 27, 39). Luke here puts together two separate regulations: the purification of the mother after childbirth (Lev. 12:1-4), which required a sacrifice of a lamb and a pigeon except in hardship cases in which two pigeons or doves would suffice (Lev. 12:6-8), and the dedication of the firstborn son to God (Exod. 13:2, 12-16). The firstborn son could be redeemed for five shekels (Num. 18:15-16). This leads to the third point of the story: nothing is said by Luke about the child Jesus being redeemed from his belonging-to-God status under the law. He is, therefore, like Samuel who was dedicated to God, who grew in wisdom, in stature, and in God's favor (I Sam. 1–2), and who lived in the temple. Clearly the Samuel story lies back of the summary statements about Jesus' growth (verses 40, 52) and the account of Jesus' regarding the temple as his Father's house (verse 49).

The importance of Simeon (verses 25-35) is that he is a devout and righteous Jew, advanced in age, inspired by the Holy Spirit and looking for the consolation of Israel. The consolation of Israel was a way of referring to the messianic age, using liberally words and phrases from Isaiah 40–55. The Nunc Dimittis (verses 29-32) might have been an early Christian hymn familiar to the Lukan church. The consolation of Israel would not be easy or without cost. On the contrary, there would be opposition, the sword, and death (verses 34-35). But even so, Judaism, as represented in this old, righteous, Spirit-filled, hopeful man, a resident in the temple area, would be fulfilled in Jesus. With the arrival of Jesus, the old can depart in peace, giving way to the new.

The importance of Anna (verses 36-38) is that she is old (the Greek text is unclear as to whether she is eighty-four or has been a widow for eighty-four years), a prophetess, devout in the practice of prayer and fasting, and a resident in the temple who is looking for the redemption of Israel. Together with Simeon, Anna represents Israel seen in the most favorable light, and Israel, as portrayed in this old woman, sees in Jesus the redemption of Israel, gives thanks to God, and witnesses concerning Jesus to all who share Israel's hope. In other words, this is a portrait of the Israel that accepted Jesus. Those who rejected Jesus were those who misunderstood and misrepresented their own tradition and, therefore, were not capable of recognizing him as the continuation and the fulfillment of their own best memory and hope.

Scripture Reading Index

SCRIPTURE READING INDEX

Table of Readings and Psalms

(Versification follows that of the *Revised Standard Version*)

	First Sunday of Advent	Second Sunday of Advent	Third Sunday of Advent	Fourth Sunday of Advent
A. Lesson 1	Isaiah 2:1-5 Psalm 122	Isaiah 11:1-10 Psalm 72:1-8	Isaiah 35:1-10 Psalm 146:5-10	Isaiah 7:10-16 Psalm 24
Lesson 2	Romans 13:11-14	Romans 15:4-13	James 5:7-10	Romans 1:1-7
Gospel	Matthew 24:36-44	Matthew 3:1-12	Matthew 11:2-11	Matthew 1:18-25
B. Lesson 1	Isaiah 63:16-64:8 Psalm 80:1-7	Isaiah 40:1-11 Psalm 85:8-13	Isaiah 61:1-4, 8-11 Luke 1:46b-55	II Samuel 7:8-16 Psalm 89:1-4, 19-24
Lesson 2	I Corinthians 1:3-9	II Peter 3:8-15a	I Thessalonians 5:16-24	Romans 16:25-27
Gospel	Mark 13:32-37	Mark 1:1-8	John 1:6-8, 19-28	Luke 1:26-38
C. Lesson 1	Jeremiah 33:14-16 Psalm 25:1-10	Baruch 5:1-9 *or* Malachi 3:1-4 Psalm 126	Zephaniah 3:14-20 Isaiah 12:2-6	Micah 5:2-5a (5:1-4a) Psalm 80:1-7
Lesson 2	I Thessalonians 3:9-13	Philippians 1:3-11	Philippians 4:4-9	Hebrews 10:5-10
Gospel	Luke 21:25-36	Luke 3:1-6	Luke 3:7-18	Luke 1:39-55

	Christmas, First Proper (Christmas Eve/Day*)	Christmas, Second Proper (Additional Lessons for Christmas Day)	Christmas, Third Proper (Additional Lessons for Christmas Day)
A. Lesson 1	Isaiah 9:2-7 Psalm 96	Isaiah 62:6-7, 10-12 Psalm 97	Isaiah 52:7-10 Psalm 98
Lesson 2	Titus 2:11-14	Titus 3:4-7	Hebrews 1:1-12
Gospel	Luke 2:1-20	Luke 2:8-20	John 1:1-14

*The readings from the second and third propers for Christmas may be used as alternatives for Christmas Day. If the third proper is not used on Christmas Day, it should be used at some service during the Christmas cycle because of the significance of John's prologue.

		First Sunday After Christmas*	January 1—Holy Name of Jesus Solemnity of Mary, Mother of God	January 1 (when observed as New Year)	Second Sunday After Christmas**
A.	Lesson 1	Isaiah 63:7-9 Psalm 111	Numbers 6:22-27 Psalm 67	Deuteronomy 8:1-10 Psalm 117	Jeremiah 31:7-14 or Ecclesiasticus 24:1-4, 12-16 Psalm 147:12-20
	Lesson 2	Hebrews 2:10-18	Galatians 4:4-7 or Philippians 2:9-13	Revelation 21:1-6a	Ephesians 1:3-6, 15-18
	Gospel	Matthew 2:13-15, 19-23	Luke 2:15-21	Matthew 25:31-46	John 1:1-18
B.	Lesson 1	Isaiah 61:10–62:3 Psalm 111		Ecclesiastes 3:1-13 Psalm 8	
	Lesson 2	Galatians 4:4-7		Colossians 2:1-7	
	Gospel	Luke 2:22-40		Matthew 9:14-17	
C.	Lesson 1	I Samuel 2:18-20, 26 or Ecclesiasticus 3:3-7, 14-17 Psalm 111		Isaiah 49:1-10 Psalm 90:1-12	
	Lesson 2	Colossians 3:12-17		Ephesians 3:1-10	
	Gospel	Luke 2:41-52		Luke 14:16-24	

*Or the readings for Epiphany.

**Or the readings for Epiphany if not otherwise used.

		Epiphany	Baptism of the Lord (First Sunday After Epiphany)*	Second Sunday After Epiphany	Third Sunday After Epiphany	Fourth Sunday After Epiphany
A.	Lesson 1	Isaiah 60:1-6 Psalm 72:1-14	Isaiah 42:1-9 Psalm 29	Isaiah 49:1-7 Psalm 40:1-11	Isaiah 9:1-4 Psalm 27:1-6	Micah 6:1-8 Psalm 37:1-11
	Lesson 2	Ephesians 3:1-12	Acts 10:34-43	I Corinthians 1:1-9	I Corinthians 1:10-17	I Corinthians 1:18-31
	Gospel	Matthew 2:1-12	Matthew 3:13-17	John 1:29-34	Matthew 4:12-23	Matthew 5:1-12
B.	Lesson 1		Genesis 1:1-5	I Samuel 3:1-10 (11-20)	Jonah 3:1-5, 10	Deuteronomy 18:15-20
	Lesson 2		Psalm 29 Acts 19:1-7	Psalm 63:1-8 I Corinthians 6:12-20	Psalm 62:5-12 I Corinthians 7:29-31 (32-35)	Psalm 111 I Corinthians 8:1-13
	Gospel		Mark 1:4-11	John 1:35-42	Mark 1:14-20	Mark 1:21-28
C.	Lesson 1		Isaiah 61:1-4	Isaiah 62:1-5	Nehemiah 8:1-4a, 5-6, 8-10	Jeremiah 1:4-10
	Lesson 2		Psalm 29 Acts 8:14-17	Psalm 36:5-10 I Corinthians 12:1-11	Psalm 19:7-14 I Corinthians 12:12-30	Psalm 71:1-6 I Corinthians 13:1-13
	Gospel		Luke 3:15-17, 21-22	John 2:1-11	Luke 4:14-21	Luke 4:21-30

*In leap years, the number of Sundays after Epiphany will be the same as if Easter Day were one day later.

	Fifth Sunday After Epiphany	Sixth Sunday After Epiphany (Proper 1)	Seventh Sunday After Epiphany (Proper 2)	Eighth Sunday After Epiphany (Proper 3)	Last Sunday After Epiphany Transfiguration
A. Lesson 1	Isaiah 58:3-9a Psalm 112:4-9	Deuteronomy 30:15-20 or Ecclesiasticus 15:15-20 Psalm 119:1-8	Isaiah 49:8-13 Psalm 62:5-12	Leviticus 19:1-2, 9-18 Psalm 119:33-40	Exodus 24:12-18 Psalm 2:6-11
Lesson 2	I Corinthians 2:1-11	I Corinthians 3:1-9	I Corinthians 3:10-11, 16-23	I Corinthians 4:1-5	II Peter 1:16-21
Gospel	Matthew 5:13-16	Matthew 5:17-26	Matthew 5:27-37	Matthew 5:38-48	Matthew 17:1-9
B. Lesson 1	Job 7:1-7 Psalm 147:1-11	II Kings 5:1-14 Psalm 32	Isaiah 43:18-25 Psalm 41	Hosea 2:14-20 Psalm 103:1-13	II Kings 2:1-12a Psalm 50:1-6
Lesson 2	I Corinthians 9:16-23	I Corinthians 9:24-27	II Corinthians 1:18-22	II Corinthians 3:1-6	II Corinthians 4:3-6
Gospel	Mark 1:29-39	Mark 1:40-45	Mark 2:1-12	Mark 2:18-22	Mark 9:2-9
C. Lesson 1	Isaiah 6:1-8 (9-13) Psalm 138	Jeremiah 17:5-10 Psalm 1	Genesis 45:3-11, 15 Psalm 37:1-11	Ecclesiasticus 27:4-7 or Isaiah 55:10-13 Psalm 92:1-4, 12-15	Exodus 34:29-35 Psalm 99
Lesson 2	I Corinthians 15:1-11	I Corinthians 15:12-20	I Corinthians 15:35-38, 42-50	I Corinthians 15:51-58	II Corinthians 3:12—4:2
Gospel	Luke 5:1-11	Luke 6:17-26	Luke 6:27-38	Luke 6:39-49	Luke 9:28-36

	Ash Wednesday	First Sunday of Lent	Second Sunday of Lent	Third Sunday of Lent	Fourth Sunday of Lent
A. Lesson 1	Joel 2:1-2, 12-17a Psalm 51:1-12	Genesis 2:4b-9, 15-17, 25–3:7 Psalm 130	Genesis 12:1-4a (4b-8) Psalm 33:18-22	Exodus 17:3-7 Psalm 95	I Samuel 16:1-13 Psalm 23
Lesson 2	II Corinthians 5:20b–6:2 (3-10)	Romans 5:12-19	Romans 4:1-5 (6-12), 13-17	Romans 5:1-11	Ephesians 5:8-14
Gospel	Matthew 6:1-6, 16-21	Matthew 4:1-11	John 3:1-17 *or* Matthew 17:1-9	John 4:5-26 (27-42)	John 9:1-41
B. Lesson 1		Genesis 9:8-17 Psalm 25:1-10	Genesis 17:1-10, 15-19 Psalm 105:1-11	Exodus 20:1-17 Psalm 19:7-14	II Chronicles 36:14-23 Psalm 137:1-6
Lesson 2		I Peter 3:18-22	Romans 4:16-25	I Corinthians 1:22-25	Ephesians 2:4-10
Gospel		Mark 1:9-15	Mark 8:31-38 *or* Mark 9:1-9	John 2:13-22	John 3:14-21
C. Lesson 1		Deuteronomy 26:1-11 Psalm 91:9-16	Genesis 15:1-12, 17-18 Psalm 127	Exodus 3:1-15 Psalm 103:1-13	Joshua 5:9-12 Psalm 34:1-8
Lesson 2		Romans 10:8b-13	Philippians 3:17–4:1	I Corinthians 10:1-13	II Corinthians 5:16-21
Gospel		Luke 4:1-13	Luke 13:31-35 *or* Luke 9:28-36	Luke 13:1-9	Luke 15:1-3, 11-32

	Fifth Sunday of Lent	Lent 6 when observed as Passion Sunday	Lent 6 when observed as Palm Sunday*
A. Lesson 1	Ezekiel 37:1-14 Psalm 116:1-9	Isaiah 50:4-9a Psalm 31:9-16	Isaiah 50:4-9a Psalm 118:19-29
Lesson 2	Romans 8:6-11	Philippians 2:5-11	Philippians 2:5-11
Gospel	John 11:(1-16), 17-45	Matthew 26:14–27:66 *or* Matthew 27:11-54	Matthew 21:1-11
B. Lesson 1	Jeremiah 31:31-34 Psalm 51:10-17	Same as A Psalm 31:9-16	Same as A Psalm 118:19-29
Lesson 2	Hebrews 5:7-10	Same as A	Same as A
Gospel	John 12:20-33	Mark 14:1–15:47 *or* Mark 15:1-39	Mark 11:1-11 *or* John 12:12-16
C. Lesson 1	Isaiah 43:16-21 Psalm 126	Same as A Psalm 31:9-16	Same as A Psalm 118:19-29
Lesson 2	Philippians 3:8-14	Same as A	Same as A
Gospel	John 12:1-8	Luke 22:14–23:56 *or* Luke 23:1-49	Luke 19:28-40

*These readings are provided for the liturgy or procession of palms for churches which have not had the tradition of readings-and-procession and also for an early "said" service in the Episcopal tradition.

HOLY WEEK

	Monday	Tuesday	Wednesday	Holy Thursday* **	Good Friday
A. Lesson 1	Isaiah 42:1-9 Psalm 36:5-10	Isaiah 49:1-7 Psalm 71:1-12	Isaiah 50:4-9a Psalm 70	Exodus 12:1-14 Psalm 116:12-19	Isaiah 52:13–53:12 Psalm 22:1-18
Lesson 2	Hebrews 9:11-15	I Corinthians 1:18-31	Hebrews 12:1-3	I Corinthians 11:23-26	Hebrews 4:14-16; 5:7-9
Gospel	John 12:1-11	John 12:20-36	John 13:21-30	John 13:1-15	John 18:1–19:42 or John 19:17-30
B. Lesson 1				Exodus 24:3-8 Psalm 116:12-19	
Lesson 2				I Corinthians 10:16-17	
Gospel				Mark 14:12-26	
C. Lesson 1				Jeremiah 31:31-34 Psalm 116:12-19	
Lesson 2				Hebrews 10:16-25	
Gospel				Luke 22:7-20	

*For those who want the feet washing emphasis every year, "A" readings are used each year.
**Psalm 116 is used at the Lord's Supper on Holy Thursday. Psalm 89:20-21, 24, 26 is used at the "chrism" service.

EASTER VIGIL*

Old Testament Readings and Psalms (A, B, C)

Genesis 1:1–2:2
Psalm 33
Genesis 7:1-5, 11-18; 8:6-18; 9:8-13
Psalm 46
Genesis 22:1-18
Psalm 16
Exodus 14:10–15:1
Exodus 15:1-6, 11-13, 17-18
Isaiah 54:5-14
Psalm 30

Isaiah 55:1-11
Isaiah 12:2-6
Baruch 3:9-15, 32–4:4
Psalm 19
Ezekiel 36:24-28
Psalm 42
Ezekiel 37:1-14
Psalm 143
Zephaniah 3:14-20
Psalm 98

Second Reading (A, B, C)
Romans 6:3-11
Psalm 114

Gospel
A. Matthew 28:1-10
B. Mark 16:1-8
C. Luke 24:1-12

*This selection of readings and psalms is provided for the Easter Vigil. A minimum of three readings from the Old Testament should be used, and this should always include Exodus 14.

	Easter* **	Second Sunday of Easter	Third Sunday of Easter	Fourth Sunday of Easter	Fifth Sunday of Easter
A. Lesson 1	Acts 10:34-43 *or* Jeremiah 31:1-6 Psalm 118:14-24	Acts 2:14a, 22-32 Psalm 16:5-11	Acts 2:14a, 36-41 Psalm 116:12-19	Acts 2:42-47 Psalm 23	Acts 7:55-60 Psalm 31:1-8
Lesson 2	Colossians 3:1-4 *or* Acts 10:34-43	I Peter 1:3-9	I Peter 1:17-23	I Peter 2:19-25	I Peter 2:2-10
Gospel	John 20:1-18 *or* Matthew 28:1-10	John 20:19-31	Luke 24:13-35	John 10:1-10	John 14:1-14
B. Lesson 1	Acts 10:34-43 *or* Isaiah 25:6-9 Psalm 118:14-24	Acts 4:32-35 Psalm 133	Acts 3:12-19 Psalm 4	Acts 4:8-12 Psalm 23	Acts 8:26-40 Psalm 22:25-31
Lesson 2	I Corinthians 15:1-11 *or* Acts 10:34-43	I John 1:1-2:2	I John 3:1-7	I John 3:18-24	I John 4:7-12
Gospel	John 20:1-18 *or* Mark 16:1-8	John 20:19-31	Luke 24:35-48	John 10:11-18	John 15:1-8

*See next page for Easter Evening.

**If the Old Testament passage is chosen for the first reading, the Acts passage is used as the second reading in order to initiate the sequential reading of Acts during the fifty days of Easter.

	Easter*	Second Sunday of Easter	Third Sunday of Easter	Fourth Sunday of Easter	Fifth Sunday of Easter
C. Lesson 1	Acts 10:34-43 *or* Isaiah 65:17-25 Psalm 118:14-24	Acts 5:27-32 Psalm 2	Acts 9:1-20 Psalm 30:4-12	Acts 13:15-16, 26-33 Psalm 23	Acts 14:8-18 Psalm 145:13b-21
Lesson 2	I Corinthians 15:19-26 *or* Acts 10:34-43	Revelation 1:4-8	Revelation 5:11-14	Revelation 7:9-17	Revelation 21:1-6
Gospel	John 20:1-18 *or* Luke 24:1-12	John 20:19-31	John 21:1-19 *or* John 21:15-19	John 10:22-30	John 13:31-35

Easter Evening*

A. Lesson 1	Acts 5:29-32 *or* Daniel 12:1-3 Psalm 150
Lesson 2	I Corinthians 5:6-8 *or* Acts 5:29-32
Gospel	Luke 24:13-49

*If the first reading is from the Old Testament, the reading from Acts should be second.

	Sixth Sunday of Easter	Ascension*	Seventh Sunday of Easter	Pentecost**	Trinity Sunday
A. Lesson 1	Acts 17:22-31 Psalm 66:8-20	Acts 1:1-11 Psalm 47	Acts 1:6-14 Psalm 68:1-10	Acts 2:1-21 *or* Isaiah 44:1-8 Psalm 104:24-34	Deuteronomy 4:32-40 Psalm 33:1-12
Lesson 2	I Peter 3:13-22	Ephesians 1:15-23	I Peter 4:12-14; 5:6-11	I Corinthians 12:3b-13 *or* Acts 2:1-21	II Corinthians 13:5-14
Gospel	John 14:15-21	Luke 24:46-53 *or* Mark 16:9-16, 19-20	John 17:1-11	John 20:19-23 *or* John 7:37-39	Matthew 28:16-20
B. Lesson 1	Acts 10:44-48 Psalm 98	Psalm 47	Acts 1:15-17, 21-26 Psalm 1	Acts 2:1-21 *or* Ezekiel 37:1-14 Psalm 104:24-34	Isaiah 6:1-8 Psalm 29
Lesson 2	I John 5:1-6		I John 5:9-13	Romans 8:22-27 *or* Acts 2:1-21	Romans 8:12-17
Gospel	John 15:9-17		John 17:11b-19	John 15:26-27; 16:4b-15	John 3:1-17

*Or on Seventh Sunday of Easter.

**If the Old Testament passage is chosen for the first reading, the Acts passage is used as the second reading.

	Sixth Sunday of Easter	Ascension*	Seventh Sunday of Easter	Pentecost**	Trinity Sunday
C. Lesson 1	Acts 15:1-2, 22-29 Psalm 67	Psalm 47	Acts 16:16-34 Psalm 97	Acts 2:1-21 *or* Genesis 11:1-9 Psalm 104:24-34	Proverbs 8:22-31 Psalm 8
Lesson 2	Revelation 21:10, 22-27		Revelation 22:12-14, 16-17, 20	Romans 8:14-17 *or* Acts 2:1-21	Romans 5:1-5
Gospel	John 14:23-29		John 17:20-26	John 14:8-17, 25-27	John 16:12-15

*Or on Seventh Sunday of Easter.

**If the Old Testament passage is chosen for the first reading, the Acts passage is used as the second reading.

		Proper 4* Sunday between May 29 and June 4 inclusive (if after Trinity Sunday)	Proper 5 Sunday between June 5 and 11 inclusive (if after Trinity Sunday)	Proper 6 Sunday between June 12 and 18 inclusive (if after Trinity Sunday)	Proper 7 Sunday between June 19 and 25 inclusive (if after Trinity Sunday)	Proper 8 Sunday between June 26 and July 2 inclusive
A.	Lesson 1	Genesis 12:1-9 Psalm 33:12-22	Genesis 22:1-18 Psalm 13	Genesis 25:19-34 Psalm 46	Genesis 28:10-17 Psalm 91:1-10	Genesis 32:22-32 Psalm 17:1-7, 15
	Lesson 2	Romans 3:21-28	Romans 4:13-18	Romans 5:6-11	Romans 5:12-19	Romans 6:3-11
	Gospel	Matthew 7:21-29	Matthew 9:9-13	Matthew 9:35–10:8	Matthew 10:24-33	Matthew 10:34-42
B.	Lesson 1	I Samuel 16:1-13 Psalm 20	I Samuel 16:14-23 Psalm 57	II Samuel 1:1, 17-27 Psalm 46	II Samuel 5:1-12 Psalm 48	II Samuel 6:1-15 Psalm 24
	Lesson 2	II Corinthians 4:5-12	II Corinthians 4:13–5:1	II Corinthians 5:6-10, 14-17	II Corinthians 5:18–6:2	II Corinthians 8:7-15
	Gospel	Mark 2:23–3:6	Mark 3:20-35	Mark 4:26-34	Mark 4:35-41	Mark 5:21-43
C.	Lesson 1	I Kings 8:22-23, 41-43 Psalm 100	I Kings 17:17-24 Psalm 113	I Kings 19:1-8 Psalm 42	I Kings 19:9-14 Psalm 43	I Kings 19:15-21 Psalm 44:1-8
	Lesson 2	Galatians 1:1-10	Galatians 1:11-24	Galatians 2:15-21	Galatians 3:23-29	Galatians 5:1, 13-25
	Gospel	Luke 7:1-10	Luke 7:11-17	Luke 7:36–8:3	Luke 9:18-24	Luke 9:51-62

*If the Sunday between May 24 and 28 inclusive follows Trinity Sunday, use Eighth Sunday After Epiphany on that day.

	Proper 9 Sunday between July 3 and 9 inclusive	Proper 10 Sunday between July 10 and 16 inclusive	Proper 11 Sunday between July 17 and 23 inclusive	Proper 12 Sunday between July 24 and 30 inclusive	Proper 13 Sunday between July 31 and Aug. 6 inclusive
A. Lesson 1	Exodus 1:6-14, 22–2:10	Exodus 2:11-22	Exodus 3:1-12	Exodus 3:13-20	Exodus 12:1-14
	Psalm 124	Psalm 69:6-15	Psalm 103:1-13	Psalm 105:1-11	Psalm 143:1-10
Lesson 2	Romans 7:14-25a	Romans 8:9-17	Romans 8:18-25	Romans 8:26-30	Romans 8:31-39
Gospel	Matthew 11:25-30	Matthew 13:1-9, 18-23	Matthew 13:24-30, 36-43	Matthew 13:44-52	Matthew 14:13-21
B. Lesson 1	II Samuel 7:1-17	II Samuel 7:18-29	II Samuel 11:1-15	II Samuel 12:1-14	II Samuel 12:15b-24
	Psalm 89:20-37	Psalm 132:11-18	Psalm 53	Psalm 32	Psalm 34:11-22
Lesson 2	II Corinthians 12:1-10	Ephesians 1:1-10	Ephesians 2:11-22	Ephesians 3:14-21	Ephesians 4:1-6
Gospel	Mark 6:1-6	Mark 6:7-13	Mark 6:30-34	John 6:1-15	John 6:24-35
C. Lesson 1	I Kings 21:1-3, 17-21	II Kings 2:1, 6-14	II Kings 4:8-17	II Kings 5:1-15ab ("... in Israel")	II Kings 13:14-20a
	Psalm 5:1-8	Psalm 139:1-12	Psalm 139:13-18	Psalm 21:1-7	Psalm 28
Lesson 2	Galatians 6:7-18	Colossians 1:1-14	Colossians 1:21-29	Colossians 2:6-15	Colossians 3:1-11
Gospel	Luke 10:1-12, 17-20	Luke 10:25-37	Luke 10:38-42	Luke 11:1-13	Luke 12:13-21

		Proper 14 Sunday between August 7 and 13 inclusive	Proper 15 Sunday between August 14 and 20 inclusive	Proper 16 Sunday between August 21 and 27 inclusive	Proper 17 Sunday between August 28 and Sept. 3 inclusive	Proper 18 Sunday between September 4 and 10 inclusive
A.	Lesson 1	Exodus 14:19-31 Psalm 106:4-12	Exodus 16:2-15 Psalm 78:1-3, 10-20	Exodus 17:1-7 Psalm 95	Exodus 19:1-9 Psalm 114	Exodus 19:16-24 Psalm 115:1-11
	Lesson 2	Romans 9:1-5	Romans 11:13-16, 29-32	Romans 11:33-36	Romans 12:1-13	Romans 13:1-10
	Gospel	Matthew 14:22-33	Matthew 15:21-28	Matthew 16:13-20	Matthew 16:21-28	Matthew 18:15-20
B.	Lesson 1	II Samuel 18:1, 5, 9-15 Psalm 143:1-8	II Samuel 18:24-33 Psalm 102:1-12	II Samuel 23:1-7 Psalm 67	I Kings 2:1-4, 10-12 Psalm 121	Ecclesiasticus 5:8-15 or Proverbs 2:1-8 Psalm 119:129-136
	Lesson 2	Ephesians 4:25–5:2	Ephesians 5:15-20	Ephesians 5:21-33	Ephesians 6:10-20	James 1:17-27
	Gospel	John 6:35, 41-51	John 6:51-58	John 6:55-69	Mark 7:1-8, 14-15, 21-23	Mark 7:31-37
C.	Lesson 1	Jeremiah 18:1-11 Psalm 14	Jeremiah 20:7-13 Psalm 10:12-18	Jeremiah 28:1-9 Psalm 84	Ezekiel 18:1-9, 25-29 Psalm 15	Ezekiel 33:1-11 Psalm 94:12-22
	Lesson 2	Hebrews 11:1-3, 8-19	Hebrews 12:1-2, 12-17	Hebrews 12:18-29	Hebrews 13:1-8	Philemon 1-20
	Gospel	Luke 12:32-40	Luke 12:49-56	Luke 13:22-30	Luke 14:1, 7-14	Luke 14:25-33

	Proper 19 Sunday between September 11 and 17 inclusive	Proper 20 Sunday between September 18 and 24 inclusive	Proper 21 Sunday between Sept. 25 and Oct. 1 inclusive	Proper 22 Sunday between October 2 and 8 inclusive	Proper 23 Sunday between October 9 and 15 inclusive
A. Lesson 1	Exodus 20:1-20 Psalm 19:7-14	Exodus 32:1-14 Psalm 106:7-8, 19-23	Exodus 33:12-23 Psalm 99	Numbers 27:12-23 Psalm 81:1-10	Deuteronomy 34:1-12 Psalm 135:1-14
Lesson 2	Romans 14:5-12	Philippians 1:21-27	Philippians 2:1-13	Philippians 3:12-21	Philippians 4:1-9
Gospel	Matthew 18:21-35	Matthew 20:1-16	Matthew 21:28-32	Matthew 21:33-43	Matthew 22:1-14
B. Lesson 1	Proverbs 22:1-2, 8-9 Psalm 125	Job 28:20-28 Psalm 27:1-6	Job 42:1-6 Psalm 27:7-14	Genesis 2:18-24 Psalm 128	Genesis 3:8-19 Psalm 90:1-12
Lesson 2	James 2:1-5, 8-10, 14-17	James 3:13-18	James 4:13-17; 5:7-11	Hebrews 1:1-4; 2:9-11	Hebrews 4:1-3, 9-13
Gospel	Mark 8:27-38	Mark 9:30-37	Mark 9:38-50	Mark 10:2-16	Mark 10:17-30
C. Lesson 1	Hosea 4:1-3, 5:15–6:6 Psalm 77:11-20	Hosea 11:1-11 Psalm 107:1-9	Joel 2:23-30 Psalm 107:1, 33-43	Amos 5:6-7, 10-15 Psalm 101	Micah 1:2; 2:1-10 Psalm 26
Lesson 2	I Timothy 1:12-17	I Timothy 2:1-7	I Timothy 6:6-19	II Timothy 1:1-14	II Timothy 2:8-15
Gospel	Luke 15:1-10	Luke 16:1-13	Luke 16:19-31	Luke 17:5-10	Luke 17:11-19

		Proper 24 Sunday between October 16 and 22 inclusive	Proper 25 Sunday between October 23 and 29 inclusive	Proper 26 Sunday between October 30 and Nov. 5 inclusive	Proper 27 Sunday between November 6 and 12 inclusive	Proper 28 Sunday between November 13 and 19 inclusive
A.	Lesson 1	Ruth 1:1-19a Psalm 146	Ruth 2:1-13 Psalm 128	Ruth 4:7-17 Psalm 127	Amos 5:18-24 Psalm 50:7-15	Zephaniah 1:7, 12-18 Psalm 76
	Lesson 2	I Thessalonians 1:1-10	I Thessalonians 2:1-8	I Thessalonians 2:9-13, 17-20	I Thessalonians 4:13-18	I Thessalonians 5:1-11
	Gospel	Matthew 22:15-22	Matthew 22:34-46	Matthew 23:1-12	Matthew 25:1-13	Matthew 25:14-30
B.	Lesson 1	Isaiah 53:7-12 Psalm 35:17-28	Jeremiah 31:7-9 Psalm 126	Deuteronomy 6:1-9 Psalm 119:33-48	I Kings 17:8-16 Psalm 146	Daniel 7:9-14 Psalm 145:8-13
	Lesson 2	Hebrews 4:14-16	Hebrews 5:1-6	Hebrews 7:23-28	Hebrews 9:24-28	Hebrews 10:11-18
	Gospel	Mark 10:35-45	Mark 10:46-52	Mark 12:28-34	Mark 12:38-44	Mark 13:24-32
C.	Lesson 1	Habakkuk 1:1-3; 2:1-4 Psalm 119:137-144	Zephaniah 3:1-9 Psalm 3	Haggai 2:1-9 Psalm 65:1-8	Zechariah 7:1-10 Psalm 9:11-20	Malachi 4:1-6 (3:19-24 in Hebrews) Psalm 82
	Lesson 2	II Timothy 3:14-4:5	II Timothy 4:6-8, 16-18	II Thessalonians 1:5-12	II Thessalonians 2:13-3:5	II Thessalonians 3:6-13
	Gospel	Luke 18:1-8	Luke 18:9-14	Luke 19:1-10	Luke 20:27-38	Luke 21:5-19

	Proper 29 (Christ the King) Sunday between November 20 and 26 inclusive	All Saints, November 1*	Thanksgiving Day**
A. Lesson 1	Ezekiel 34:11-16, 20-24 / Psalm 23	Revelation 7:9-17 / Psalm 34:1-10	Deuteronomy 8:7-18 / Psalm 65
Lesson 2	I Corinthians 15:20-28	I John 3:1-3	II Corinthians 9:6-15
Gospel	Matthew 25:31-46	Matthew 5:1-12	Luke 17:11-19
B. Lesson 1	Jeremiah 23:1-6 / Psalm 93	Revelation 21:1-6a / Psalm 24:1-6	Joel 2:21-27 / Psalm 126
Lesson 2	Revelation 1:4b-8	Colossians 1:9-14	I Timothy 2:1-7
Gospel	John 18:33-37	John 11:32-44	Matthew 6:25-33
C. Lesson 1	II Samuel 5:1-5 / Psalm 95	Daniel 7:1-3, 15-18 / Psalm 149	Deuteronomy 26:1-11 / Psalm 100
Lesson 2	Colossians 1:11-20	Ephesians 1:11-23	Philippians 4:4-9
Gospel	John 12:9-19	Luke 6:20-36	John 6:25-35

*Or on first Sunday in November.
**Readings *ad libitum*, not tied to A, B, or C.

	Presentation February 2	Holy Cross September 14
A. Lesson 1	Malachi 3:1-4 / Psalm 84 *or* 24:7-10	Numbers 21:4b-9 / Psalm 98:1-5 *or* 78:1-2, 34-38
Lesson 2	Hebrews 2:14-18	I Corinthians 1:18-24
Gospel	Luke 2:22-40	John 3:13-17

	Annunciation March 25	Visitation May 31
A. Lesson 1	Isaiah 7:10-14 / Psalm 45 *or* 40:6-10	I Samuel 2:1-10 / Psalm 113
Lesson 2	Hebrews 10:4-10	Romans 12:9-16b
Gospel	Luke 1:26-38	Luke 1:39-57

Titles of Seasons, Sundays, and Special Days

Advent Season

First Sunday of Advent...The Sunday occurring November 27 to December 3
Second Sunday of Advent..The Sunday occurring December 4 to December 10
Third Sunday of Advent...The Sunday occurring December 11 to December 17
Fourth Sunday of Advent...The Sunday occurring December 18 to December 24

Christmas Season

Christmas Eve/Day..December 24/25
First Sunday After Christmas.....................................The Sunday occurring December 26 to January 1
New Year's Eve/Day...December 31 to January 1
Second Sunday After Christmas.....................................The Sunday occurring January 2 to January 5

Epiphany Season

Epiphany...January 6 or first Sunday in January
First Sunday After Epiphany (Baptism of the Lord).................The Sunday occurring January 7 to January 13
Second Sunday After Epiphany..................................The Sunday occurring January 14 to January 20
Third Sunday After Epiphany.....................................The Sunday occurring January 21 to January 27
Fourth Sunday After Epiphany*..................................The Sunday occurring January 28 to February 3
Fifth Sunday After Epiphany*....................................The Sunday occurring February 4 to February 10
Sixth Sunday After Epiphany (Proper 1)*....................The Sunday occurring February 11 to February 17
Seventh Sunday After Epiphany (Proper 2)*.................The Sunday occurring February 18 to February 24
Eighth Sunday After Epiphany (Proper 3)*...................The Sunday occurring February 25 to February 29
Last Sunday After Epiphany (Transfiguration Sunday)

*Except when this Sunday is the Last Sunday After Epiphany.

Lenten Season

Ash Wednesday: Seventh
  Wednesday Before Easter
First Sunday of Lent
Second Sunday of Lent
Third Sunday of Lent
Fourth Sunday of Lent
Fifth Sunday of Lent

Holy Week

Passion/Palm Sunday
Monday in Holy Week
Tuesday in Holy Week
Wednesday in Holy Week
Holy Thursday
Good Friday
(Holy Saturday)

Easter Season

Easter Vigil
Easter
Easter Evening
Second Sunday of Easter
Third Sunday of Easter
Fourth Sunday of Easter
Fifth Sunday of Easter
Sixth Sunday of Easter
Ascension (fortieth day, sixth Thursday of Easter)
Seventh Sunday of Easter
Pentecost

Season After Pentecost

Trinity Sunday (First Sunday After Pentecost)
Propers 4-28 (See note below.)
Proper 29, Christ the King: the Sunday occurring
  November 20 to 26

Special Days

Some special days observed by many churches are included in the table, with appropriate readings and psalms.

NOTE: Easter is a movable feast, and can occur as early as March 22 and as late as April 25. When Easter is early, it encroaches on the Sundays after Epiphany, reducing their number, as necessary, from as many as nine to as few as four. In similar fashion the date of Easter determines the number of Sunday Propers after Pentecost. When Easter is as early as March 22, the numbered Proper for the Sunday following Trinity Sunday is Proper 3.